Crochet
for a Quiet Evening™

Edited by Laura Scott

HOUSE of
WHITE
BIRCHES
PUBLISHERS
SINCE 1947

Crochet for a Quiet Evening

Editor: Laura Scott
Associate Editor: Cathy Reef
Managing Editor: Jacqueline Stetter
Design Associate: Vicki Blizzard
Technical Editor: Agnes Russell
Book and Cover Design: Jessi Butler
Copy Editors: Marla Freeman, Nicki Lehman, Mary Martin
Publications Coordinator: Tanya Turner

Photography: Jeff Chilcote, Tammy Christian, Kelly Heydinger, Justin P. Wiard
Photography Assistant: Linda Quinlan

Production Coordinator: Brenda Gallmeyer
Graphic Arts Supervisor: Ronda Bechinski
Graphic Artist: Pam Gregory
Production Assistants: Janet Bowers, Marj Morgan
Traffic Coordinator: Sandra Beres
Technical Artists: Liz Morgan, Mitchell Moss, Travis Spangler, Chad Summers

Publishers: Carl H. Muselman, Arthur K. Muselman
Chief Executive Officer: John Robinson
Publishing Marketing Director: David J. McKee
Book Marketing Manager: Craig Scott
Product Development Director: Vivian Rothe
Publishing Services Manager: Brenda R. Wendling

Printed in the United States of America
First Printing: 2002
Library of Congress Number: 2001089860
ISBN: 1-882138-84-8

Every effort has been made to ensure the accuracy and completeness of the instructions
in this book. However, we cannot be responsible for human error or for the results when using
materials other than those specified in the instructions, or for variations in individual work.

Special thanks to Swiss Village Retirement Community for the photo locations.

A Note From the Editor

Hundreds of crocheters from across the United States and Canada have told us what they love most about crochet. One avid crocheter from Pennsylvania wrote, "More than anything else, I love to spend my evenings winding down from a busy day with my latest crochet project." Her letter and many others inspired this book of all-new crochet patterns you hold in your hands.

There is something so very soothing about the steady pace of crocheting stitch by stitch. All of the day's worries seem to melt away as the yarn pulls out of the skein, wraps around the hook and is worked into the piece of crochet. For hundreds, maybe even thousands of years, women of all ages and walks of life have found enormous pleasure and peace in the yarn and hook.

As for patterns, we've brought you all your favorites in this book—gorgeous afghans perfect for warming a sick child or loved one, attractive home accents, sweet and soft baby items, one-of-a-kind gifts sure to be appreciated and enjoyed for years to come, delightful toys and dolls for the young and young-at-heart, and handsome garments for you and yours to wear throughout the year. With our full-color photos, large pages and easy-to-follow instructions, each pattern is perfect for that evening of quiet relaxation.

So, go pick out several skeins of your favorite yarn, sit back in your favorite chair, turn on the television or some favorite music, and spend a blissful evening with your crochet!

With warm regards,

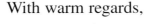

Laura Scott

Conte

1 Afghan Keepsakes

2 Home Sweet Home

3 Baby Boutique

nts

Afghan Keepsakes

Whether you lovingly crochet one of these beautiful afghans for yourself or to give as a cherished gift, you're sure to find the perfect one for any occasion from our selection of keepsake afghans!

Tea Rose Trellis

Design by Jo Hanna Dzikowski

Skill Level: Beginner

Size: 40 x 58 inches

Materials

► Caron Simply Soft worsted weight yarn (6 oz per skein): 4 skeins plum wine #9722, 1 skein bone #9703

► Size I/9 crochet hook or size needed to obtain gauge

► Tapestry needle

For an elegant look and wonderfully soft feel, crochet this beautiful afghan in soft yarn in shades of plum and bone!

Gauge

Square = 9 inches; 4 dc = 1½ inches

Check gauge to save time.

Pattern Notes

Weave in loose ends as work progresses.

Sl st to join each rnd in top of beg st.

Pattern Stitches

3-dc cl: [Yo hook, insert hook in indicated sp, yo, draw up a lp, yo draw through 2 lps on hook] 3 times in same sp, yo, draw through all 4 lps on hook.

Beg 3-dc cl: Sl st into indicated ch sp, ch 2 (counts as first dc), [yo hook, insert hook in indicated sp, yo, draw up a lp, yo, draw through 2 lps on hook] twice in same sp, yo, draw through all 3 lps on hook.

Square

Make 24

Rnd 1 (RS): With plum wine, ch 4, sl st to join to form a ring, [ch 3, 2 dc in ring, sl st in ring] 4 times. (4 petals)

Rnd 2: [Sl st into center dc of 3-dc group, ch 3] 4 times, sl st in same st as beg sl st. (4 ch sps)

Rnd 3: Sl st into ch-3 sp, [beg 3-dc cl, ch 1, 3-dc cl] in same ch-3 sp, ch 5, [{3-dc cl, ch 1, 3-dc cl} in next ch-3 sp, ch 5] rep around, join in top of beg cl.

Rnd 4: Sl st into ch-1 sp, [beg 3-dc cl, ch 3, 3-dc cl] in same ch-1 sp, *ch 1, 3 dc in next ch-5 sp, ch 1 **, [3-dc cl, ch 3, 3-dc cl] in next ch-1 sp, rep from * around, ending last rep at **, join in top of beg cl.

Rnd 5: Sl st into ch-3 sp, [beg 3-dc cl, ch 3, 3-dc cl] in same ch-3 sp, *ch 2, dc in next ch-1 sp, dc in each of next 3 dc, dc in next ch-1 sp, ch 2 **, [3-dc cl, ch 3, 3-dc cl] in next ch-3 sp, rep from * around, ending last rep at **, join in top of beg cl.

Rnd 6: Sl st into ch-3 sp, [beg 3-dc cl, ch 3, 3-dc cl] in same ch-3 sp, *ch 2, dc in next ch-2 sp, dc in each of next 5 dc, dc in next ch-2 sp, ch 2 **, [3-dc cl, ch 3, 3-dc cl] in next ch-3 sp, rep from * around, ending last rep at **, join in top of beg cl.

Rnd 7: Sl st into ch-3 sp, [beg 3-dc cl, ch 3, 3-dc cl] in same ch-3 sp, *ch 2, dc in next ch-2 sp, dc in each of next 7 dc, dc in next ch-2 sp, ch 2 **, [3-dc cl, ch 3, 3-dc cl] in next ch-3 sp, rep from * around, ending last rep at **, join in top of beg cl.

Rnd 8: Sl st into ch-3 sp, [beg 3-dc cl] in same ch-3 sp, *ch 2, dc in next ch-2 sp, dc in each of next 4 dc, ch 2, sk next dc, dc in each of next 4 dc, dc in next ch-2 sp, ch 2 **, [3-dc cl, ch 3, 3-dc cl] in next ch-3 sp, rep from * around, ending last rep at **, join in top of beg cl, fasten off.

Joining one edge

Rnd 8: Sl st into ch-3 sp, beg 3-dc cl, ch 2, sl st in ch-3 sp of previous square, ch 2, 3-dc cl in same ch-3 sp of working square, ch 2, dc in next ch-2 sp, dc in each of next 4 dc, ch 1, sl st in ch-2 sp of previous square, ch 1, sk next dc on working square, dc in each of next 4 dc, dc in next ch-2 sp, 3-dc cl in next ch-3 sp, ch 2, sl st in ch-3 sp of previous square, ch 2, 3-dc cl in same ch-3 sp of working square, *ch 2, dc in next ch-2 sp, dc in each of next 4 dc, ch 2, sk next dc, dc in each of next 4 dc, dc in next ch-2 sp, ch 2 **, [3-dc cl, ch 3, 3-dc cl] in next ch-3 sp, rep from * around, ending last rep at **, join in top of beg cl, fasten off.

Joining two edges

Rnd 8: Sl st into ch-3 sp, beg 3-dc cl, ch 2, sl st in ch-3 sp of previous squares, ch 2, 3-dc cl in same ch-3 sp on working square, [ch 2, dc in next ch-2 sp, dc in each of next 4 dc, ch 1, sl st in ch-2 sp of previous square, ch 1, sk next dc on working square, dc in each of next 4 dc, dc in next ch-2 sp, {3-dc cl, ch 2, sl st in ch-3 sp of previous square, ch 2, 3-dc cl} in same ch-3 sp of working square] twice, *ch 2, dc in next ch-2 sp, dc in each of next 4 dc, ch 2, sk next dc, dc in each of next 4 dc, dc in next ch-2 sp, ch 2 **, [3-dc cl, ch 3, 3-dc cl] in next ch-3 sp, rep from * around, ending last rep at **, join in top of beg cl, fasten off.

Continue to make squares, joining in 6 rows of 4 each.

Continued on page 41

Frosty Morn

*Design by Carol Alexander
for Crochet Trends and Traditions*

Skill Level: Intermediate

Size: 54 x 75 inches

Materials

► Coats & Clark Red Heart Fiesta worsted weight yarn (6 oz per skein): 7 skeins millennium #6341

► Coats & Clark Red Heart Super Saver worsted weight yarn (8 oz per skein): 1 skein black #312, 3 skeins white #311

► Size H/8 crochet hook or size needed to obtain gauge

► Yarn needle

Chase away the chill as you watch the early morning sunrise snuggled in this beautiful granny square afghan. Don't forget that morning cup of coffee!

Gauge

Rnd 1 of square = 2 inches; square = 7¾ inches; fill-in motif = 2¾ inches

Check gauge to save time.

Pattern Notes

Weave in loose ends as work progresses.

Where joining is indicated, join with sl st unless otherwise indicated.

Ch-3 counts as first dc throughout.

Ch-2 counts as first hdc throughout.

Pattern Stitches

Long sc: Insert hook in indicated st, yo, draw up a lp level with working rnd, yo, draw through 2 lps on hook.

2-tr cl: [Yo hook twice, insert hook in indicated st, yo, draw up a lp, {yo, draw through 2 lps on hook} twice] twice, yo, draw through all 3 lps on hook.

Puff st: [Yo, insert hook in indicated st, yo, draw up a ½-inch lp] 4 times, yo, draw through all 9 lps on hook.

Dc dec: Retaining last lp of each dc on hook, work 2 dc in each of next 2 ch-2 sps, yo, draw through all 5 lps on hook.

First Square
Center puff stitch

With millennium, leaving a 6 inch length at beg, ch 2, puff st in 2nd ch from hook, ch 1 tightly to lock, leaving a 6 inch length fasten off. Set aside.

Rnd 1 (RS): With white, ch 5, sl st to join to form a ring, ch 3 ,[dc, ch 1, 2 dc] in ring, ch 3, [{2 dc, ch 1, 2 dc} in ring, ch 3] 3 times, join in top of beg ch-3, fasten off.

Rnd 2: Attach millennium in any corner ch-3 sp, ch 3, [2 dc, ch 3, 3 dc] in same ch sp, *ch 4, long sc in center ring covering next ch-1 sp on Rnd 1, ch 4 **, [3 dc, ch 3, 3 dc] in next corner ch-3 sp, rep from * around, ending last rep at **, join in top of beg ch-3, fasten off.

Rnd 3: Attach black in any corner ch-3 sp, ch 1, [{2 sc, ch 1, 2 sc} in corner ch-3 sp, sc in each of next 3 dc, ch 1, tr in next long sc, ch 1, sc in each of next 3 dc] rep around, join in beg sc, fasten off.

Rnd 4: Attach white in corner ch-1 sp, ch 4, [tr, {ch 2, 2-tr cl} twice] in same ch sp, ch 1, sk next sc, tr in each of next 4 sc, ch 2, puff st in next tr, ch 2, tr in each of next 4 sc, ch 1, sk next sc **, [2-tr cl, {ch 2, 2-tr cl} twice] in next corner ch-1 sp, rep from * around, ending last rep at **, join in top of beg cl, fasten off.

Thread both yarn ends of set-aside puff st onto yarn needle and insert through center ring of square. Pull puff st firmly into place over center ring on RS, hold firmly in place while weaving 1 yarn tail 3 times around center ring on WS of square, going under bottom of lps of each long sc; then weave other yarn length in the opposite direction in same manner, catching a lp or 2 on underside of puff st

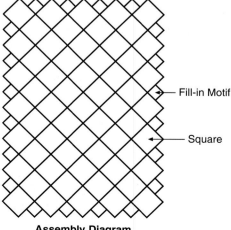

Fill-in Motif

Square

Assembly Diagram

through center opening. Secure ends and fasten off.

Rnd 5: Attach millennium in first ch-2 sp of any corner, ch 3, dc in same ch sp, *[2 dc, ch 2, 2 dc] in center 2-tr cl of corner, 2 dc in next corner ch-2 sp, dc in next 2-tr cl, dc in next ch-1 sp after 2-tr cl, dc in each of next 4 tr, dc dec, dc in each of next 4 tr, dc in ch-1 sp before next 2-tr cl, dc in next 2-tr cl **, 2 dc in next corner ch-2 sp, rep from * around, ending last rep at **, join in top of beg ch-3.

Rnd 6: Sl st in each of next 3 dc, sl st into corner ch-2 sp, ch 2, [2 hdc, ch 3, 3 hdc] in same ch sp, *ch 1, sk next 2 dc, [{2 hdc, ch 1, 2 hdc} in next dc, ch 1, sk next 3 dc] 4 times, [2 hdc, ch 1, 2 hdc] in next dc, ch 1, sk next 2 dc **, [3 hdc, ch 3, 3 hdc] in next corner ch-2 sp, rep from * around, ending last rep at **, join in top of beg ch-2, fasten off.

Second Square
Center puff stitch

Rep instructions for center puff stitch for first square.

Rnds 1–5: Rep Rnds 1–5 of first square.

Rnd 6: Sl st in each of next 3 dc, sl st in corner ch-2 sp, ch 2, 2 hdc in same sp, ch 1, with WS of squares tog, sl st in corresponding corner ch-2 sp on previous square, ch 1, 3 hdc in same corner ch-2 sp on working square, ch 1, sk next 2 dc, [2 hdc in next dc, sl st in corresponding ch-1 sp on previous square, 2 hdc in same dc on working square, ch 1, sk next 3 dc] 4 times, 2 hdc in next dc, sl st in corresponding ch-1 sp on previous square, 2 hdc in same dc on working square, ch 1, sk next 2 dc, 3 hdc in next corner ch-2 sp, ch 1, sl st in corresponding corner ch-2 sp on previous square, 3 hdc in same corner ch-2 sp on working square, complete rem of rnd the same as for first square.

Using diagram as a guide, make and join 57 more squares the same as 2nd square.

Note: When joining a corner to previously joined corners, work joining sl st into center of previous joining.

Fill-in Motif
Make 20

Rnd 1: Rep Rnd 1 of first square.

Note: Use diagram as a guide for motif placement.

Rnd 2: Attach millennium in any corner ch-3 sp, ch 2, hdc in same sp, ch 1, sl st in corner joining of squares on edge of afghan, ch 1, 2 hdc in same corner sp on motif, 2 hdc in next ch-1 sp on motif, sl st in ch-1 sp of corresponding shell on square, 2 hdc in same ch-1 sp on motif, 2 hdc in next corner ch-3 sp on motif, ch 1, sl st

Continued on page 40

Rustic Ripple

Design by Darla Fanton

Skill Level: Intermediate

Size: 42 x 72 inches

Materials

- ► Coats & Clark Red Heart Soft worsted weight yarn: 15 oz navy #7855, 14 oz each rust #7285, country blue #7883 and light wheat #7320
- ► Size K/10½ flexible double-ended crochet hook or size needed to obtain gauge
- ► Crochet hooks sizes K/10½ and N/15
- ► Tapestry needle

Create these warm and earthy country-inspired ripples to warm a loved one during the cold winter months.

Gauge

2 puff sts = 1 inch; 4 rows = 1 inch

Check gauge to save time.

Pattern Notes

Weave in loose ends as work progresses.

Due to multiple yarn-overs required, this project can only be done on a flexible hook.

Crochet hook size N is used only to get the foundation ch loose enough.

Crochet hook size K is used only for final edging of afghan.

Carry unused yarn along side edge, working over it before beg ch-1 in order to lock in place.

Afghan

Row 1: With hook size K and navy, ch 278 loosely, working through both lps of ch, draw up a lp in 2nd ch from hook, yo, draw up a lp in same ch, [sk next ch, draw up a lp in next ch, yo, draw up a lp in same ch] rep across. Slide all sts to opposite end of hook, turn. (418 lps on hook)

Row 2: To work lps off hook, place rust on hook with sl knot, working from left to right draw through first lp on hook, [ch 1, yo, draw through 4 lps] rep across until 1 lp is left on hook, do not turn.

Row 3: Working right to left, with rust, ch 1, sk first ch-1 sp, *[draw up a lp in next ch-1 sp, yo, draw up a lp in same sp] 5 times, draw up a lp in next ch-1 sp, yo, draw up a lp in same sp, [yo hook twice, draw up a lp in same sp] twice, [draw up a lp in next ch-1 sp, yo, draw up a lp in same sp] 5 times, sk next ch-1 sp, draw up a lp in next ch-1 sp, yo,

draw up a lp in same sp, sk next ch-1 sp, rep from * ending with draw up a lp in last ch-1 sp. Slide all sts to opposite end of hook, turn. (419 lps on hook)

Row 4: Place country blue on hook with a sl knot, draw through first lp, [ch 1, yo, draw through 4 lps on hook] rep across, ending with ch 1, yo, draw through last 2 lps, do not turn.

Row 5: With country blue, rep Row 3.

Row 6: With light wheat, rep Row 4.

Row 7: With light wheat, rep Row 3.

Row 8: Pick up navy, yo and draw through first lp, [ch 1, yo, draw through 4 lps] rep across, ending with ch 1, yo, draw through last 2 lps, do not turn.

Row 9: With navy, rep Row 3.

Row 10: With rust, rep Row 8.

Rows 11–264: Rep Rows 3–10, ending last rep after a Row 8.

Row 265: Bind off as follows: with navy and working right to left, ch 1, sk first ch-1 sp, *[draw up a lp in next ch-1 sp, yo, draw up a lp in same sp, yo and draw through all 4 lps on hook, ch 1] 11 times, sk next ch-1 sp, draw up a lp

in next ch-1 sp, yo, draw up a lp in same sp, yo and draw through all 4 lps on hook, ch 1, sk next ch-1 sp, rep from * across, ending with draw up a lp in last ch-1 sp, yo and draw through both lps on hook, transfer last navy lp to size K hook to work side edging, fasten off rem yarn colors.

Edging

Note: Edging is worked on each long edge of afghan only.

Row 1: Working across side edge of afghan, ch 1, hdc evenly sp across edge, sl st in foundation ch, fasten off.

Row 2: Attach navy with sl st in opposite end of foundation ch, ch 1, hdc evenly sp across edge, sl st in end st of last row of afghan, fasten off. ✄

Blue Skies, Spring Flowers

Design by Anne Halliday

Skill Level: Beginner

Size: 46 x 66 inches

Materials

► Coats & Clark Red Heart TLC worsted weight yarn: 30 oz medium blue #5823 (MC), 10 oz each butterscotch #5263 (A) and natural #5017 (B)

► Size I/9 crochet hook or size needed to obtain gauge

► Yarn needle

Gauge

Large square = 6½ inches; small square = 3¼ inches

Check gauge to save time.

Pattern Notes

Weave in loose ends as work progresses.

Join each rnd with a sl st unless otherwise stated.

Ch-3 counts as first dc throughout.

Small Square A

Make 116

Rnd 1 (RS): With A, ch 4, 2 dc in 4th ch from hook, ch 3, [3 dc in same ch, ch 3] 3 times, join in top of beg ch-4, fasten off. (4 corner ch-3 sps)

Rnd 2 (RS): Attach MC in corner ch-3 sp, [ch 3, 2 dc, ch 3, 3 dc] in same corner ch-3 sp, ch 1, [{3 dc, ch 3, 3 dc} in next ch-3 sp, ch 1] rep around, join in top of beg ch-3, fasten off. (24 dc; 4 ch-1 sps; 4 corner ch-3 sps)

Small Square B

Make 35

Rnd 1: With B, rep Rnd 1 of small square A.

Rnd 2: Rep Rnd 2 of small square A.

Large Square

Make 24

Rnd 1 (RS): Rep Rnd 1 of small square A.

Rnd 2 (RS): Attach MC in any corner ch-3 sp, [ch 3, 2 dc, ch 1, 3 dc] in same ch-3 sp, ch 5, [{3 dc, ch 1, 3 dc} in next corner ch-3 sp, ch 5] rep around, join in top of beg ch-3, fasten off.

Rnd 3 (RS): Attach B in corner ch-1 sp, ch 1, sc in same corner ch-1 sp, *ch 2, [ch 3, 2 dc, ch 3, 3 dc] in next ch-5 sp, ch 2 **, sc in next corner ch-1 sp, rep from * around, ending last rep at **, join in top of beg sc.

Rnd 4 (RS): Sl st into next ch-2 sp, ch 3, 2 dc in same ch-2 sp, ch 1, *[3 dc, ch 3, 3 dc] in next corner ch-3 sp, ch 1 **, [3 dc in next ch-2 sp, ch 1] twice, rep from * around, ending last rep at **, 3 dc in next ch-2 sp, ch 1, join in top of beg ch-3, fasten off.

Rnd 5 (RS): Attach MC in corner ch-3 sp, [ch 3, 2 dc, ch 3, 3 dc] in same ch-3 sp, *ch 1, [3 dc in next ch-1 sp, ch 1] 3 times **, [3 dc, ch 3, 3 dc] in next corner ch-3 sp, rep from * around, ending last rep at **, join in top of beg ch-3, fasten off. (60 dc; 4 corner ch-3 sps; 16 ch-1 sps)

Assembly

Using diagram as a guide, working through both lps of sts, sew squares tog.

Edging

Rnd 1 (RS): Attach MC in any corner ch-3 sp, ch 1, *[sc, ch 2, sc] in corner ch-3 sp, ch 1, sk next dc, sc in next dc, ch 1, sc in next ch-1 sp, ch 1, sk next dc, sc in next dc, ch 1, [{sc in next ch sp, ch 1} twice, sk next dc, sc in next dc, ch 1, sc in next ch-1 sp, ch 1, sk next dc, sc in next dc, ch 1] rep across to next corner ch-3 sp, rep from * around entire outer edge of afghan, join in beg sc.

Rnd 2: Sl st into corner ch-2 sp, ch 1, *[sc, ch 3, sc] in corner ch-2 sp, ch 1, [sc in next ch-1 sp, ch 1] rep across to next corner ch-2 sp, rep from * around, join in beg sc.

Rnd 3: Sl st into corner ch-3 sp, [ch 3, 2 dc, ch 3, 3 dc] in same corner ch-3 sp, *ch 1, sk next ch-1 sp, [3 dc in next ch-1 sp, ch 1, sk next ch-1 sp] rep across to next corner ch-3 sp **, [3 dc, ch 3, 3 dc], rep from * around, ending last rep at **, omit last ch-1 and replace with sc in top of beg ch-3 to position hook to start following rnd.

Rnd 4: Ch 1, sc in same sp over last joining sc of previous rnd, sk next dc, [dc, ch 2, dc] in next dc, sk next dc, *[sc, dc, ch 2, dc, sc] in next corner ch-3 sp, sk next dc, [dc, ch 2, dc] in next dc, sk next dc, [sc in next ch-1 sp, sk next dc, {dc, ch 2, dc} in next dc, sk next dc] rep across to next corner ch-3 sp, rep from * around, join in beg sc, fasten off. ✂

Assembly Diagram

Bring the beauty of spring indoors with this cheery afghan stitched in shades of blue and yellow and reminiscent of spring flowers against a brilliant blue sky.

Aran Squares

Design by Angela Tate

Skill Level: Beginner

Size: 51 x 72 inches, excluding fringe

Materials

▶ Coats & Clark Red Heart Super Saver worsted weight yarn: 64 oz Aran #313

▶ Size J/10 crochet hook or size needed to obtain gauge

▶ Tapestry needle

Squares of ribbing with popcorn accents create a wonderfully warm, beautiful afghan!

Gauge

Motif = 9 inches square; Rnds 1 and 2 of motif or 13 dc = 4 inches

Check gauge to save time.

Pattern Notes

Weave in loose ends as work progresses.

Join each rnd with a sl st unless otherwise stated.

Ch-3 counts as first dc throughout.

Pattern Stitch

Popcorn (pc): 5 dc in indicated st, draw up a lp, remove hook, insert hook in first dc of 5-dc group, pick up dropped lp and draw through st on hook, ch 1 to lock.

Motif

Make 35

Rnd 1 (RS): Ch 10, sl st to join to form a ring, ch 3, 19 dc in ring, join in top of beg ch-3. (20 dc)

Rnd 2: Ch 3, dc in same st, 2 dc in next st, pc in next st, [2 dc in each of next 2 sts, ch 3 (for corner), 2 dc in each of next 2 sts, pc in next st] 3 times, 2 dc in each of next 2 sts, ch 3, join in top of beg ch-3. (32 dc; 4 pc; 4 ch-3 corner sps)

Rnd 3: Ch 3, dc in each dc and each pc around, working [3 dc, ch 3, 3 dc] in each corner ch-3 sp, join in top of beg ch-3. (60 dc)

Rnd 4: Ch 3, fpdc around next dc, [bpdc around next dc, fpdc around next dc] 5 times, *5 sc in next corner ch-3 sp **, fpdc around next dc, [bpdc around next dc, fpdc around next dc] 7 times, rep from * around, ending last rep at **, fpdc around next dc, bpdc around next dc, fpdc around next dc, join in top of beg ch-3. (80 sts)

Rnd 5: Ch 3, fpdc around next st, [bpdc around next st, fpdc around next st] 5 times, *sc in each of next 2 sc, 3 sc in next sc, sc in each of next 2 sc **, fpdc around next st, [bpdc around next st, fpdc around next st] 7 times, rep from * around, ending last rep at **, fpdc around next st, bpdc around next st, fpdc around next st, join in top of beg ch-3. (88 sts)

Rnd 6: Ch 3, fpdc around next st, [bpdc around next st, fpdc around next st] 5 times, *sc in each of next 3 sc, 3 sc in next sc, sc in each of next 3 sc **, fpdc around next st, [bpdc around next st, fpdc around next st] 7 times, rep from * around, ending last rep at **, fpdc around next st, bpdc around next st, fpdc around next st, join in top of beg ch-3. (96 sts)

Rnd 7: Ch 3, dc in each st around, working [3 dc, ch 3, 3 dc] in 5th sc of each corner 9-sc group, join in top of beg ch-3, fasten off. (116 dc)

Assembly

With RS facing, working in back lps only, using tapestry needle and yarn, whipstitch motifs tog in 5 rows of 7 motifs each.

Border

Rnd 1 (RS): Attach yarn with a sl st in first dc after corner of afghan, ch 3, dc in each dc around, working 3 dc in corner ch-3 sp of each motif and 5 sc at each corner of afghan, join in top of beg ch-3.

Rnd 2: Ch 3, [{fpdc around next st, bpdc around next st} rep across to next corner sc sts, sc in each of next 2 sc, 3 sc in next sc, sc in each of next 2 sc] rep around, join in top of beg ch-3.

Rnd 3: Ch 3, [{fpdc around next st, bpdc around next st} rep across to next corner sc sts, sc in each of next 3 sc, 3 sc in next sc, sc in each of next 3 sc] rep around, join in top of beg ch-3.

Rnd 4: Ch 3, [{fpdc around next st, bpdc around next st} rep across to next corner sc sts, sc in each of next 4 sc, 3 sc in next sc, sc in each of next 4 sc] rep around, join in top of beg ch-3.

Rnd 5: Ch 1, sc in each st around entire outer edge, working 3 sc in 6th sc of each corner 11-sc group, join in beg sc, fasten off.

Fringe

Cut 2 (8-inch) strands of yarn; fold strands in half. Insert hook in first sc and draw fold of yarn through sc st on hook; draw cut ends through lp on hook and pull ends to secure to complete a lark's head knot. Rep in every other sc st around entire outer edge of afghan. Trim ends evenly. ✄

Easy Ombre Afghan

Design by Margret Willson

Skill Level: Beginner

Size: 42 x 58 inches, excluding fringe

Materials

▶ Coats & Clark Red Heart Super Saver worsted weight yarn: 30 oz sage mary #997, 14 oz dark plum #533

▶ Size H/8 crochet hook or size needed to obtain gauge

▶ Yarn needle

Gauge

Rows 2–10 = 4 inches; 11 dc = 3 inches

Check gauge to save time.

Pattern Notes

Weave in loose ends as work progresses.

Ch-3 counts as first dc throughout.

Warm up on those cold winter nights with this cozy afghan. Deep, rich colors are sure to soothe body and spirit!

Afghan

Row 1: With dark plum, ch 216, dc in 4th ch from hook, dc in each rem ch across, changing to sage mary yarn in last yo of last dc st, turn. (214 dc)

Row 2: Ch 1, sc in first dc, [ch 2, sk next 2 dc, sc in next dc] rep across, turn. (72 sc; 71 ch-2 sps)

Row 3: Ch 3, dc in first sc, [3 dc in next sc] rep across to last sc, 2 dc in last sc, turn. (214 dc)

Row 4: Ch 1, sc in first dc, ch 2, [sc in center dc of next 3-dc group, ch 2] rep across, ending with sc in last dc, turn.

Rows 5–9: Rep Rows 3 and 4 changing to dark plum at end of Row 9, turn.

Row 10: Ch 3, [2 dc in next ch-2 sp, dc in next sc] rep across, changing to sage mary in last yo of last dc, turn.

[Rep Rows 2–10] 9 times. At the end of last rep, fasten off.

Border

Note: Border is worked across short sides of afghan only.

Working around ends of rows, attach dark plum in first row, ch 3, 2 dc in same row, ch 1, [2 dc around end of next row, ch 1] rep across, ending with 3 dc in last row, fasten off.

Fringe

Note: Fringe is attached in each ch-1 sp of border.

Cut 18-inch strands of dark plum yarn. [Fold 6 strands of dark plum yarn in half, insert hook in ch-1 sp, draw strands through at fold to form a lp on hook, draw cut ends through lp on hook, pull to secure] rep across each side of border. Trim ends evenly. ✂

Bounteous Blue

Design by Christine Grazioso

Skill Level: Intermediate

Size: 43 x 57 inches

Materials

► Coats & Clark Red Heart Super Saver worsted weight yarn: 41 oz country blue #382

► Size I/9 crochet hook or size needed to obtain gauge

► Yarn needle

Add warmth and country charm to your home decor in just a weekend with this beautiful afghan stitched in country blue!

Gauge

Rows 1–5 = 2½ inches; finished panel = 3¾ inches wide

Check gauge to save time.

Pattern Note

Weave in loose ends as work progresses.

Pattern Stitches

Sc cl: [Insert hook in indicated st, yo, draw up a lp, yo, draw through 1 lp on hook] 3 times in next st, yo, draw through all 4 lps on hook.

Bptr tog: Yo hook twice, insert hook around post of 2nd sc, yo, draw up a lp, [yo, draw through 2 lps on hook] twice, 2 lps rem on hook, sk next sc, sk next sc cl, sk next sc, yo hook twice, insert hook around post of next sc, yo, draw up a lp, [yo, draw through 2 lps on hook] twice, yo, draw through rem 3 lps on hook. *Note: In Row 5, bptr tog are worked around bptr tog of Row 3.*

Afghan Panels

Make 12

Row 1: Ch 164 loosely, sc in 2nd ch from hook, sc in each of next 2 chs, [sc cl in next ch, sc in each of next 3 chs] rep across, turn. (40 sc cls)

Row 2: Ch 3, dc in each st across, turn.

Note: Mark Row 2 as RS and bottom edge.

Row 3: Ch 1, sc in next dc, sc cl in next dc, sc in next dc, [bptr tog, sk next dc, sc in next dc, sc cl in next dc, sc in next dc] rep across, turn.

Row 4: Ch 3, dc in each st across, turn.

Row 5: Ch 1, sc in next dc, bptr around bptr tog 2 rows down, sk next dc, sc in next dc, sc cl in next dc, sc in next dc, [work bptr tog, sk next dc, sc in next dc, sc cl in next dc, sc in next dc] rep across, ending with bptr around bptr tog 2 rows down, sk next dc, sc in last dc, turn.

Panel Border

Rnd 1: Ch 3, 2 dc in same st, dc in each rem st across, 3 dc in last sc, 3 dc in dc of Row 4, 2 dc in sc of Row 3, 3 dc in dc of Row 2, 3 dc in beg ch of Row 1, dc in each free lp across, 3 dc in beg ch, 3 dc in dc of Row 2, 2 dc in sc of Row 3, 3 dc in dc of Row 4, sl st to join in top of beg ch-3, fasten off.

Assembly

With WS and bottom edges tog, whipstitch from bottom edge to top edge. Rep joining panels in same manner until all 12 panels are joined.

Border

Attach yarn with sl st in any dc, ch 1, sc in same st as beg ch-1, sc in each dc around, working sc dec over each joining, join in beg sc, fasten off. ✄

Double Aran

Design by Angela Tate

Skill Level: Beginner

Size: 48 x 63 inches, excluding tassels

Materials

► Coats & Clark Red Heart Super Saver worsted weight yarn: 64 oz Aran #313

► Size N/15 crochet hook or size needed to obtain gauge

► Tapestry needle

Alternating bands of two deeply textured ribbings create a beautiful afghan. Two strands of yarn add extra body, but you can finish it fast!

Gauge

Rows 1–9 = 5 inches; 11 dc = 5 inches

Check gauge to save time.

Pattern Notes

Weave in loose ends as work progresses.

Afghan is worked holding 2 strands of yarn tog throughout.

Ch-3 counts as first dc throughout.

Afghan

Row 1 (RS): Ch 102 loosely, dc in 4th ch from hook, dc in each rem ch across, turn. (100 dc)

Row 2: Working in back lps for this row only, ch 1, sl st in each dc across, turn.

Row 3: Working in rem front lps of 2nd row below, ch 3, dc in each st across, turn.

Rows 4–9: Rep Rows 2 and 3.

Row 10: Ch 3, dc in each st across, turn.

Row 11: Ch 3, [fpdc around next st, bpdc around next st] rep across, turn.

Rows 12–14: Ch 3, [fpdc around each fpdc, bpdc around each bpdc] rep across, turn.

Row 15: Rep Row 10.

Rows 16–99: [Rep Rows 2–15] 6 times.

Rows 100–107: Rep Rows 2–9, at the end of Row 107, fasten off.

Tassels

Note: Attach tassels with a lark's head knot, beg 3 inches from corner and rep every 3 inches around outer edge.

Cut 10 (8-inch) strands of yarn; holding strands tog, fold in half. Insert hook in edge of afghan and draw fold through to form a lp on hook; draw cut ends of strands through lp on hook and gently pull ends to secure (lark's head knot). Trim ends evenly. ✄

Hearts & Flowers Delight

Design by Carol Alexander
for Crochet Trends and Traditions

Skill Level: Intermediate

Size: 55 x 66 inches

Materials

▶ Coats & Clark Red Heart Super Saver worsted weight yarn (8 oz per skein): 4 skeins soft white #316, 2 skeins each rose pink #372 and medium sage #632, 1 skein each country rose #374 and dark sage #633

▶ Size G/6 crochet hook or size needed to obtain gauge

▶ Yarn needle

Gauge

Flower motif = 3 inches; heart motif = 3½ x 4 inches; square = 11 inches

Check gauge to save time.

Pattern Notes

Weave in loose ends as work progresses.

Join each rnd with a sl st unless otherwise stated.

Pattern Stitches

Sc p: Ch 2, sc around top of post of last tr made.

Beg tr shell: Ch 5 (counts as first tr, ch-1), [tr, ch 1] 5 times in same st as beg ch-5.

Tr shell: [Tr, ch 1] 6 times in indicated st.

Dc shell: [Dc, ch 1] 4 times in indicated st.

Puff st: [Yo, insert hook in indicated st, yo, draw up a lp] 3 times, yo, draw through all 7 lps on hook.

First Square
Flower

Rnd 1: With country rose, ch 5, sl st to join to form a ring, ch 1, work 16 sc in ring, join in front lp only of beg sc. (16 sc)

Rnd 2: Working in front lps for this rnd only, ch 3, sk next st, [sl st in next st, ch 3, sk next st] 8 times, ending with last sl st in same st as beg ch-3.

Rnd 3: Sl st into ch-3 sp, [ch 2, {dc, tr, dc} in same ch-3 sp, ch 2, sl st in next ch-3 sp] rep around, ending with sl st between last and first petals. (8 petals)

Rnd 4: Ch 1, sl st to lower center back of first petal,

ch 3, [sl st to lower center back of next petal, ch 3] 7 times, join in base of beg ch-3, fasten off.

Leaves

Attach dark sage in any ch-3 sp of Rnd 4, *ch 3, [2 tr, sc p, tr, ch 3, sl st] in same ch-3 sp, fasten off to complete first leaf. [Sk next ch-3 sp of Rnd 4, attach dark sage in next ch-3 sp, rep from * of first leaf, fasten off] 3 times. (4 leaves)

First heart motif

Rnd 1: With rose pink, ch 12 loosely, sc in 2nd ch from hook, sc in each of next 3 chs, draw up a lp in each of next 3 chs, yo, draw through all 4 lps on hook, sc in each of next 3 chs, 3 sc in last ch, working on opposite side of foundation ch, sc in next 4 chs, 3 sc in next ch (bottom tip of heart), sc in each of next 4 chs, 2 sc in last ch, join in beg sc. (24 sc)

Rnd 2: Ch 1, sc in same st as beg ch, 2 dc in each of next 2 sts, dc in next st, draw up a lp in each of next 2 sts at top center of heart, yo, draw through all 3 lps on hook, dc in next st, 2 dc in each of next 2 sts, sc in next st.

Rnd 3: Continuing from last sc of Rnd 2, ch 1, [sc, ch 1] in each of next 14 sc, [sc, ch 1] in first sc at top right corner of heart and in next dc, [hdc, ch 1] in each of next 3 dc, draw up a lp in each of next 3 sts, yo, draw through all 4 lps on hook,

ch 1 (center between lobes), [hdc, ch 1] in each of next 3 dc, [sc, ch 1] in next dc, sl st in next sc, fasten off.

Rnd 4: Working in back lps for this rnd only, attach soft white at center dec at top of heart between lobes, [ch 3, sk next 2 sts, sc in next st] twice, [ch 3, sk next st, sc in next st] 3 times, [ch 3, sk next 2 sts, sc in next st] 4 times, ch 1, with WS of flower facing, sl st in any unused ch-3 sp of Rnd 4 on back of flower, ch 1, sk next st at center bottom of heart, sc in next st, [ch 3, sk next 2 sts, sc in next st] 4 times, [ch 3, sk next st, sc in next st] 3 times, ch 3, sk next 2 sts, sc in next st, ch 3, sk last 2 sts, sl st in base of beg ch-3, fasten off.

Second heart motif

Rnds 1–3: Rep Rnds 1–3 of first heart motif.

Rnd 4: Working in back lps for this rnd only, attach soft white in center st at top of heart between lobes, [ch 3, sk next 2 sts, sc in next st] twice, [ch 3, sk next st, sc in next st] 3 times, [ch 1, sl st in corresponding ch-3 sp on right edge of previous heart motif, ch 1, sk 2 sts, sc in next st] 3 times, ch 3, sk next 2 sts, sc in next st, ch 1, sl st in next free ch-3 sp of Rnd 4 on back of flower, ch 1, sk next st at bottom corner of heart, sc in next st *, [ch 3, sk next 2 sts, sc in next st] 4 times, [ch 3, sk

Continued on page 41

Visions of Autumn

Design by Anne Halliday

Skill Level: Beginner

Size: 56 x 70 inches

Materials

► Coats & Clark Red Heart Fiesta worsted weight yarn: 7 skeins soft white #6316 (MC)

► Coats & Clark Red Heart Super Saver worsted weight yarn: 12 oz each burgundy #376 (A) and gold #321 (B)

► Size I/9 crochet hook or size needed to obtain gauge

► 2 safety pins

► Yarn needle

Create this granny-square afghan in burgundy and gold colors as shown, or select coordinating colors to match your favorite chair or sofa!

Gauge

Square = 7¼ inches
Check gauge to save time.

Pattern Notes

Weave in loose ends as work progresses.

Join each rnd with a sl st unless otherwise stated.

Ch-3 counts as first dc throughout.

Make a total of 63 squares: 32 squares with A and 31 squares with B as indicated.

Granny Square

Rnd 1 (RS): With A (B), ch 4, 2 dc in 4th ch from hook, ch 3, [3 dc in same ch, ch 3] 3 times, join in top of beg ch-4, fasten off. (4 corner ch-3 sps)

Rnd 2: Attach MC in any corner ch-3 sp, [ch 3, 2 dc, ch 3, 3 dc] in same ch-3 sp, ch 1, [{3 dc, ch 3, 3 dc} in next ch-3 sp, ch 1] rep around, join in top of beg ch-3. (24 dc; 4 corner ch-3 sps; 4 ch-1 sps)

Rnd 3 (RS): Ch 1, sk joining dc, [sc in next dc, ch 1, {sc, ch 2, sc} in next corner ch-3 sp, ch 1, sk next dc, sc in next dc, ch 1, sc in next ch-1 sp, ch 1, sk next dc] rep around, join in beg sc, turn.

Rnd 4 (WS): Ch 1, sk joining sc, [sc in next ch-1 sp, ch 1] 3 times, [sc, ch 2, sc] in corner ch-2 sp, ch 1, *[sc in next ch-1 sp, ch 1] 4 times, [sc, ch 2, sc] in next corner ch-2 sp, ch 1, rep from * twice, sc in next ch-1 sp, ch 1, join in beg sc, drop MC, secure lp on hook with safety pin on WS of square, turn.

Rnd 5 (RS): Attach A (B), in ch-1 sp to the right of any corner ch-2 sp, ch 1, sc in same ch-1 sp, ch 1, [sc, ch 2, sc] in next corner ch-2 sp, ch 1, *[sc in next ch-1 sp, ch 1] 5 times, [sc, ch 2, sc] in next ch-2 sp, ch 1, rep from * twice, [sc in next ch-1 sp, ch 1] 4 times, join in beg sc, drop A (B), secure lp on hook with safety pin on WS of square, turn.

Rnd 6 (WS): Remove safety pin from MC lp, insert hook in lp, ch 2, sc in ch-1 sp behind ch-2 just made, ch 1, [sc in next ch-1 sp, ch 1] 3 times, [sc, ch 3, sc] in next corner ch-2 sp, ch 1, *[sc in next ch-1 sp, ch 1] 6 times, [sc, ch 3, sc] in next corner ch-2 sp, ch 1, rep from * twice, [sc in next ch-1 sp, ch 1] twice, join in beg sc, fasten off, turn.

Rnd 7 (RS): Remove safety pin from A (B) lp, insert hook in 2nd ch-1 sp from corner ch-3 sp, [ch 3, 2 dc] in same ch-1 sp, ch 1, sk next ch-1 sp, [3 dc, ch 3, 3 dc] in next corner ch-3 sp, ch 1, sk next ch-1 sp, *[3 dc in next ch-1 sp, ch 1, sk next ch-1 sp] 3 times, [3 dc, ch 3, 3 dc] in next corner ch-3 sp, ch 1, sk next ch-1 sp, rep from * twice, [3 dc in next ch-1 sp, ch 1, sk next ch-1 sp] twice, join in top of beg ch-3, fasten off. (60 dc; 16 ch-1 sps; 4 corner ch-3 sps)

Rnd 8 (RS): Attach MC in corner ch-3 sp, [ch 3, 2 dc, ch 3, 3 dc] in same corner ch-3 sp, ch 1, *[3 dc in next ch-1 sp, ch 1] 4 times **, [3 dc, ch 3, 3 dc in next ch-3 corner sp, ch 1, rep from * around, ending last rep at **, join in top of beg ch-3, fasten off. (72 dc; 20 ch-1 sps; 4 ch-3 sps)

Assembly

With MC, beg in top left corner with an A square and alternating A and B squares, whipstitch tog in 9 rows of 7 squares each.

Edging

Rnd 1 (RS): Attach MC in any corner ch-3 sp, ch 1, *[sc, ch 3, sc] in corner ch-3 sp, ch 1, sk next dc, sc in next dc, ch 1, [sc in next ch-1 sp, ch 1, sk next dc, sc in next dc, ch 1] 5 times, [{sc in next ch sp, ch 1} twice, sk next dc, sc in next dc, ch 1, {sc in next ch-1 sp, ch 1, sk next dc, sc in next dc, ch 1} 5 times] rep across to next corner ch-3 sp, rep from * around, join in beg sc, turn.

Rnd 2 (WS): Ch 1, sk joining sc, *[sc in next ch-1 sp, ch 1] rep across to corner ch-2 sp, [sc, ch 2, sc] in corner ch-2 sp, ch 1, rep from * around, join in beg sc, fasten off, turn.

Rnd 3 (RS): Attach B in any corner ch-2 sp, ch 1, *[sc, ch 2, sc] in corner ch-2

sp, [sc in next ch-1 sp, ch 1] rep across to next corner ch-2 sp, rep from * around, join in beg sc, fasten off, turn.

Rnd 4: (WS): Attach MC in any corner ch-2 sp, ch 1, *[sc, ch 3, sc] in corner ch-2 sp, [sc in next ch-1 sp, ch 1] rep across to corner ch-2 sp, rep from * around, join in beg sc, fasten off, turn.

Rnd 5 (RS): Attach B in any corner ch-3 sp, [ch 3, 2 dc, ch 3, 3 dc] in same corner ch-3 sp, *ch 1, sk next ch-1 sp, [3 dc in next ch-1 sp, ch 1, sk next ch-1 sp] rep across to next corner ch-3 sp **, [3 dc, ch 3, 3 dc] in next corner ch-3 sp, rep from * around, ending last rep at **, join in

top of beg ch-3, fasten off.

Rnd 6 (RS): Attach MC in any corner ch-3 sp, ch 6 (counts as first dc, ch 3), 3 dc in same ch-3 sp, ch 1, *[3 dc in next ch-1 sp, ch 1] rep across to next corner ch-3 sp **, [3 dc, ch 3, 3 dc] in next corner ch-3 sp, rep from * around, ending last rep at **, 2 dc in same

ch-3 sp as beg ch-6, join in 3rd ch of beg ch-6.

Rnd 7 (RS): Ch 1, *[sc, dc, ch 2, dc, sc] in corner ch-3 sp, sk next dc, [dc, ch 2, dc] in next dc, [sc in next ch-1 sp, sk next dc, {dc, ch 2, dc} in next dc] rep across to next corner ch-3 sp, rep from * around, join in beg sc, fasten off. ✂

Spiraling Bars & Squares

Design by Anne Halliday

Skill Level: Beginner

Size: 53 x 73 inches

Materials

▶ Coats & Clark Red Heart Classic worsted weight yarn: 24½ oz white #1, 10½ oz each pink #737 and grenadine #730, 7 oz soft navy #853

▶ Size I/9 crochet hook or size needed to obtain gauge

▶ Yarn needle

Gauge

Square = 3¼ inches; bar = 3¼ x 6½ inches; block = 9¾ inches

Check gauge to save time.

Pattern Notes

Weave in loose ends as work progresses.

Join rnds with a sl st unless otherwise stated.

Ch-3 counts as first dc throughout.

Pattern Stitches

3-dc cl: [Yo hook, insert hook in indicated st, yo, draw up a lp, yo, draw through 2 lps on hook] 3 times, yo, draw through all 4 lps on hook.

Beg 3-dc cl: Ch 2, [yo, insert hook in next dc, yo, draw up a lp, yo, draw through 2 lps on hook] twice, yo, draw through all 3 lps on hook.

P: Ch 3, yo, insert hook in 3rd ch from hook, yo, draw up a lp, yo, draw through 2 lps on hook, yo, insert hook in same ch, yo, draw up a lp, yo, draw through 2 lps on hook, yo, draw through all 3 lps on hook.

Square C

Make 35

Rnd 1 (RS): With soft navy, ch 4, 2 dc in 4th ch from hook, ch 1, [3 dc in same ch, ch 3] 3 times, join in top of beg ch-4, fasten off. (4 corner ch-3 sps)

Rnd 2 (RS): Attach white in any corner ch-3 sp, [ch 3, 2 dc, ch 3, 3 dc] in same ch-3 sp, ch 1, [{3 dc, ch 3, 3 dc} in next ch-3 sp, ch 1] rep around, join in top of beg ch-3, fasten off. (24 dc; 4 corner ch-3 sp, 4 ch-1 sps)

Bar A

Make 70

Rnd 1 (RS): With soft navy, ch 15, dc in 5th ch from hook (4 skipped chs count as first ch-4 sp), dc in each of next 2 chs, [ch 1, sk next ch, dc in each of next 3 chs] twice, ch 4, sl st in same ch as last dc, fasten off. (9 dc; 4 ch-1 sps; 2 ch-4 sps)

Rnd 2 (RS): Attach pink in ch-4 sp at end, [ch 3, 2 dc, {ch 3, 3 dc} twice] in same ch-4 sp, ch 1, [3 dc in next ch-1 sp, ch 1] twice, [3 dc, {ch 3, 3 dc} twice] in next ch-4 sp, ch 1, [3 dc in next ch-1 sp, ch 1] twice, join in top of beg ch-3, fasten off. (30 dc; 4 ch-3 sps; 6 ch-1 sps)

Rnd 3 (RS): Holding bar vertically, attach white in corner ch-3 sp at top right corner, [ch 3, 2 dc, ch 3, 3 dc] in same ch-3 sp, *ch 1, [3 dc, ch 3, 3 dc] in next ch-3 sp, ch 1, [3 dc in next ch-1 sp, ch 1] 3 times *, [3 dc, ch 3, 3 dc] in next corner ch-3 sp, rep from * to *, join in top of beg ch-3, fasten off. (42 dc; 4 ch-3 sps; 10 ch-1 sps)

Bar B

Make 70

Rnd 1: With soft navy, rep Rnd 1 of bar A.

Rnd 2: With grenadine, rep Rnd 2 of bar A.

Rnd 3: With white, rep Rnd 3 of bar A.

Assembly

Using diagram as a guide,

Assembly Diagram

with MC, matching sts and sewing through both lps of each st, sew bars and squares tog to form 35 blocks.

Sew blocks tog in 7 rows of 5 blocks each.

Edging

Rnd 1 (RS): Attach white in any corner ch-3 sp, ch 1, *[sc, ch 3, sc] in corner ch-3 sp, ch 1, sk next dc, sc in next dc, ch 1, [sc in next ch-1 sp, ch 1, sk next dc, sc in next dc, ch 1] 4 times, [sc in next ch sp, ch 1] twice, sk next dc, sc in next dc, ch 1, sc in next ch-1 sp, ch 1, sk next dc, sc in next dc, ch 1, [{sc in next ch sp, ch 1} twice, sk next dc, sc in next dc, ch 1, {sc in next ch-1 sp, ch 1, sk next dc, sc in next dc, ch 1} 4 times, {sc in next ch sp, ch 1} twice, sk next dc, sc in next dc, ch 1, sc in next ch-1 sp, ch 1, sk next dc, sc in next dc, ch 1] rep across to next corner ch-3 sp, rep from * around, join in beg sc.

Rnds 2 & 3: Ch 1, *[sc, ch 3, sc] in corner ch-3 sp, ch 1, [sc in next ch-1 sp, ch 1] rep across to next corner ch-3 sp, rep from * around, join in beg sc.

Rnd 4: Sl st into corner ch-3 sp, [ch 3, 2 dc, ch 3, 3 dc] in same corner ch-3 sp, *ch 1, sk next ch-1 sp, [3 dc in next ch-1 sp, ch 1, sk next ch-1 sp] rep across to next corner ch-3 sp **, [3 dc, ch 3, 3 dc] in next ch-3 corner sp, rep from * around, ending last rep at **, join in top of beg ch-3.

Rnd 5: Beg 3-dc cl over next 3 dc sts, p, [dc, p, dc] in next corner ch-3 sp, *p, [3-dc cl over next 3 dc, p] rep across to next corner ch-3 sp, [dc, p, dc] in next ch-3 sp, rep from * twice, work p, [3-dc cl over next 3 dc, p] rep from * twice, p, [3-dc cl over next 3 dc, p] rep across to beg cl, join in top of beg cl, fasten off. ✂

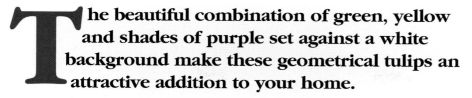

Tulip Garden

The beautiful combination of green, yellow and shades of purple set against a white background make these geometrical tulips an attractive addition to your home.

Design by Martha Stein

Skill Level: Beginner

Size: 58 x 78 inches

Materials

▶ Coats & Clark Red Heart Classic and Super Saver worsted weight yarn: 43 oz white #311, 9 oz grass green #687, 7 oz purple #596, 6 oz lavender #584, 1½ oz yellow #230

▶ Size I/9 crochet hook or size needed to obtain gauge

▶ Yarn needle

Gauge

Square = 2¾ inches
Check gauge to save time.

Pattern Notes

Weave in loose ends as work progresses.

Join each rnd with a sl st unless otherwise stated.

Ch-2 counts as first dc throughout.

Granny Square

Note: Make solid-colored granny squares of 271 white, 48 lavender, 24 each purple and grass green, and 12 yellow.

Rnd 1 (RS): Ch 4, sl st to join to form a ring, ch 2, 2 dc in ring, [ch 2, 3 dc in ring] 3 times, hdc in top of beg ch-2 to position hook in corner to start following rnd.

Rnd 2: Ch 2, 2 dc in corner sp, *ch 1, [3 dc, ch 2, 3 dc] in next corner ch-2 sp, rep from * twice, ch 1, 3 dc in same beg corner sp, ch 2, join in top of beg ch-2, leaving an 8-inch length of yarn, fasten off.

Two-Color Granny Square

Note: Make 2-color granny squares of 24 white/purple, 48 white/grass green and 24 grass green/purple.

Rnd 1: With lighter color, ch 4, sl st to join to form a ring, ch 3, sl st in 2nd ch from hook holding lp made to right of chs, work [2 dc, ch 2, 3 dc] in ring, leaving a 3-inch length, fasten off, pick up darker color and leaving a 3-inch length at beg, sl st, ch 1, [3 dc, ch 2, 3 dc] in ring, sl st to join in top of beg ch-3, fasten off. Tie ends of color changes tog in square knot.

Rnd 2: In last corner joined, pick up lighter color with sl st, ch 3, sl st in 2nd ch from hook, work 2 dc in same corner sp, ch 1, [3 dc, ch 2, 3 dc] in next corner, ch 1, 3 dc in next corner, leaving a 3-inch length, fasten off, pick up darker color, leaving a 3-inch length at beg, sl st, ch 1, 3 dc in same corner sp, ch 1, [3 dc, ch 2, 3 dc] in next corner sp, ch 1, 3 dc in beg corner sp, join in side lp of beg ch-3, leaving an 8-inch length of yarn, fasten off. Tie ends of color change tog in a square knot.

Assembly

Following assembly diagram, with RS tog and working through back lps only whipstitch squares tog.

Border

Rnd 1 (RS): Working in back lps for this rnd only, attach white with sl st in back lp of 2nd ch of any corner ch-2 sp, ch 1, sc in same st, *[sc in each of next 3 dc, sc in ch sp, sc in each of next 3 dc, sc in ch sp, sk joining sts, sc in ch sp of next square] rep across to next corner ch-2 sp, working in corner ch-2 sp, sc in first ch **, ch 2, sc in 2nd ch, rep from * around, ending last rep at **, hdc in beg sc.

Rnd 2: Ch 1, sc in corner sp, ch 1, *[sk next sc, sc in next sc, ch 1] rep across to next corner ch-2 sp **, work [sc, ch 2, sc] in corner ch-2 sp, ch 1, rep from * around, ending last rep at **, sc in same corner sp as beg sc, ch 2, join in beg sc, fasten off.

Rnd 3: Attach grass green in any corner ch-2 sp, ch 1, sc in same corner sp, ch 1, *[sc in next ch sp, ch 1] rep across to corner ch-2 sp **, [sc, ch 2, sc] in corner ch-2 sp, ch 1, rep from * around, ending last rep at **, sc in same beg corner ch-2 sp, ch 2, join in beg sc, fasten off.

Rnd 4: Attach white in corner ch-2 sp, ch 3 (counts as first dc), *[[dc, ch 2, dc] in next ch-1 sp] rep in each ch-1 sp to next corner ch-2 sp **, [[dc, ch 2] twice and dc] in next corner ch-2 sp, rep from * around, ending last rep at **, sp [dc, ch 2] twice in same corner ch-2 sp as beg ch-3, join in top of beg ch-3, fasten off. ✂

COLOR KEY	
■	Purple
▨	Lavender
□	Yellow
▦	Grass green
□	White

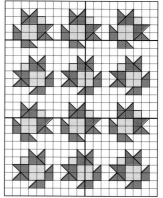

Assembly Diagram

Crocus in the Snow

Design by Susan Peak

Skill Level: Beginner

Size: 44 x 67 inches

Materials

► Coats & Clark Red Heart Super Saver worsted weight yarn (8 oz per skein): 3 skeins each soft white #316 (A) and dark plum #533 (B)

► Size N/15 crochet hook or size needed to obtain gauge

► Yarn needle

Gauge

5 sc = 2 inches; 6 rows = 4 inches

Check gauge to save time.

Pattern Notes

Weave in loose ends as work progresses.

Work with 2 strands of yarn held tog throughout.

Alternate working 6 rows each color.

Pattern Stitch

Long dc: [Yo hook, insert hook in same st as 3-sc group 2 rows below, yo, draw up a lp level with working row, {yo, draw through 2 lps on hook} twice] 3 times in same sp.

Rich plum in contrast with a snow white gives an elegant touch to this basic ripple pattern—much like the effect of a crocus blooming in the early spring snow!

Afghan

Row 1 (RS): With A, ch 121 loosely, sc in 3rd ch from hook, sc in each of next 6 chs, 3 sc in next ch, [sc in each of next 7 chs, sk next 2 chs, sc in each of next 7 chs, 3 sc in next ch] 6 times, sc in each of next 8 chs, turn. (120 sc)

Row 2: Working in back lps only, ch 1, sk first 2 sc, sc in each of next 7 sc, 3 sc in next sc, *sc in each of next 7 sc, sk next 2 sc, sc in each of next 7 sc, 3 sc in next sc] rep across to last 8 sc, sc in each of next 8 sc, turn.

Rows 3–6: Rep Row 2. At the end of Row 6, fasten off A, change to B, turn.

Row 7: Working in back lps only, ch 1, sk first 2 sc, sc in each of next 7 sc, long dc in indicated sp, [sc in each of next 7 sc, sk next 2 sc, sc in each of next 7 sc, long dc in indicated sp] rep across to last 8 sc, sc in each of next 8 sc, turn.

Rows 8–12: Rep Row 2. At the end of Row 12, fasten off B; change to A, turn.

Row 13: Rep Row 7.

Rows 14–18: Rep Rows 3–6.

Rep Rows 7–18 until a total of 8 dark plum and 9 soft-white groups are completed. ✄

Rings in Hexagon Motifs

Design by Anne Halliday

Skill Level: Beginner

Size: 43 x 56 inches

Materials

► Coats & Clark Red Heart Super Saver worsted weight yarn (8 oz per skein): 3 skeins white #311 (MC), 1 skein each hot red #390 (A), skipper blue #384 (B), grass green #687 (C) and bright yellow #324 (D)

► Size I/9 crochet hook or size needed to obtain gauge

► Yarn needle

Gauge

Motif = 5 inches corner to corner across center; 3 sc = 1 inch

Check gauge to save time.

Pattern Notes

Weave in loose ends as work progresses.

Join each rnd with a sl st unless otherwise stated.

Ch-3 counts as first dc throughout.

Pattern Stitches

Dc dec: *Yo hook, insert hook in next ch sp, yo, draw up a lp, yo, draw through 2 lps on hook *, sk next seam, rep from * to *, yo, draw through all 3 lps on hook.

Sc dec: Draw up a lp in each of next 2 ch-1 sps, yo, draw through all 3 lps on hook.

Motif

Note: Rnd 3 of each motif is worked with a CC; make 32 motifs with A, 31 motifs with B and 24 motifs each with C and D.

Rnd 1 (RS): With MC, ch 2, 6 sc in 2nd ch from hook, join in beg sc. (6 sc)

Rnd 2 (RS): Ch 3, dc in same st 3 dc in each of next 5 sts, dc in same st as beg ch-3, join in top of beg ch-3, fasten off. (18 dc)

Rnd 3 (RS): Attach CC in beg ch-3 of previous rnd, ch 4 (counts as first tr), tr in same st, 2 tr in each rem st around, join in top of beg ch-4, fasten off. (36 tr)

Rnd 4 (RS): Attach MC in beg ch-4 of previous rnd, ch 1, beg in same st as beg ch-1, [sc in each of next 3 tr, hdc in next tr, {dc, ch 1, dc} in next tr, hdc in next tr] rep around, join in beg sc, fasten off. (42 sts; 6 ch-1 sps)

Half Motif

Make 12

Row 1 (WS): With MC, ch 4, 6 dc in 4th ch from hook, turn. (7 dc)

Row 2 (RS): Ch 2 (counts as first hdc), hdc in same st as beg ch-2, 2 hdc in each of next 5 sts, hdc in last st, turn. (13 hdc)

Row 3 (WS): Ch 3, dc in same st as beg ch-3, [dc in next st, 2 dc in next st] 5 times, dc in each of next 2 sts, turn. (19 dc)

Row 4 (RS): Ch 3, dc in same st as beg ch-3, hdc in next st, sc in each of next 3 sts, hdc in next st, [{dc, ch 1, dc} in next st, hdc in next st, sc in each of next 3 sts, hdc in next st] twice, 2 dc in last st, fasten off. (23 sts; 2 ch-1 sps)

Assembly

Using diagram as a guide, with RS facing and working through both lps, whip-stitch motifs tog.

COLOR KEY
A Hot red
B Skipper blue
C Grass green
D Bright yellow

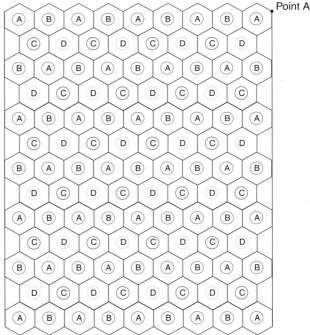

Point A

Assembly Diagram

Edging

Rnd 1 (RS): Attach MC with a sl st in ch-1 sp indicated on diagram at A, ch 4 (counts as first dc, ch-1), dc in same sp, ch 1, *sk next st, [dc in next st, ch 1, sk next st] 3 times, [dc, ch 1] twice in next ch-1 sp, sk next st, [dc in next st, ch 1, sk next st] 3 times, [dc dec, ch 1, sk next st, {dc in next st, ch 1, sk next st} 3 times, {dc, ch 1} twice in next ch-1 sp, sk next st, {dc in next st, ch 1, sk next st} 3 times] 8 times, [dc, ch 1] twice in next ch-1 sp, sk next st, [dc in next st, ch 1, sk next st] 3 times, [dc in next ch sp, ch 1, working across next half motif in sps at ends of rows, {hdc in next row, ch 1} 8 times, working across next motif, dc in next ch sp, ch 1, sk next st, {dc in next st, ch 1, sk next st} 3 times] 6 times *, dc in next ch-1 sp, ch 1 (mark ch-1 sp just made for st placement), dc in same sp, ch 1, rep from * to *, join in 3rd ch of beg ch-4.

Rnd 2: Ch 1, [sc, ch 1] twice in next ch-1 sp, *[sc in next ch-1 sp, ch 1] 4 times, [sc, ch 1] twice in next ch-1 sp, [{sc in next ch-1 sp, ch 1} 3 times, work sc dec, ch 1, {sc in next ch-1 sp, ch 1} 3 times, {sc, ch 1} twice in next ch-1 sp] 8 times, [sc in next ch-1 sp, ch 1] 4 times, [sc, ch 1] twice in next ch-1 sp *, [sc in next ch-1 sp, ch 1] rep across to marked sp, [sc, ch 1] twice in marked sp, rep from * to *, [sc in next ch-1 sp, ch 1] rep across to beg, join in beg sc.

Rnd 3: Ch 1, [sc in next ch-1 sp, ch 1] rep around, join in beg sc.

Rnd 4: Ch 1, hdc in same sc, [sl st, ch 1, hdc] in each sc around, ending with sl st in same st as beg ch-1, fasten off. ✄

Climbing Flowers

Design by Rena Stevens

Skill Level: Advanced

Size: 51 x 72 inches, excluding fringe

Materials

► Patons Canadiana worsted weight yarn: 45½ oz Aran #104, 17½ oz dark jade #48, 10½ oz each light jade #46 and cranberry #13, 7 oz floral rose #167

► Size I/9 crochet hook or size needed to obtain gauge

► Tapestry needle

Whether you lovingly stitch this exquisite afghan for yourself or to give as a gift, the beautiful flowers that adorn this project will make it a treasure to be cherished for generations!

Gauge

4 dc worked in 1 lp only = 1 inch; 2 rows = 1 inch

Check gauge to save time.

Pattern Notes

Weave in loose ends as work progresses.

Ch-3 counts as first dc throughout.

Afghan is worked vertically from right to left.

"Drop yarn" means to remove hook from lp, but do not fasten off.

"Pick up yarn" means to insert hook in dropped lp and work as indicated.

Pattern Stitches

Right bud: Working on RS of afghan, yo, turn and insert hook into both lps of free dc just passed 2 rows below, yo and draw up a lp, yo, insert hook in same place, yo and draw up a lp, yo and draw through all 5 lps on hook.

Right small leaf: Working on RS of afghan, yo hook 3 times, turn and insert hook into both lps of free dc just passed in same row as bud tip, yo and draw up a lp, yo and draw through 2 lps on hook (mark lp on hook just drawn up), [yo and draw through 2 lps on hook] twice, yo, insert hook in lp just marked and draw up a lp, remove marker, yo and draw through 2 lps on hook, yo and draw through all 3 lps on hook.

Left bud: Working on RS of afghan, yo and insert hook in both lps on next free st in designated row, yo and draw up a lp, yo, insert hook in same place, yo and draw up a lp, yo and draw through 4 lps on hook, yo and draw through 2 lps on hook.

Left small leaf: Working on RS of afghan in front of next 4 sts, yo hook 3 times, insert hook in both lps on next free st in designated row (same row as buds), yo and draw up a lp, yo and draw through 2 lps on hook, yo hook twice and insert hook in same place, yo and draw up a lp, [yo and draw through 2 lps on hook] twice, yo and draw through 3 lps on hook, [yo and draw through 2 lps on hook] twice.

Top and two right petals: Yo hook 5 times, turn afghan and insert hook on current row into both lps of 5th cranberry sl st from hook, yo and draw up a lp, [yo and draw through 2 lps on hook] 5 times, *yo hook 4 times, insert hook in same place behind and to your right of post just made, yo and draw up a lp, [yo, draw through 2 lps on hook] 4 times *, rep from * to *, working on RS of afghan, yo hook 3 times, insert hook in designated st, yo, draw up a lp, [yo, draw through 2 lps on hook] 3 times, **yo hook 4 times, insert hook in same place to your right of post just made, yo, draw up a lp, [yo, draw through 2 lps on hook] 4 times **, rep from

** to **, working on RS of afghan and working each post to left of post last made, †yo hook 4 times, fold last dc row out of the way away from you and insert hook in normal manner into designated st, yo, draw up a lp, [yo, draw through 2 lps on hook] 4 times, rep from †, yo hook 5 times, insert hook in same place, yo, draw up a lp, [yo, draw through 2 lps on hook] 5 times, yo, draw through all 10 lps on hook, ch 1 (mark last ch made as center of flower).

3-yo (4-yo) stem: Working on RS of afghan, yo hook 3 (4) times, turn, insert hook in designated place, yo, draw up a lp, [yo, draw through 2 lps on hook] 3 (4) times, turn, insert hook in back lp of next sc of current row, yo, draw lp through the sc and the 2 lps on hook.

Right large leaf: Working on RS of afghan, yo hook 5 times, turn, insert hook from top down into both lps of free sc just passed 4 rows below, yo, draw up a lp, [yo, draw through 2 lps on hook] 5 times, *yo hook 4 times, insert hook in same place to your right of post just made, yo, draw up a lp, [yo, draw through 2 lps on hook] 4 times *, rep from * to *, yo, draw through all 4 lps on hook.

Upper left petal: Working on RS of afghan and inserting each post to the left of the last post made, *yo hook 4 times, insert hook into both lps of marked flower center ch st, remove marker, yo, draw up a lp, [yo, draw through 2 lps on hook] 4 times *, rep * to * twice, yo and draw through all 4 lps on hook.

Lower left petal: Working on RS of afghan and inserting each post above (to your right of) the last post made, *yo hook 4 times, turn and insert hook from top down into same place as last petal made, yo, draw up a lp, [yo, draw through 2 lps on hook] 4 times *, rep from * to *, yo hook 5 times, insert hook into same place as last post made, yo, draw up a lp, [yo, draw through 2 lps on hook] 5 times, yo, draw through all 4 lps on hook.

Left large leaf: Working on RS of afghan and inserting each post to the left of last post made, *yo hook 4 times, insert hook in designated place, yo, draw up a lp, [yo, draw through 2 lps on hook] 4 times *, rep from * to * twice, yo, draw through all 4 lps on hook.

3-yo (4-yo, 6-yo) connecting stem: Yo hook 3 (4, 6) times, insert hook in desig-nated place on flower stem 3 Aran rows below, yo, draw up a lp, [yo, draw through 2 lps on hook] 3 (4, 6) times to 2 lps left on hook, insert hook in back lp of next st on current row, yo, draw lp through the st and the 2 lps on hook.

Afghan

Row 1 (RS): With light jade, ch 266, dc in 4th ch from hook, dc in each rem ch across, turn. (264 dc)

Row 2: Working in back lps only, ch 3, dc in each dc across, turn.

Row 3: Working in front lps only, ch 1, sc in next dc, *ch 1, sk next dc, sc in each of next 2 dc, [ch 1, sk next dc, sc in each of next 4 dc] twice, rep from * across, ending with ch 1, sk next dc, sc in last dc, drop light jade, do not turn.

Row 4 (RS): Work sl sts loosely in back lps only, attach floral rose with a sl st in first st, ch 1, sl st in each of next 3 sts, *work right bud, on current row, sl st in next 13 sts, rep from * across, fasten off floral rose, turn.

Row 5: Pick up light jade, ch 1, working in back lps only of previous light jade row (to hide floral rose sl sts), [sc in each of next 12 sts, ch 1, sk next bud and the st under it] rep across, ending with sc in last 3 sts, fasten off light jade, turn.

Row 6: Work sl sts loosely in back lps only, attach dark jade with sl st in first sc, ch 1, *sl st in next 2 sc, sl st in next ch-1 sp, sl st in next 4 sc, work right small leaf, on current row, sk next sc, sl st in next 4 sc, work right small leaf, on current row, sk next sc, rep from * across, ending on current row after last leaf with sk next sc, sl st in last 3 sc, fasten off dark jade, do not turn.

Row 7: Working behind dark jade sl sts in both lps of same light jade row just worked in, attach Aran with sl st in first sc, ch 1, sc in each of next 5 sts, *[ch 1, sk next st, sc in each of next 4 sts] twice, ch 1, sk next st, sc in each of next 2 sts, rep from * across, ending with [ch 1, sk next st, sc in each of next 4 sts] twice, sc in last st, drop Aran, do not turn.

Row 8: Work sl sts loosely in back lps only, attach floral rose with sl st in first st, ch 1, sl st in next 3 sts, [work left bud into last light jade row, on current row, sl st in next 13 sts] rep across, fasten off floral rose, turn.

Row 9: Pick up Aran, ch 1, work in back lps only of previous Aran row, sc in next 10 sts, [ch 1, sk next bud and the st under it, sc in next 12 sts] rep across, ending with sc in last 5 sts, drop Aran, turn.

Row 10: Work sl sts loose-ly in back lps only, attach dark jade with sl st in first sc, ch 1, sl st in next 6 sts, [work left small leaf in next free st of last light jade row, on current row, sk next st, sl st in next 4 sts, work left small leaf in next free st of last light jade row, on current row, sk next st, sl st in next 7 sts] rep across, ending with; on current row after last leaf with sk next st, sl st in last 9 sts, fasten off dark jade, do not turn.

Row 11: Pick up Aran, ch 3, work in front lps only of previous Aran row, dc in next 7 sts, [sk next leaf tip, dc in next st (under leaf) and in next 4 sts, sk next leaf tip, dc in next st (under leaf) and in next 7 sts] rep across, ending with sk last leaf tip, dc in next st (under leaf) and in last 3 sts, turn.

Row 12: Working in back lps only, ch 3, dc in each st across, turn.

Row 13: Working in front lps only, ch 3, dc in each st across, turn.

Row 14: Rep Row 12.

Row 15: Working in front lps only, ch 1, sc in each st across, turn.

Row 16: Working in both lps, ch 1, sc in each of next 32 sts, [ch 1, sk next st, sc in each of next 31 sts] rep across, ending with after last ch 1, sk next st, sc in last 6 sts, turn.

Row 17: Working in front lps only, ch 3, dc in each of next 12 sts, [ch 1, sk next st, dc in next st, {ch 1, sk next st, dc in each of next 4 sts} twice, ch 1, sk next st, dc in each of next 19 sts] rep across, ending with dc in last 14 sts, turn.

Row 18: Rep Row 12, end-ing with drop Aran, turn.

Row 19 (RS): Work sl sts loosely in back lps only, attach cranberry with sl st in first st, ch 1, sl st in next 7 sts, *work top and two right petals as follows: work top petal as instructed; work first right petal in both lps on free sc just passed 4 rows below; work 2nd right petal in next free sc 3 rows below; on current row, sk next st, mark st just skipped, do not remove marker until instructed, sl st in next 31 sts, rep from * across, fasten off carnberry, do not turn.

Row 20: Pick up Aran, ch 1, working in front lps only of previous Aran row, sc in next 2 sts, *ch 1, sk next petal tip and the st under st, sc in next 4 sts, ch 1, sk next flower center and the marked st under it, sc in next 26 sts, rep from * across, sc in last 31 sts, drop Aran, do not turn.

Row 21: Work sl sts loosely in back lps only, attach dark jade with sl st in first st, ch 1, sl st in next 11 sts, *work a 3-yo stem into both lps of free marked dc under flower center, remove this marker, sl st in next 3 sts, work a 3-yo stem around last stem made, [sl st in next 2 sts, work large right leaf, on current row, sk next st, sl st in next st, work a 4-yo stem around last stem made] 3 times, sl st in next 12 sts, rep from * across, ending with last rep by omitting 12 sl sts and replacing with sl st in next 4 sts, work a 4-yo stem around last stem made, sl st in last 3 sts, fasten off dark jade, turn.

Row 22: Pick up Aran, ch 3, working in back lps only of previous Aran row, dc in next 3 sts, sk stem end, pushing stems out of the way on RS of afghan, work in front of stems throughout, dc in next 5 sts, *[sk stem end, dc in next st, ch 1, sk leaf and the st under it, dc in next 3 sts] 3 times, sk stem end, dc in next 4 sts, sk stem end, dc in next 13 sts, rep from * across, dc in last 12 sts, turn.

Row 23: Working in front lps only, ch 1, sc in each st across, drop Aran, do not turn.

Row 24: Work sl sts loosely in back lps only, attach cranberry with sl st in first st, ch 1, sl st in next 5 sts, *work upper left petal, on current row, sk next st, sl st in next 5 sts, work lower left petal, on current row, sk next st, sl st in next 25 sts, rep from * across, sl st in last 27 sts, fasten off cranberry, turn.

Row 25: Pick up Aran, ch 3, work in back lps only of previous Aran row, dc in next 8 sts, *ch 1, sk next st, dc in next 7 sts, ch 1, sk next st, dc in next 9 sts, ch 1, sk next petal tip and the st under it, dc in next 5 sts, ch 1, sk next petal tip and the st under it, dc in next 7 sts, rep from * across, dc in last 6 sts, drop Aran, turn.

Row 26: Work sl sts loosely in back lps only, attach dark jade with sl st in first st, ch 1, sl st in next 13 sts, *work left large leaf into 2 lps of stem below, just above (to right of) base of upper right large leaf, on current row, sk next st, sl st in next 3 sts, work a 4-yo

connecting stem into 2 lps of stem below, halfway between bases of upper and middle right large leaves, on current row, sl st in next 18 sts, turn and work a 6-yo connecting stem around base just passed of stem below, on current row, sl st in next 8 sts, rep from * across, end after last 4-yo connecting stem with sl st in next 21 sts, fasten off dark jade, do not turn.

Row 27: Pick up Aran, ch 3, work in front lps only of previous Aran row, dc in next 13 sts, *ch 1, sk next leaf tip and the st under it, dc in next 4 sts, sk next connecting stem, dc in next 10 sts, ch 1, sk next st, dc in next 7 sts, sk next connecting stem, dc in next 9 sts, rep from * across, end after last ch 1, sk next st with dc in last 10 sts, turn.

Row 28: Ch 1, working in back lps only, sc in each st across, drop Aran, turn.

Row 29: Work sl sts loosely in back lps only, attach dark jade with sl st in first st, ch 1, sl st in next 9 sts, turn and work a 3-yo stem into 2 lps of 3rd dark jade sl st from hook, *on current row, sl st in next 3 sts, work a 3-yo stem around stem just made, work a 3-yo connecting stem around next connecting stem 3 Aran rows below, on current row, sl st in next 12 sts, work a 3-yo stem into RS of afghan lp only of 4th dark jade sl st from hook, sl st in next 3 sts, work a 3-yo stem around last stem made, sl st in next st, work right large leaf into free sc just passed 4 rows below,

working over the cranberry sl st, on current row, sk next st, sl st in next 2 sts, work a 4-yo stem around last stem made on current row, on current row, sl st in next 2 sts, work a 4-yo connecting stem around connecting stem just passed 3 rows below, on current row, sl st in next st, work a 4-yo stem around last stem made on current row, rep from * across, end after last 4-yo stem (made after last large right leaf) with sl st in last 2 sts, fasten off dark jade, do not turn.

Row 30: Pick up Aran, ch 1, working in front lps only of previous row, keep stems on right side of afghan throughout, sc in next 7 sts, sk next stem, sc in next 3 sts, *sk next stem, sc in next 3 sts, sc in next st under stem, ch 1, sk next stem, sk next connecting stem and sk the st under connecting stem, sc in next 8 sts, ch 1, sk next stem and the st under it, [sc in next 3 sts, sc in next st under stem, sk next stem] twice, sc in next st, ch 1, sk next leaf and the st under it, sc in next 2 sts, sc in next st under stem, sk next stem, sc in next 2 sts, ch 1, sk next connecting stem and the st under it, sc in next st, sc in next st under stem, rep from * across, end after skipping last stem with sc in last 2 sts, drop Aran, do not turn.

Row 31: Work sl sts loosely in back lps only, attach cranberry with sl st in first st, ch 1, sl st in next 23 sts, *work top and two right petals as follows: work top petal as instructed, work first right petal into 2 lps of cranberry sl st showing through ch-1 sp 4 Aran rows below, work 2nd right petal in next free dc 4 rows below, working over dark jade sl st, on current row, sk next st, sl st around stem and into both lps of next (to pull top of dark green stem into better position), sc around same stem and into both lps of next st, with stem on right side of afghan, sl st in next 29 sts, rep from * across, sl st in last 13 sts, fasten off cranberry, turn.

Row 32: Pick up Aran, ch 3, work in back lps of previous row, dc in next 12 sts, *ch 3, sk next 3 sts at flower center, keeping petal on RS of afghan, dc in next 4 sts, ch 1, sk next petal tip and the st under it, dc in next 24 sts, rep from * across, dc in last 19 sts, turn.

Row 33: Ch 1, working in front lps only, sc in each st across, drop Aran, do not turn.

Row 34: Work sl sts loosely in back lps only, attach dark jade with sl st in first st, ch 1, sl st in next 3 sts, work left large leaf into 2 lps at top of stem 4 Aran rows below, *on current row, sk next st, sl st in next 4 sts, work left large leaf into 2 lps of stem 4 Aran rows below, just above (to your right of) next connecting stem, on current row, sk next st, sl st in next 21 sts, work left large leaf into 2 lps of stem 4 Aran rows below, just below (to your left of) base of next right large leaf, on current row, sk next st, sl st in next 4 sts, work left large leaf into 2 lps of stem below, at point where next connecting stem joins main stem, rep from * across, end after last flower with working 1 last upper left large leaf, on current row, sk next st, sl st in last 8 sts, fasten off dark jade, turn.

Row 35: Pick up Aran, ch 1, work in back lps only of previous row, sc in next 7 sts, *ch 1, sk next leaf and the st under it, sc in next 21 sts, [ch 1, sk next leaf and the st under it, sc in next 4 sts] twice, rep from * across, end after last leaf with sl st in last 4 sts, drop Aran, turn.

Row 36: Work sl sts loosely in back lps only, attach cranberry with sl st in first st, ch 1, sl st in next 21 sts, *work upper left petal, on current row, sk next st, sl st in next 5 sts, work lower left petal, on current row, sk next st, sl st in next 25 sts, rep from * across, end on current row after working last lower left petal with sk next st, sl st in last 11 sts, fasten off cranberry, do not turn.

Row 37: Pick up Aran, ch 3, work in front lps only of previous row, dc in next 21 sts, *ch 1, sk next petal and the st under it, dc in next 5 sts, ch 1, sk next petal and the st under it, dc in next 25 sts, rep from * across, end dc in last 11 sts, turn.

Rows 38 & 39: Rep Rows 12 and 13.

Row 40: Rep Row 12.

Row 41: Continuing to work with Aran, rep Row 3.

Row 42: Rep Row 4.

Row 43: Continuing with Aran and working in previous Aran row, rep Row 5, fasten off Aran, turn.

Row 44: Rep Row 6.

Row 45: With light jade and working in previous Aran row, rep Row 7, drop light jade, do not turn.

Row 46: Working buds into last Aran row, rep Row 8.

Row 47: With light jade and working in previous light jade row, rep Row 9.

Row 48: Working leaves in front of light jade rows and into last Aran row, rep Row 10.

Row 49: With light jade and working in front lps only of previous light jade row, rep Row 11.

[Rep Rows 2–49] 3 times

Rep Row 2, fasten off.

Fringe

Work 33 groups of fringe evenly sp across each end of afghan: Cut Aran yarn into 20-inch lengths; holding 10 strands tog, fold in half. Insert hook into edge of afghan and draw strands through at fold; draw cut end through lp on hook and gently pull to secure. Trim ends evenly. ✂

Frosty Morn

Continued from page 11

in ch-1 sp of corresponding shell on square, ch 1, 2 hdc in same corner sp on motif, [2 hdc, ch 1, 2 hdc] in next ch-1 sp, [2 hdc, ch 3, 2 hdc] in next corner ch-3 sp, [2 hdc, ch 1, 2 hdc] in next ch-1 sp, 2 hdc in next corner ch-3 sp on motif, ch 1, sl st in ch-1 sp of corresponding shell on square, ch 1, 2 hdc in same corner sp on motif, 2

hdc in next ch-1 sp on motif, sl st in ch-1 sp of corresponding shell on square, 2 hdc in same ch-1 sp on motif, join in top of beg ch-2, fasten off.

Tassel

Make 18

Cut 25 strands of millennium each 12 inches in length. Holding all strands tog, tie a separate length of yarn tightly around strands at center. Fold strands in half at tied point and tie a 12-inch length of yarn tightly around folded strands 1¼ inch below top. Blend ends of tying strand in with tassel strands.

Sew one tassel securely to bottom point of each square and each fill-in motif across short ends of afghan. ✂

Tea Rose Trellis

Continued from page 8

Rosettes

Make 15

Rnd 1: With bone, ch 4, sl st to join to form a ring, [ch 3, 2 dc in ring, sl st in ring] 5 times, leaving a long length of yarn, fasten off. (5 petals)

With RS facing, sew a rosette to the junction of each 4 square joining.

Border

Rnd 1: Attach bone in corner ch-3 sp, ch 1, [5 sc in corner ch-3 sp, sc in top of 3-dc cl, 2 sc in next ch-2 sp, sc

in each of next 5 dc, 3 sc in next ch-2 sp, sc in each of next 5 dc, 2 sc in next ch-2 sp, sc in next 3-dc cl, 4 sc in next ch sp of joining of squares] rep in this manner around entire outer edge of afghan, join in beg sc.

Rnd 2: Working in back lps for this rnd only, ch 1, [sc in each of next 7 sc, {sc, ch 7, sc} in next sc] rep around, join in beg sc.

Rnd 3: Sl st in next 2 sc, ch 1, sc in same sc as beg ch-1, dc in next sc, sc in next sc, 9 sc over next ch-7 sp, [sk next 3 sc, sc in next sc, dc in next sc, sc in next sc, sk next 3 sc, 9 sc over next ch-7 sp] rep around, join in beg sc.

Rnd 4: Sl st into next dc, ch 1, [sc in dc, ch 4, {sc, ch 5, sc} in 5th sc of 9-sc group, ch 4] rep around, join in beg sc.

Rnd 5: Ch 1, beg in same sc as beg ch-1, [sc in next sc, 3 sc in next ch-4 sp, 5 sc in next ch-5 sp, 3 sc in next ch-4 sp] rep around, join in beg sc, fasten off. ✁

Hearts & Flowers Delight

Continued from page 24

next st, sc in next st] 3 times, ch 3, sk next 2 sts, sc in next st, ch 2, sk last st, sl st in base of beg ch-3, fasten off.

Third heart motif

Rep 2nd heart motif.

Fourth heart motif

Rnds 1–3: Rep Rnds 1–3 of first heart motif.

Rnd 4: Rep Rnd 4 of 2nd heart motif to *, ch 3, sk next 2 sts, sc in next st, [ch 1, sl st in corresponding ch-3 sp on left edge of first heart motif, ch 1, sk next 2 sts, sc in next st] 3 times, [ch 3, sk 1 st, sc in next st] 3 times, ch 3, sk next 2 sts, sc in next st, ch 2, sk last st, sl st in base of beg ch-3, fasten off.

On WS of piece, tack the 2 free ch lps of Rnd 4 at bottom of each heart motif to back of leaves at each juncture.

Background

Rnd 1: Attach soft white in the last ch-2 sp of Rnd 4 at top of any heart motif, ch 1, sc in same sp, *[ch 3, sc in next ch-3 sp] 5 times on same heart motif, holding back last lp of each tr on hook, work 1 tr in each of the next 2 joined ch-3 sps between heart motifs, yo, draw through all 3 lps on hook, sc in next ch-3 sp on next heart motif, [ch 3, sc in next ch-3 sp] 3 times, ch 3 **, sc in next ch-2 sp at top of heart motif, rep from * 3 times, ending last rep at **, join in beg sc. (36 ch-3 sps)

Rnd 2: Sl st in first ch-3 sp, ch 5 (counts as first dtr), [2 dtr, ch 2, 3 dtr] in same ch sp (beg corner), *2 tr in next ch-3 sp, 2 dc in next ch-3 sp, 2 hdc in each of next 2 ch-3 sps, 2 dc

in next tr dec, dc in next sc, 2 hdc in each of next 2 ch-3 sps, 2 dc in next ch-3 sp, 2 tr in next ch-3 sp **, [3 dtr, ch 2, 3 dtr] in next ch-3 sp (corner), rep from * 3 times, ending last rep at **, join in top of beg ch-5. (100 sts; 4 ch-2 sps)

Rnd 3: Sl st into corner ch-2 sp, ch 3, [2 dc, ch 2, 3 dc] in same ch-2 sp, *dc in each of next 4 sts, hdc in each of next 17 sts, dc in each of next 4 sts **, [3 dc, ch 2, 3 dc] in next corner ch-2 sp, rep from * 3 times, ending last rep at **, join in top of beg ch-3, fasten off. (124 sts; 4 ch-2 sps)

Rnd 4: Attach medium sage in any corner ch-2 sp, beg tr shell in same ch-2 sp, *sk next 3 sts of corner group, [puff st around front of post of next st, ch 1, sk next 2 sts, dc shell in next st, sk next 2 sts] 4 times, puff st around front of post of next st, ch 1, sk last 3 sts before corner sp **, tr shell in corner ch-2 sp, rep from * 3 times, ending last rep at **, join in 4th ch of beg ch-5, fasten off.

Second square

Rep first square through Rnd 3 of background.

Rnd 4 (Joining rnd): Work same as Rnd 4 of background of first square to first corner of joining side; join shells on joining side as follows: Work the 4th and 5th ch-1 sps of first corner tr shell as a sl st in corresponding ch-1 sps of corner tr shell on previous square; work the 2nd ch-1 of each dc shell as a sl st in the corresponding ch-1 sp of dc shell on previous square; work the first and 2nd ch-1 sps of 2nd corner tr shell as a sl st in corresponding ch-1 sps of corner tr shell on previous square. Work rem of rnd same as Rnd 4 of previous square.

Make and join 28 more squares in same manner as 2nd square in a pattern of 5 squares across and 6 squares down. ✁

Home Sweet Home

Crocheted items have long been valued for their functionality as well as their attractive appearance. Crochet these patterns to spruce up your own home or to give as special gifts.

Scalloped Pineapple Doily

Design by Valmay Flint

Skill Level: Beginner

Size: 10½ inches in diameter

Materials

► Crochet cotton size 20: 200 yds ecru

► Size 9 steel crochet hook or size needed to obtain gauge

Pineapple motifs surrounding a center motif, and scalloped edging give this beautiful doily added appeal!

Gauge

Rnds 1–3 = 2 inches; 6 tr = ½ inch

Check gauge to save time.

Pattern Notes

Weave in loose ends as work progresses.

Join rnds with a sl st unless otherwise stated.

Pattern Stitches

3-tr cl: *Yo hook twice, insert hook in indicated st, yo, draw up a lp, [yo, draw through 2 lps on hook] twice, rep from * twice, yo, draw through all 4 lps on hook.

Beg 3-tr cl: Ch 3 (counts as first tr), *yo hook twice, insert hook in indicated st, yo, draw up a lp, [yo, draw through 2 lps on hook] twice, rep from * once, yo, draw through all 3 lps on hook.

Tr dec: *Yo hook twice, insert hook in indicated st, yo, draw up a lp, [yo, draw through 2 lps on hook] twice, rep from * once, yo, draw through all 3 lps on hook.

Beg tr dec: Ch 3 (counts as first tr), yo hook twice, insert hook in indicated st, yo, draw up a lp, [yo, draw through 2 lps on hook] 3 times.

Doily

Rnd 1 (RS): Ch 8, sl st to join to form a ring, beg 3-tr cl in ring, ch 4, [3-tr cl in ring, ch 4] 7 times, join in top of beg cl. (8 cls; 8 ch-4 sps)

Rnd 2: Ch 1, sc in top of cl, ch 5, sc in next ch-4 sp, [ch 5, sc in top of next cl, ch 5, sc in next ch-5 sp] rep around, ending with ch 2, dc in beg sc to form last ch-5 sp. (16 ch-5 sps)

Rnd 3: Beg 3-tr cl in same ch sp, ch 4, [3-tr cl in next ch-5 sp, ch 4] rep around, join in top of beg cl. (16 cls; 16 ch-4 sps)

Rnd 4: Ch 1, sc in top of cl, ch 5, sc in next ch-4 sp, [ch 5, sc in top of next cl, ch 5, sc in next ch-4 sp] rep around, ending with ch 3, dc in beg sc. (16 ch-5 sps)

Rnd 5: Ch 1, sc in same sp, ch 3, sc in next ch sp, [ch 6, sc in next ch sp, ch 3, sc in next ch sp] rep around, ending with ch 3, dc in beg sc to form last ch-6 sp.

Rnd 6: Ch 4 (counts as first tr throughout), 2 tr in same sp as beg ch-4, ch 5, sk next ch-3 sp, [3 tr in next ch-6 sp, ch 5, sk next ch-3 sp] rep around, join in top of beg ch-4.

Rnd 7: Beg 3-tr cl over next 3 tr, ch 9, [3-tr cl over next 3 tr, ch 9] rep around, join in top of beg cl.

Rnd 8: Sl st into ch-9 sp, ch 4, 10 tr in same ch sp, 11 tr in each rem ch-9 sp around, join in top of beg ch-4. (16 pineapple bases)

Rnd 9: Beg tr dec over next 2 tr, *tr in each of next 7 tr, tr dec over next 2 tr, ch 3 **, tr dec over next 2 tr, rep from * around, ending last rep at **, join in top of beg dec.

Rnd 10: Beg tr dec over next 2 tr, *tr in each of next 5 tr, tr dec over next 2 tr, ch 5, sc in next ch sp, ch 5 **, tr dec over next 2 tr, rep from * around, ending last rep at **, join in top of beg tr dec.

Rnd 11: Beg tr dec over next 2 tr, *tr in each of next 3 tr, tr dec over next 2 tr, [ch 5, sc in next ch sp] twice, ch 5 **, tr dec over next 2 tr, rep from * around, ending last rep at **, join in top of beg tr dec.

Rnd 12: Beg tr dec over next 2 tr, *tr in next tr, tr dec over next 2 tr, [ch 5, sc in next ch sp] 3 times, ch 5 **, tr dec over next 2 tr, rep from * around, ending last rep at **, join in top of beg tr dec.

Rnd 13: Beg 3-tr cl over next 3 tr, *[ch 5, sc in next ch sp] 4 times, ch 5 **, 3-tr cl over next 3 tr, rep from * around, ending last rep at **, join in top of beg cl.

Rnd 14: Ch 1, sc in top of cl, *[ch 5, sc in next ch sp] 5 times, ch 5 **, sc in top of next cl, rep from * around, ending last rep at **, join in beg sc.

Rnd 15: Sl st into next ch sp, ch 4, 10 tr in same ch sp, *ch 2, sk next 2 ch sps, 3 dc in next ch sp, ch 2, sk next 2 ch sps **, 11 tr in next ch sp, rep from * around, ending last rep at **, join in top of beg ch-4.

Rnd 16: Ch 5 (counts as first tr, ch 1), tr in next tr, [ch 1, tr in next tr] 9 times, *ch 2, [yo hook, insert hook in next dc, yo, draw up a lp, yo, draw through 2 lps on hook] 3 times, yo, draw through all 4 lps on hook, ch 2 **, tr in next tr,

[ch 1, tr in next tr] 10 times, rep from * around, ending last rep at **, join in 4th ch of beg ch-5.

Rnd 17: Sl st into ch-1 sp, ch 1, sc in same ch-1 sp, *[ch 5, sc in next ch-1 sp] 9 times, ch 2, sk next 2 ch-2 sps **, sc in next ch-1 sp, rep from * around, ending last rep at **, join in beg sc.

Rnd 18: Sl st into next ch sp, ch 1, sc in same ch sp, *[ch 6, sc in next ch-5 sp] 8 times **, sc in next ch-5 sp, rep from * around, ending last rep at **, join in beg sc, fasten off. ✂

Rose Pocket Place Mats

Design by Carol Alexander
for Crochet Trends and Traditions

Skill Level: Beginner

Size: 13¼ x 17¾ inches

Materials

▶ J. & P. Coats Knit-Cro-Sheen crochet cotton size 10: 675 yds white #1, 450 yds spruce #179, small amount of each mid rose #46A and forest green #49

▶ Size G/6 crochet hook or size needed to obtain gauge

▶ 2½ yds ⅜-inch-wide pink ribbon

▶ ½-inch decorative button

▶ Tapestry needle

Gauge

2 shells = 2¼ inches; 2 pattern rows = 1 inch; rose motif measures 3½ inches in diameter

Check gauge to save time.

Pattern Notes

Weave in loose ends as work progresses.

All rows are worked on RS.

Work with 3 strands cotton held tog throughout.

Ch 3 counts as first dc throughout.

Join rnds with a sl st unless otherwise stated.

Pattern Stitches

V-st: [Dc, ch 2, dc] in indicated st.

Half shell: 3 dc in indicated st.

Beg half shell: Ch 3, 2 dc in same st.

Place Mat

Row 1: With spruce, ch 74, sc in 2nd ch from hook, [sk next 2 chs, V-st in next ch, sk next 2 chs, sc in next ch] rep across, fasten off. (12 V-sts)

Row 2: Attach white in first sc at beg of previous row, beg half shell in same st, sc in next V-st, [shell in next sc, sc in next V-st] 11 times, half shell in last sc, fasten off white. (11 shells; 2 half shells)

Row 3: Attach spruce in 3rd ch of beg ch-3 of previous row, ch 1, sc in same st, V-st in next sc, [sc in 3rd dc of next shell, V-st in next sc] 11 times, sc in last dc of half shell, fasten off.

Rows 4–33: Rep Rows 2 and 3.

Border

Rnd 1: Attach white in corner at beg of last row (Row 33), ch 3, 2 dc in same st, dc in first sc of last row, [2 dc in next V-st, 2 dc in next sc] 12 times, 2 dc in next V-st, dc in last sc, 3 dc in corner, [2 dc around post of outside dc of next 3-dc group] 16 times across short side, 3 dc in corner, [2 dc in next skipped ch-2 sp of foundation ch] 24 times, 3 dc in corner, [2 dc around post of outside dc of next 3-dc group] 16 times across short side, join in 3rd ch of beg ch-3. (172 dc)

Rnd 2: Sl st in next (corner) dc, ch 3, [dc, ch 2, 2 dc] in same st, *dc in each dc across to next corner st **, [2 dc, ch 2, 2 dc] in corner st, rep from * around, ending last rep at **, join in 3rd ch of beg ch-3, fasten off.

Note: On the following rnd when working between [ ] on each side, adjust spacing of sts as needed to accommodate st sequence, keeping sts consistent between opposite sides.

Rnd 3: Attach forest green in corner ch-2 sp at right end of long side, ch 3, work 6 dc in same sp, *sk 1 st, sc in next st, [sk next 2 sts, 5 dc in next st, sk next 2 sts, sc in next st] rep across, ending in 3rd st from next corner sp, sk next 2 sts **, work 7 dc in corner sp, rep from * around, ending last rep at **, join, fasten off.

Rose Motif

Rnd 1: With mid rose, ch 6, sl st to join to form a ring, ch 1, working over beg tail, work 16 sc in ring, join in beg sc. (16 sc)

Rnd 2: Ch 6 (counts as first dc, ch 3), sk 1 sc, [dc in next sc, ch 3, sk 1 sc] 7 times, join in 3rd ch of beg ch-6. (8 dc; 8 ch-3 sps)

Rnd 3: For outer petals, working in each ch-3 sp around, ch 1, [sc, 3 dc, ch 1, sl st in back lp of last dc, 3 dc, sc] in each ch-3 sp around, join in beg sc. (8 petals)

Rnd 4: For inner petals, working around dc post of Rnd 2 directly below, ch 1, [sc, 2 dc, ch 1, sl st in back lp of last dc, 2 dc, sc] around each of 8 dc sts of Rnd 2, join in beg sc. (8 petals)

Rnd 5: For rose center, continue from joining of inner petals, ch 1, sc in next sk sc of Rnd 1 below, ch 3, [sc in next sk sc of Rnd 1, ch 3] 7 times, join in beg

sc, fasten off. (8 ch-3 sps)

Leaf
Make 2

With forest green, ch 5, working in first ch of ch-5, [2 dtr, ch 1, sl st in top of last dtr, 2 dtr, ch 4, sl st] all in same first ch, fasten off.

Finishing

With 2 outside petals of rose centered at top, sew leaves to back of rose at lower right and upper left outside edges. Sew button to center of rose.

Position rose motif to lower right corner of place mat as shown, with edge of rose approximately 1 inch from base of place mat border at right and bottom sides; pin in place to hold. Leaving top open, stitch motif to place mat, sewing just underneath edge of outside rose petals around sides and bottom of motif.

Beg at top left corner of place mat and leaving approximately a 12-inch end at beg, weave ribbon through sps along base of place mat border completely around, ending with a 12-inch rem length. Tie ends into a bow, tack bow through center knot to place mat.

Insert small folded napkin and silverware inside pocket. ✂

Patchwork Heart Rug

Design by Donna Collinsworth

Skill Level: Beginner

Size: 25 x 35 inches, excluding fringe

Materials

► Coats & Clark Red Heart Classic worsted weight yarn (3½ oz per skein): 12 oz skipper blue #848, 12 oz cherry red #912, 8 oz cornmeal #220

► Sizes F/5 and J/10 crochet hooks or sizes needed to obtain gauge

► Tapestry needle

Two strands held together in contrasting colors gives this patchwork rug a woven look. Add crocheted hearts for that extra-special touch!

Gauge

J hook, 3 hdc = 1 inch; 2 hdc rows = 1 inch; each block = 5 inches square

F hook, 4 sc = 1 inch; 4 sc rows = 1 inch

Check gauge to save time.

Pattern Note

Weave in loose ends as work progresses.

Basic Block

Make 35

Row 1: With 2 strands of yarn held tog and crochet hook size J, ch 13, hdc in 2nd ch from hook, hdc in each rem ch across, turn. (12 sts)

Rows 2–10: Ch 2 (counts as first hdc throughout), hdc in each hdc across, turn. At the end of Row 10, fasten off.

Rug

Make 10 basic blocks using 1 strand each cherry red and skipper blue.

Make 6 basic blocks using 1 strand each cornmeal and skipper blue.

Make 7 basic blocks using 1 strand each cornmeal and cherry red.

Make 2 basic blocks using 2 strands cornmeal.

Make 6 basic blocks using 2 strands cherry red.

Make 4 basic blocks using 2 strands skipper blue.

Using diagram as a guide, sew basic blocks together.

Heart

Make 6 each cherry red, skipper blue & cornmeal

Row 1: With 1 strand of yarn and crochet hook size F, ch 2, sc in 2nd ch from hook, turn. (1 sc)

Row 2: Ch 1, 3 sc in sc, turn. (3 sc)

Row 3: Ch 1, 2 sc in first sc, sc in each rem sc across, turn. (4 sc)

Row 4: Rep Row 3. (5 sc)

Row 5: Ch 1, sc in each sc across, turn.

Rows 6–11: Rep Row 3. (11 sc)

Row 12: Ch 1, sc in first st, [hdc, dc] in next st, 2 tr in next st, [dc, hdc] in next st, sc in next st, sl st in next st, sc in next st, [hdc, dc] in next st, 2 tr in next st, [dc, hdc] in next st, sc in next st, leaving a length of yarn, fasten off.

Using rug diagram as a guide, sew hearts centered to basic blocks as indicated.

Fringe

Working along short ends of rug as indicated in rug placement diagram, cut 4 (8-inch) strands of yarn, fold strands in half, insert J hook in indicated st on rug, draw fold through to form a lp on hook, draw cut ends through lp on hook, pull gently to secure.

Trim ends evenly. ✂

HEART PLACEMENT KEY
♥ Blue heart
♡ Yellow heart
♥ Red heart

Fringe	Blue	Red/Blue	Blue/Yellow	Red/Blue	Blue/Yellow	Red/Blue	Blue	Fringe
	Red/Blue	Red	Red/Yellow	Red	Red/Yellow	Red	Red/Blue	
	Blue/Yellow	Red/Yellow	Yellow	Red/Yellow	Yellow	Red/Yellow	Blue/Yellow	
	Red/Blue	Red	Red/Yellow	Red	Red/Yellow	Red	Red/Blue	
	Blue	Red/Blue	Blue/Yellow	Red/Blue	Blue/Yellow	Red/Blue	Blue	

Rug Placement

Pretty Roses Blender Cover

Design by Beverly Mewhorter

Skill Level: Beginner

Size: Fits standard-size blender

Materials

► Worsted weight yarn: 4½-oz off-white, ½ oz each red and green

► Size H/8 crochet hook or size needed to obtain gauge

► Hot-glue gun

► Tapestry needle

Gauge

3 dc = 1 inch; 5 dc rnds = 3 inches

Check gauge to save time.

Pattern Notes

Weave in loose ends as work progresses.

Join rnds with a sl st unless otherwise stated.

Ch 3 counts as first dc throughout.

Blender Cover

Rnd 1 (RS): With off-white, ch 4, 13 dc in 4th ch from hook, join in top of beg ch-4. (14 dc)

Rnd 2: Ch 3, dc in same st as beg ch, 2 dc in each rem dc around, join in top of beg ch-3. (28 dc)

Rnd 3: Ch 3, dc in same st as beg ch, dc in next dc, [2 dc in next dc, dc in next dc] rep around, join in top of beg ch-3. (42 dc)

Rnd 4: Ch 3, dc in same st as beg ch, dc in each of next 2 dc, [2 dc in next dc, dc in each of next 2 dc] rep around, join in top of beg ch-3. (56 dc)

Rnd 5: Ch 3, dc in same st as beg ch, dc in each of next 3 dc, [2 dc in next dc, dc in each of next 3 dc] rep around, join in top of beg ch-3. (70 dc)

Rnd 6: Ch 3, dc in same st as beg ch, dc in each of next 4 dc, [2 dc in next dc, dc in each of next 4 dc] rep around, join in top of beg ch-3. (84 dc)

Rnds 7–24: Ch 3, dc in each dc around, join in top of beg ch-3.

Rnd 25: Sl st in each dc around, fasten off.

Rose

Make 7

Row 1: With red, ch 19, [sc, ch 1, sc] in 2nd ch from hook, [sc, ch 1, sc] in each rem ch across, leaving a length of yarn, fasten off.

Starting at first group of sts of row, roll piece to form rose, with rem length of yarn, weave through foundation ch to secure rose.

Leaf

Make 14

Row 1: With green, ch 9, sl st in 2nd ch from hook, sc in next ch, dc in each of next 6 chs, fasten off.

With 2 leaves to each rose, arrange on front of cover and glue in place. ✂

Flower Basket Guest Towel Set

Designs by Michele Wilcox

Skill Level: Intermediate

Size:

Towel: 16 x 29 inches

Washcloth: 13 inches square

Materials

► Cotton sport weight yarn: 1 oz lemon, small amounts bright pink, blue and green

► Size F/5 crochet hook or size needed to obtain gauge

► 16 x 29-inch white hand towel

► 13-inch-square white washcloth

► Sewing needle and thread

► Tapestry needle

Your guests will want to stay forever when you dress up their bath with this bright and cheery guest set adorned with a colorful basket of flowers!

Gauge

5 dc = 1 inch

Check gauge to save time.

Pattern Note

Weave in loose ends as work progresses.

Basket

Row 1: With lemon beg at bottom of basket, ch 13, sc in 2nd ch from hook, sc in each rem ch across, turn. (12 sc)

Row 2: Ch 1, sc in each st across, turn.

Row 3: Ch 3, dc in same st as beg ch, dc in each st across to last st, 2 dc in last st, turn. (14 dc)

Row 4: Rep Row 3. (16 dc)

Rows 5 & 6: Rep Row 2.

Rows 7 & 8: Rep Row 3. (20 dc)

Rows 9 & 10: Rep Row 2.

Rows 11 & 12: Rep Row 3. (24 dc)

Rows 13 & 14: Ch 1, 2 sc in first st, sc in each st across to last st, 2 sc in last st, turn. (28 sc)

Row 15: Ch 1, [sk 1 sc, 5 dc in next sc, sk 1 sc, sc in next sc] rep across, fasten off. (7 groups of 5-dc)

Position basket on towel, leaving top open (Row 15), with sewing needle and thread sew rem of basket to towel.

Handle

Row 1: With lemon, ch 57, sc in 2nd ch from hook, sc in each rem ch across, turn. (56 sc)

Row 2: Sl st in first 2 sc, [ch 3, sl st in next 2 sc] rep across, fasten off.

Position handle in arch shape above basket, with sewing needle and thread sew handle to towel.

Flower

Make 1 blue & 2 each lemon & bright pink

Ch 3, in first ch of ch-3 work [dc, ch 2, sl st] all in same ch, [ch 2, {dc, ch 2, sl st} in same first ch of beg ch-3] 3 times, fasten off.

With tapestry needle, embroider a lemon French knot in the center of each blue and bright pink flowers and bright pink French knot in the center of lemon flowers.

Using photo as a guide, sew flowers to washcloth.

Leaf Group

Make 2

With green, ch 4, [tr, ch 3, sl st] twice in first ch of ch-4, fasten off. Sew a leaf group at each outer edge. Fold washcloth and place in basket as shown. ✂

Lacy Lamp Shade Cover

Design by Josie Rabier

Skill Level: Intermediate

Size: Fits 6-inch-deep lamp shade with 16½-inch circumference at opening at top and 25¼-inch circumference around bottom

Materials

▶ Crochet cotton size 10: 650 yds white

▶ Size 7 steel crochet hook or size needed to obtain gauge

▶ Starch

▶ Plastic bag

▶ Tapestry needle

Gauge

6 knit sts = 1½ inches; 4 rows = 1 inch

Check gauge to save time.

Pattern Notes

Weave in loose ends as work progresses.

Join rnds with a sl st unless otherwise stated.

Pattern Stitches

Shell: [2 dc, ch 3, 2 dc] in indicated sp.

Beg shell: Sl st into ch-3 sp, [ch 3, dc, ch 3, 2 dc] in same ch sp.

Popcorn (pc): 5 dc in indicated st, draw up a lp, remove hook, insert hook in first dc of 5-dc group, pick up dropped lp, draw through st on hook, ch 1 to lock.

Beg pc: Ch 3, 4 dc in same st, draw up a lp, remove hook, insert hook in top of beg ch-3, pick up dropped lp, draw through st on hook, ch 1 to lock.

Reverse pc: 5 dc in indicated st, draw up a lp, remove hook, insert hook from back to front through first dc of 5-dc group, pick up dropped lp, draw through st on hook, ch 1 to lock. (This places the popcorn on RS of work).

Lamp-Shade Cover

Rnd 1: Ch 96, using care not to twist ch, sl st to join in beg ch to form a ring, ch 1, hdc in each ch around, join in top of beg hdc. (96 hdc)

Rnd 2: [Ch 7, 2 dtr in same st, sk next 2 hdc, sl st in next hdc] rep around, ending with sl st into base of beg ch-7, working behind lps, sl st into next sk hdc.

Rnd 3: Ch 3 (counts as first dc throughout), ch 3, 2 dc in next sk hdc, [2 dc in next sk hdc, ch 3, 2 dc in next sk hdc] rep around, join in top of beg ch-3. (32 ch-3 sps)

Rnd 4: Beg shell in first ch-3 sp, shell in each ch-3 sp around, join in top of beg ch-3. (32 shells)

Rnds 5–9: Rep Rnd 4.

Rnd 10: Sl st into next ch-3 sp, [beg pc, ch 3, pc] in same ch-3 sp, [{pc, ch 3, pc} in next ch-3 sp] rep in each ch-3 sp around, join in top of beg pc.

Rnds 11 & 12: Rep Rnd 10.

Rnd 13: Sl st into next ch-3 sp, [beg pc, ch 3, pc] in same ch-3 sp, *[5 dc in next ch-3 sp] 3 times **, [pc, ch 3, pc] in next ch-3 sp, rep from * around, ending last rep at **, join in top of beg pc.

Rnd 14: Sl st into ch-3 sp, [beg pc, ch 3, pc] in same ch-3 sp, *dc in each of next 7 dc, sk next dc, dc in each of next 7 dc **, [pc, ch 3, pc] in next ch-3 sp, rep from * around, ending last rep at **, join in top of beg pc.

Rnd 15: Sl st into ch-3 sp, [beg pc, ch 3, pc] in same sp, *dc in each of next 6 dc, sk next 2 dc, dc in each of next 6 dc **, [pc, ch 3, pc] in next ch-3 sp, rep from * around, ending last rep at **, join in top of beg pc.

Rnd 16: Sl st into ch-3 sp, beg pc in ch-3 sp, [ch 3, pc] twice in same ch-3 sp, *dc in each of next 5 dc, sk next 2 dc, dc in each of next 5 dc **, pc in next ch-3 sp, [ch 3, pc] twice in same ch-3 sp, rep from * around, ending last rep at **, join in top of beg pc.

Row 17 (RS): Sl st across into 2nd ch-3 sp, ch 4 (counts as first tr throughout), [pc, ch 3, pc] in same ch-3 sp, dc in each of next 4 dc, sk next 2 dc, dc in each of next 4 dc, [pc, ch 3, pc, tr] in next ch-3 sp, turn.

Row 18 (WS): Sl st into next ch-3 sp, ch 4, [reverse pc, ch 3, reverse pc] in same ch-3 sp, dc in each of next 3 dc, sk next 2 dc, dc in each of next 3 dc, [reverse pc, ch 3, reverse pc, tr] in next ch-3 sp, turn.

Row 19 (RS): Sl st into ch-3 sp, [ch 4, pc, ch 3, pc] in same ch-3 sp, dc in each of next 2 dc, sk next 2 dc, dc in each of next 2 dc, [pc, ch 3, pc, tr] in next ch-3 sp, turn.

Row 20 (WS): Sl st into ch-3 sp, [ch 4, reverse pc,

ch 3, reverse pc] in same ch-3 sp, dc in next dc, sk next 2 dc, dc in next dc, [reverse pc, ch 3, reverse pc, tr] in same ch-3 sp, turn.

Row 21 (RS): Sl st into ch-3 sp, [ch 4, pc] in same ch-3 sp, sk next 2 dc, [pc, tr] in next ch-3 sp, fasten off.

[With finished point to the right and with RS facing, attach cotton in next ch-3 sp between pc sts, rep Rows 17–21] 7 times.

Bottom Edging

Rnd 1 (RS): Working over beg ch-4 and end tr sts, attach cotton with sl st in first row of any section, *ch 5, tr in same sp, [sl st into next row, ch 5, tr in same sp] 4 times, pc in sp between 2 pc sts of Row 21, ch 6, tr in 6th ch from hook, sl st in next row, [ch 5, tr in same sp, sl st in next row] 4 times, sl st in first row of next section, rep from * around, join, fasten off.

Top Edging

Rnd 1 (RS): Working on opposite side of foundation ch, attach cotton with sl st in same hdc as sl st directly below, [ch 7, 2 dtr in same sp, sk 2 hdc, sl st in next hdc] rep around, ending with sl st into base of beg ch-7, fasten off.

Finishing

Cover lamp shade with plastic bag; secure opening at top so that no starch will stain shade. Saturate lampshade cover with starch; place over shade and shape. Allow to dry completely before removing. ✂

Tabletop Ecru Doily

Design by Josie Rabier

Skill Level: Intermediate

Size: 34 inches in diameter

Materials

► J. & P. Coats Knit-Cro-Sheen crochet cotton size 10 (325 yds per ball): 3 balls new ecru #61

► Size 7 steel crochet hook or size needed to obtain gauge

► Tapestry needle

Create this tabletop doily for a quiet area where you can sit and relax. A beautiful flower center is the focal point in this stunning piece!

Gauge

Rnds 1 and 2 = 1½ inches; 7 tr = 1 inch

Check gauge to save time.

Pattern Notes

Weave in loose ends as work progresses.

Join rnds with a sl st unless otherwise stated.

Doily

Rnd 1 (RS): Ch 6, sl st to join to form a ring, ch 4 (counts as first tr throughout), 23 tr in ring, join in top of beg ch-4. (24 tr)

Rnd 2: Ch 4, tr in same st, 2 tr in each tr around, join in top of beg ch-4. (48 tr)

Rnd 3: Ch 4, tr in each of next 5 tr, ch 7, [tr in each of next 6 tr, ch 7] rep around, join in top of beg ch-4.

Rnd 4: Sl st into ch-7 sp, ch 4, 15 tr in same ch sp, 16 tr in each ch-7 sp around, join in top of beg ch-3.

Rnd 5: Sl st into 9th tr, ch 4, tr in each of next 6 tr, *sk next 2 tr, tr in each of next 7 tr, ch 5 **, tr in each of next 7 tr, rep from * around, ending last rep at **, join in top of beg ch-4.

Rnd 6: Ch 4, tr in each of next 5 tr, *sk next 2 tr, tr in each of next 6 tr, ch 5, sl st in ch-5 sp, ch 5 **, tr in each of next 6 tr, rep from * around, ending last rep at **, join in top of beg ch-4.

Rnd 7: Ch 4, tr in each of next 4 tr, *sk next 2 tr, tr in each of next 5 tr, [ch 7, sl st in next ch-5 sp] twice,

ch 7 **, tr in each of next 5 tr, rep from * around, ending last rep at **, join in top of beg ch-4.

Rnd 8: Ch 4, tr in each of next 3 tr, *sk next 2 tr, tr in each of next 4 tr, [ch 7, sl st in next ch-7 sp] 3 times, ch 7 **, tr in each of next 4 tr, rep from * around, ending last rep at **, join in top of beg ch-4.

Rnd 9: Ch 3, holding back the last lp of each tr, tr in next 2 tr, sk next 2 tr, tr in each of next 3 tr, yo, draw through all 6 lps on hook, ch 1 to lock, *[ch 7, 2 tr in 4th ch of next ch-7 sp] 4 times **, holding back last lp of each tr, tr in next 3 tr, sk next 2 tr, tr in each of next 3 tr, yo, draw through all 7 lps on hook, ch 1 to lock, rep from * around, ending last rep at **, join in top of beg cl.

Rnd 10: Sl st into 4th ch of next ch-7 sp, ch 4, tr in same st, ch 7, [2 tr in 4th ch of next ch-7 sp, ch 7] rep around, join in top of beg ch-4.

Rnd 11: Ch 4, tr in next tr, *5 tr in 4th ch of next ch-7 sp **, tr in each of next 2 tr, rep from * around, ending last rep at **, join in top of beg ch-4.

Rnd 12: Ch 4, tr in next tr, ch 3, holding back last lp of each st, tr in next 5 tr, yo, draw through all 6 lps on hook (5-tr cl), ch 3 [tr in each of next 2 tr, ch 3, 5-tr cl over next 5 tr, ch 3] rep around, join in top of beg ch-4.

Rnd 13: Ch 4, tr in next tr, *ch 3, 2 tr in top of cl, ch 3 **, tr in each of next 2 tr, rep from * around, ending

last rep at **, join in top of beg ch-4.

Rnd 14: Ch 4, 4 tr in same st as beg ch, *ch 5, 5 tr in next tr, sl st in each of next 2 tr, [ch 7, sl st in each of next 2 tr] 3 times **, 5 tr in next tr, rep from * around, ending last rep at **, join in top of beg ch-4.

Rnd 15: Ch 4, tr in each of next 4 tr, *ch 5, 7 tr in next ch-5 sp, ch 5, tr in each of next 5 tr, sl st in next ch-7 sp, [ch 7, sl st in next ch-7 sp] twice **, tr in each of next 5 tr, rep from * around, ending last rep at **, join in top of beg ch-4.

Rnd 16: Ch 4, tr in each of next 4 tr, *ch 5, tr in each of next 3 tr, [2 tr, ch 5, 2 tr] in next tr, tr in each of next 3 tr, ch 5, tr in each of next 5 tr, sl st in next ch-7 sp, ch 7, sl st in next ch-7 sp **, tr in next 5 tr, rep from * around, ending last rep at **, join in top of beg ch-4.

Rnd 17: Ch 4, tr in each of next 4 tr, *5 tr in next ch-5 sp, tr in next 5 tr, ch 3, sl st in next ch-5 sp, ch 3, tr in each of next 5 tr, 5 tr in next ch-5 sp, tr in each of next 5 tr, sl st in next ch-7 sp **, tr in each of next 5 tr, rep from * around, ending last rep at **, join in top of beg ch-4, fasten off.

Row 18: With RS facing, sk ch-3 sp, attach cotton with sl st in next ch-3 sp, ch 4, 3 tr in same ch sp, tr in each of next 13 tr, sk next 4 tr, tr in each of next 13 tr, 4 tr in next ch-3 sp, turn.

Row 19: Ch 4, tr in each of next 14 tr, sk next 4 tr, tr in each of next 15 tr, turn.

Row 20: Ch 4, tr in each

Continued on page 74

Beaded Potpourri Bowl

Design by Tammy Hildebrand

Skill Level: Beginner

Size: Fits 5½-inch potpourri container

Materials

► Crochet cotton size 10: 45 yds pale pink

► Size B/1 crochet hook or size needed to obtain gauge

► 28 (5mm) iridescent beads

► 5 (½-inch) burgundy ribbon roses

► 24 inches ¼-inch-wide burgundy ribbon

► 24 inches ⅛-inch-wide green ribbon

► 16-inch strand 3mm pearl beads

► Craft glue

► Potpourri

► 5½-inch tall glass ivy bowl with 4-inch top opening

► Bead needle

Showcase your crochet skills and add fragrance to any room with this beautiful potpourri bowl. Beads, ribbons and tiny rosettes add that final finishing touch!

Gauge

Rnds 1–3 = 2½ inches

Check gauge to save time.

Pattern Notes

Weave in loose ends as work progresses.

Join rnds with a sl st unless otherwise stated.

String all 28 iridescent beads onto crochet cotton.

Pattern Stitches

3-dc cl: [Yo hook, insert hook in indicated st, yo, draw up a lp, yo, draw through 2 lps on hook] 3 times in indicated st, yo, draw through all 4 lps on hook.

Beg 3-dc cl: Ch 2 (counts as first dc), [yo hook, insert hook in indicated st, yo, draw up a lp, yo, draw through 2 lps on hook] twice, yo, draw through all 3 lps on hook.

Bowl Cover

Rnd 1 (RS): Ch 3, sl st to join to form a ring, beg 3-dc cl in ring, ch 3, push up 1 bead next to work, sc in first ch of ch-3, [3-dc cl in ring, ch 3, push up 1 bead next to work, sc in first ch of ch-3] rep around, join in top of beg cl. (8 cls)

Rnd 2: Ch 1, sc in same st as beg ch-1, ch 5, [sc in top of next cl, ch 5] rep around, join in beg sc.

Rnd 3: Sl st into ch-5 sp, ch 3 (counts as first dc throughout), 4 dc in same ch sp, 5 dc in each rem ch-5 sp around, join in top of beg ch-3. (40 dc)

Rnd 4: Ch 1, sc in same st as beg ch-1, [ch 3, sk next st, sc in next st] twice, [sc in next st, {ch 3, sk next st, sc in next st} twice] rep around, join in beg sc. (16 ch-3 sps)

Rnd 5: Sl st into ch-3 sp, ch 3, 2 dc in same ch-3 sp, ch 3, push up 1 bead, sc in first ch of ch-3, *3 dc in next ch-3 sp, sc in sp between next 2 sc, *3 dc in next ch-3 sp, ch 3, push up 1 bead, sc in first ch of ch-3, rep from * around, ending last rep at **, join in top of beg ch-3.

Rnd 6: Sl st into 3rd dc, ch 1, sc in same dc as beg ch-1, *ch 5, sc in next dc, ch 5, sk next 2 dc, sk next sc, sk next 2 dc **, sc in next dc, rep from * around, ending last rep at **, join in beg sc. (16 ch-5 sps)

Rnd 7: Sl st into next ch-5 sp, ch 3, 2 dc in same sp, 3 dc in each rem ch-5 sp around, join in top of beg ch-3. (48 dc)

Rnds 8 & 9: Ch 1, sc in each st around, join in beg sc.

Rnd 10: Ch 2 (counts as first hdc throughout), hdc in same st as beg ch-2, sk next st, [2 hdc in next st, sk next st] rep around, join in top of beg ch-2. (48 hdc)

Rnd 11: Ch 2, hdc in same st as beg ch-2, *2 hdc in next st, sk next hdc, sc in sp between next 2 hdc, sk next hdc **, 2 hdc in next hdc, rep from * around, ending last rep at **, join in top of beg ch-2. (48 hdc; 12 sc)

Rnd 12: Ch 3, dc in same st as beg ch-3, *2 dc in next st, dc in sp before next st, 2 dc in each of next 2 sts, sc in next sc **, 2 dc in next st, rep from * around, ending last rep at **, join in top of beg ch-3.

Rnd 13: Ch 1, sc in same st as beg ch-1, [ch 3, sk next st, sc in next st] 4 times, sc in next sc, [sc in next dc, {ch 3, sk next st, sc in next st} 4 times, sc in next sc] rep around, join in beg sc.

Rnd 14: Sl st in next ch-3 sp, ch 1, sc in same ch-3 sp, [ch 3, sc in next ch-3 sp] 3 times, [sc, ch 3, sc] in next sc, [sc in next ch-3 sp, {ch 3, sc in next ch-3 sp} 3

times, {sc, ch 3, sc} in next sc] rep around, join in beg sc. (64 ch-3 sps)

Rnd 15: Sl st into next ch-3 sp, ch 1, sc in same ch-3 sp, [ch 3, sc in next ch-3 sp] twice, 5 dc in next ch-3 sp, [sc in next ch-3 sp, {ch 3, sc in next ch-3 sp} twice, 5 dc in next ch-3 sp] rep around, join in beg sc.

Rnd 16: Sl st into next ch-3 sp, ch 1, sc in same ch-3

sp, ch 5, sc in next ch sp, *2 dc in each of next 5 dc **, sc in next ch-3 sp, ch 5, sc in next ch-3 sp, rep from * around, ending last rep at **, join in beg sc.

Rnd 17: Sl st into next ch-5 sp, ch 3, [2 dc, ch 3, push up 1 bead, sc in first ch of ch-3, 3 dc] in same ch-5 sp, sk next dc, sc in next dc, sk next 2 dc, [3 dc, ch 3, push up 1 bead, sc in first ch of

ch-3, 3 dc] in next dc, sk next 2 dc, sc in next dc, [{3 dc, ch 3, push up 1 bead, sc in first ch of ch-3, 3 dc} in next ch-5 sp, sk next dc, sc in next dc, sk next 2 dc, {3 dc, ch 3, push up 1 bead, sc in first ch of ch-3, 3 dc} in next dc, sk next 2 dc, sc in next dc] rep around, join in top of beg ch-3, fasten off.

Finishing

Place potpourri in ivy

bowl. Holding burgundy and green ribbons tog, weave through Rnd 10, place crocheted piece over top opening of ivy bowl, pull ribbon ends to gather, tie ends in a double bow. Cut pearl bead strand in half. Holding both strands tog, glue to center of double bow. Glue burgundy ribbon roses centered over pearl strands. ✂

Kitchen Dress-Ups

Designs by Lori Zeller

Skill Level: Beginner

Size:

Hot Pad: 8 inches long

Coaster: 4½ inches long

Magnet: 2 inches long

Materials

► Crochet cotton size 10: 300 yds mauve (MC), 150 yds cream (CC)

► Size 5 steel crochet hook or size needed to obtain gauge

► ½-inch magnet strip

► Hot-glue gun

► Tapestry needle

L ike three sisters all dressed up for a party, this hot pad, coaster and magnet set will make a pretty addition to any kitchen. You'll love the charm and style!

Gauge

5 dc = ½ inch

Check gauge to save time.

Pattern Notes

Weave in loose ends as work progresses.

Join rnds with a sl st unless otherwise stated.

Hot Pad

Rnd 1: With MC, ch 40, sl st to join to form a ring, ch 3 (counts as first dc throughout), dc in same ch as beg ch, dc in next ch, [2 dc in next ch, dc in next ch] rep around, join in top of beg ch-3.

Rnd 2: Ch 3, dc in each dc around, join in top of beg ch-3.

Rnd 3: Ch 1, sc in same st as beg ch, ch 3, sk next st, [sc in next st, ch 3, sk next st] rep around, join in beg sc. (30 ch-3 sps)

Rnd 4: Sl st into ch-3 sp, ch 1, [sc, ch 3, sc] in same ch-3 sp, [sc, ch 3, sc] in each rem ch-3 sp around, join in beg sc, fasten off.

Rnd 5: Attach CC in first ch-3 sp of previous rnd, ch 1, [sc, ch 3, sc] in same ch-3 sp, ch 1, [{sc, ch 3, sc} in next ch-3 sp, ch 1] rep around, join in beg sc, fasten off.

Rnd 6: With MC, rep Rnd 5, do not fasten off.

Rnds 7 & 8: Sl st into ch-3 sp, ch 1, [sc, ch 3, sc] in same ch-3 sp, ch 2, [{sc, ch 3, sc} in next ch-3 sp, ch 2] rep around, join in beg sc.

Rnd 9: Sl st into ch-3 sp, ch 3, 2 dc in same ch-3 sp, dc in next ch-2 sp, [3 dc in next ch-3 sp, dc in next ch-2 sp] rep around, join in top of beg ch-3. (120 dc)

Rnd 10: Rep Rnd 3. (60 ch-3 sps)

Rnd 11: Sl st into ch-3 sp, ch 1, sc in same ch-3 sp, [ch 3, sc in each next ch-3 sp] rep around, join in beg sc.

Rnd 12: Sl st into ch-3 sp, ch 1, [sc, ch 3, sc] in same ch-3 sp, [sc, ch 3, sc] in each rem ch-3 sp around, join in beg sc.

Rnds 13 & 14: Rep Rnd 12. At the end of Rnd 14, fasten off.

Rnd 15: Attach CC in first ch-3 sp of previous rnd, ch 1, [sc, ch 3, sc] in same ch-3 sp, [sc, ch 3, sc] in each rem ch-3 sp around, join in beg sc, fasten off.

Rnd 16: Attach MC in first ch-3 sp of previous rnd, ch 1, [sc, ch 3, sc] in same ch-3 sp, [sc, ch 3, sc] in each of next 6 ch-3 sps, sk next 16 ch-3 sps, [sc, ch 3, sc] in next 14 ch-3 sps, sk next 16 ch-3 sps, [sc, ch 3, sc] in each of next 7 ch-3 sps, join in beg sc. (28 ch-3 sps)

Rnd 17: Sl st into next ch-3 sp, ch 3, 2 dc in same ch-3 sp, 3 dc in each rem ch-3 sp around, join in top of beg ch-3. (84 dc)

Rnd 18: Ch 1, sc in same st as beg ch, ch 3, sk next st, [sc in next st, ch 3, sk next st] rep around, join in beg sc. (42 ch-3 sps)

Rnds 19 & 20: Rep Rnd 11.

Rnds 21–24: Rep Rnd 12.

Rnds 25–29: Sl st into ch-3 sp, ch 1, [sc, ch 3, sc] in same ch-3 sp, ch 1, [{sc, ch 3, sc} in next ch-3 sp, ch 1] rep around, join in beg sc.

Rnd 30: Rep Rnd 11. (126 dc)

Rnd 31: Rep Rnd 18. (63 ch-3 sps)

Rnds 32 & 33: Rep Rnds 11 and 12.

Rnd 34: Rep Rnd 4.

Rnd 35: Attach CC in first ch-3 sp of previous rnd, ch 1, [sc, ch 3, sc] in same ch-3 sp, [sc, ch 3, sc] in each rem ch-3 sp around, join in beg sc.

Rnd 36: Sl st into ch-3 sp, ch 1, [sc, ch 3, sc] in same ch-3 sp, [sc, ch 3, sc] in each rem ch-3 sp around, join in beg sc, fasten off.

Rnd 37: Attach MC in first ch-3 sp of previous rnd, ch 1, [sc, ch 3, sc] in same ch-3 sp, [sc, ch 3, sc] in each rem ch-3 sp around, join in beg sc.

Rnds 38–41: Rep Rnd 25. At the end of Rnd 41, fasten off.

Rnd 42: Attach CC in first ch-3 sp of previous rnd, ch

1, [sc, ch 3, sc] in same ch-3 sp, ch 1, [{sc, ch 3, sc} in next ch-3 sp, ch 1] rep around, join in beg sc, fasten off.

Neck Trim

Rnd 1: Attach CC in opposite side of foundation ch, ch 1, [sc, ch 3, sc] in same ch, sk next ch, [{sc, ch 3, sc} in next ch, sk next ch] rep around, join in beg sc, fasten off.

Coaster

Make 2

Note: *Make first coaster as pattern indicates; make 2nd coaster reversing the colors.*

Rnd 1: With MC, ch 30, sl st to join to form a ring,

ch 3, dc in same ch as beg ch-3, dc in each of next 2 chs, [2 dc in next ch, dc in each of next 2 chs] rep around, join in top of beg ch-3. (40 dc)

Rnd 2: Ch 1, sc in same st as joining, ch 3, sk next st, [sc in next st, ch 3, sk next st] rep around, join in beg sc. (20 ch-3 sps)

Rnd 3: Sl st into ch-3 sp, ch 1, [sc, ch 3, sc] in same ch-3 sp, [sc, ch 3, sc] in each rem ch-3 sp around, join in beg sc. (20 ch-3 sps)

Rnd 4: Rep Rnd 3.

Rnd 5: Sl st into ch-3 sp, ch 1, [sc, ch 3, sc] in same ch-3 sp, ch 1, [{sc, ch 3, sc} in next ch-3 sp, ch 1]

rep around, join in beg sc.

Rnd 6: Sl st into ch-3 sp, ch 1, [sc, ch 3, sc] in same ch-3 sp, ch 2, [{sc, ch 3, sc} in next ch-3 sp, ch 2] rep around, join in beg sc.

Rnd 7: Sl st into ch-3 sp, ch 1, [sc, ch 3, sc] in same ch-3 sp, ch 3, [{sc, ch 3, sc} in next ch-3 sp, ch 3] rep around, join in beg sc.

Rnd 8: Attach CC in first ch-3 sp of previous rnd, ch 1, [sc, ch 3, sc] in same ch-3 sp, [sc, ch 3, sc] in each ch-3 sp around, join in beg sc, fasten off.

Rnd 9: Attach MC in first ch-3 sp of previous rnd, ch 1, [sc, ch 3, sc], [sc, ch 3, sc] in each of next 4 ch-3

sps, sk next 10 ch-3 sps, [sc, ch 3, sc] in each of next 10 ch-3 sp, sk next 10 ch-3 sps, [sc, ch 3, sc] in each of next 5 ch-3 sps, join in beg sc. (20 ch-3 sps)

Rnd 10: Sl st into ch-3 sp, ch 3, 2 dc in same ch sp, 3 dc in each rem ch-3 sp around, join in beg sc. (60 dc)

Rnd 11: Rep Rnd 2. (30 ch-3 sps)

Rnd 12: Sl st into ch-3 sp, ch 1, sc in same ch-3 sp, ch 3, [sc in next ch-3 sp, ch 3] rep around, join in beg sc.

Rnds 13–18: Rep Rnd 3. At the end of Rnd 18, fasten off.

Continued on page 74

Three Napkin Rings

Designs by Maggie Petsch

Ribbon Napkin Ring

Skill Level: Intermediate

Size: 2 inches wide

Materials

► Crochet cotton size 30: small amount each white (A) and light blue (B)

► Kreinik Metallic Blending Filament: 55 yd spool of each white #100 (BFA) and sky blue #014 (BFB)

► Size 10 steel crochet hook or size needed to obtain gauge

► 18 inches ¼-inch-wide light blue satin ribbon

► Starch

► Sewing needle

These delicate napkin rings graced the table of many a 1918 homemaker. A little metallic blending filament will add an extra touch of elegance to your table.

Gauge

7 dc = ⁷⁄₁₆ inch

Check gauge to save time.

Pattern Notes

Weave in loose ends as work progresses.

Join rnds with a sl st unless otherwise stated.

Pattern Stitch

P: Ch 4, sl st in last sc made.

Napkin Ring

Row 1 (RS): With 1 strand each A and BFA held tog, ch 23, dc in 8th ch from hook, ch 2, sk next 2 chs, dc in next ch, ch 5, sk next 5 chs, dc in next ch, [ch 2, sk next 2 chs, dc in next ch] twice, turn. (2 ch-2 sps; 1 ch-5 sp; 2 ch-2 sps)

Row 2: Ch 5 (counts as first dc, ch 2 throughout), sk next ch-2 sp, dc in next dc, ch 2, dc in next dc, 5 dc in ch-5 sp, [dc in next dc, ch 2] twice, sk next 2 chs, dc in next ch, turn.

Row 3: Ch 5, sk next ch-2 sp, dc in next dc, ch 2, dc in next dc, ch 5, sk next 5 dc, [dc in next dc, ch 2] twice, sk next 2 chs, dc in next ch, turn.

Rows 4–31: Rep Rows 2 and 3.

Row 32: Rep Row 2, leaving a length of threads, fasten off.

Matching sts, sew opposite side of foundation ch to Row 32.

Border

With RS facing, attach 1 strand each B and BFB held tog with a sl st in end sp of any row on either side of napkin ring, ch 1, [sc, p, sc] in same sp, *3 sc in next sp, [sc, p, sc] in next sp, 2 sc in next sp, ch 7, turn; sk p, sc in center sc of next 3-sc group, ch 1, turn; [{3 sc, p} 3 times, 3 sc] in ch-7 sp, sc in same row end sp as last 2 sc made **, [sc, p, sc] in next sp, rep from * around, ending last rep at **, join in beg sc, fasten off.

Beg over end sp on opposite side of same row as beg sc of first side, rep on rem side of napkin ring.

Starch napkin ring lightly.

Weave ribbon through ch-5 sps; tie ends in a bow.

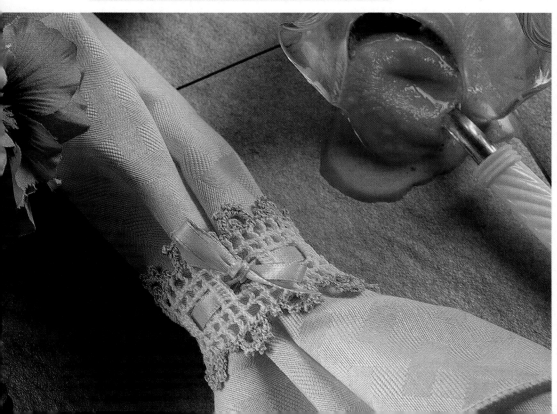

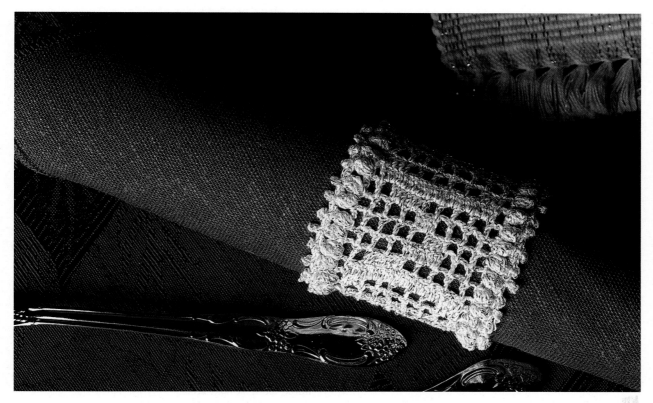

Monogrammed Napkin Ring

Skill Level: Intermediate

Size: 2¼ inches wide

Materials

▶ Crochet cotton size 10: small amount white

▶ Kreinik Metallic Blending Filament: 55 yds spool silver #001

▶ Size 10 steel crochet hook or size needed to obtain gauge

▶ Starch

▶ Sewing needle

Gauge

5 sps = 1 inch in filet mesh
Check gauge to save time.

Pattern Notes

Weave in loose ends as work progresses.

Napkin ring is worked with 1 strand each crochet cotton and blending filament held tog throughout.

When working from chart, read all odd-numbered RS row from right to left, all even-numbered WS rows from left to right.

Pattern Stitches

Popcorn (pc): 6 dc in indicated st or sp, remove hook from lp, insert hook from RS to WS in top of first dc of 6-dc group, pick up dropped lp, draw through st on hook, ch 1 tightly to lock.

Beg pc: [Ch 3, 5 dc] in indicated st or sp, remove hook from lp, insert hook from RS to WS in 3rd ch of beg ch-3, pick up dropped lp, draw through st on hook, ch 1 tightly to lock.

P: Ch 4, sl st in last sc made.

Napkin Ring

Row 1 (RS): Ch 32, dc in 8th ch from hook, [ch 2, sk 2 chs, dc in next ch] rep across, turn. (9 sps)

Rows 2–10: Ch 5 (counts as first dc, ch 2 throughout), sk next ch-2 sp, dc in next dc, [ch 2, dc in next dc] rep across, ending with ch 2, sk 2 chs, dc in next ch, turn. (9 ch-2 sps)

Rows 11–26: Work from chart for desired initial. At the end of Row 26, leaving a length of threads, fasten off.

Matching sts, sew opposite side of foundation ch to Row 26.

Border

Rnd 1 (RS): Attach thread with sl st in top of any row end st on either edge of napkin ring, beg pc in same st, ch 2, [pc in top of end st of next row, ch 2] rep around, join in top of beg pc.

Rnd 2: [{2 sc, p, sc} in next ch-2 sp] rep around, join in beg sc, fasten off.

Rep Rnds 1 and 2 on opposite side of napkin ring. Starch lightly.

Irish Rose Napkin Ring

Skill Level: Intermediate

Size: 1¾ inches wide

Materials

▶ Crochet cotton size 10: Small amount each white (A) and shaded yellows (B)

▶ Kreinik Metallic Blending Filament: 55 yd spool each white #100 (BFA) and star yellow #091 (BFB)

▶ Size 9 steel crochet hook or size needed to obtain gauge

▶ 5mm pearl bead

▶ Starch

▶ Sewing needle and thread

Gauge

Irish rose = 1½ inches in diameter

Check gauge to save time.

Pattern Notes

Weave in loose ends as work progresses.

Join rnds with a sl st unless otherwise stated.

Napkin Ring

Row 1 (WS): With 1 strand each A and BFA held tog, ch 12, dc in 4th ch from hook, ch 6, sk next 6 chs, dc in each of next 2 chs, turn. (2 dc; ch-6 sps; 2 dc)

Row 2: Ch 3 (counts as first dc throughout), dc in next dc, 6 dc over ch-6 sp, dc in each of next 2 dc, ch 5, sl st over end st of last row, turn. (10 dc)

Row 3: Ch 1, [5 sc, ch 4, 5 sc] in ch-5 sp, sl st in next dc, ch 3, dc in next dc, ch 6, sk next 6 dc, dc in each of next 2 dc, ch 5, sl st over end st of last row, turn.

Row 4: Ch 1, [5 sc, ch 4, 5 sc] in ch-5 sp, sl st in next dc, ch 3, dc in next dc, 6 dc over ch-6 sp, dc in each of next 2 dc, ch 5, sl st over

end st of last row, turn.

Rows 5–22: Rep Rows 3 and 4.

Row 23: Ch 1, [5 sc, ch 4, 5 sc] in ch-5 sp, holding RS tog and working through both thicknesses of Row 22 and opposite side of foundation ch, sl st in each st across, sl st in ch-3 sp at end of last row, ch 5, turn, sl st in top of end st of Row 1, ch 1, turn, [5 sc, ch 4, 5 sc] in ch-5 sp, sl st in ch-3 sp at base of ch-5, fasten off. Turn napkin ring RS out.

Irish Rose

Rnd 1: With 1 strand each B and BFB held tog throughout, ch 8, sl st to join to form a ring, ch 1, 18 sc in ring, join in beg sc. (18 sc)

Rnd 2: Ch 3, sk next 2 sc, [sl st in next sc, ch 3, sk next 2 sc] rep around, ending with join at base of beg ch-3. (6 ch-3 sps)

Rnd 3: [Sc, 6 dc, sc] in each ch-3 sp around, do not join. (6 petals)

Rnd 4: Working behind petals of last rnd, sl st around post of first sl st of Rnd 2, ch 4, [sl st around post of next sl st of Rnd 2, ch 4] rep around, join in sl st at base of beg ch-4.

Rnd 5: [Sc, dc, 8 tr, dc, sc] in each ch-4 sp around, join in beg sc, fasten off.

Place bead at center of rose and sew bead and rose to center of napkin ring. Starch lightly. ✂

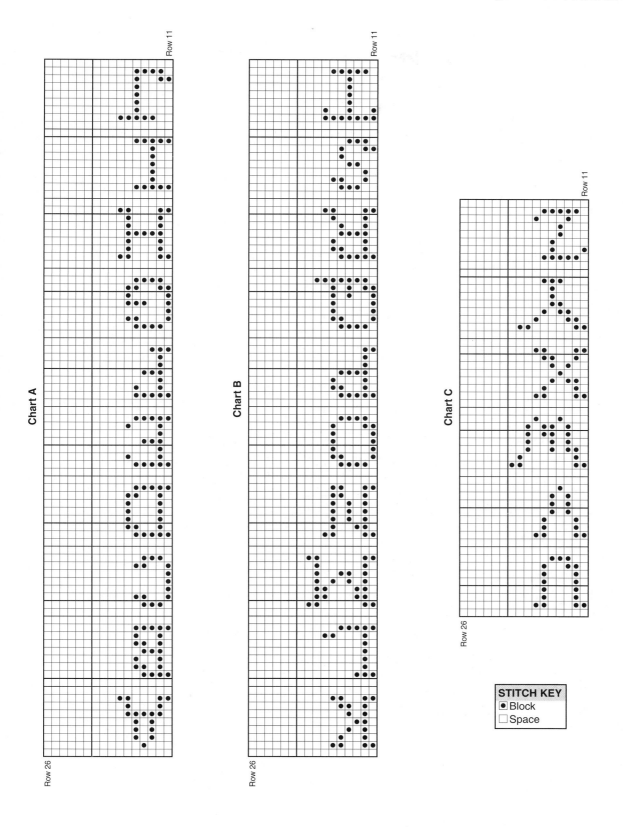

Chart A

Row 11

Row 26

Chart B

Row 11

Row 26

Chart C

Row 11

Row 26

STITCH KEY
- Block
- Space

Braided-Look Oval Rug

Design by Sue Childress

Skill Level: Beginner

Size: 26 x 32 inches

Materials

▶ Sirdar Chenille DK yarn (50 grams per ball): 3 balls cream #530, 1 ball each lilac #541, mauve #532, green #539, yellow #533, tan #531 and burgundy #551

▶ Size G/6 crochet hook or size needed to obtain gauge

▶ Tapestry needle

T
ake away the chill on early morning floors with this beautiful rug. Use the colors indicated or select colors to match your decor. Two contrasting strands held together throughout gives it a unique braided look!

Gauge

3 dc = 1 inch

Check gauge to save time.

Pattern Notes

Weave in loose ends as work progresses.

Work with 2 strands of yarn held together throughout.

Join rnds with a sl st unless otherwise stated.

Pattern Stitches

Cl: [Yo hook, insert hook in indicated st, yo, draw up a lp, yo, draw through 2 lps on hook] 5 times, yo, draw through all 6 lps on hook.

Beg cl: Ch 2 (counts as first dc), [yo hook, insert hook in indicated st, yo, draw up a lp, yo, draw through 2 lps on hook] 4 times, yo, draw through all 5 lps on hook.

Rug

Rnd 1: Holding 1 strand each cream and lilac tog, ch 26, 4 hdc in 3rd ch from hook, hdc in each of next 21 chs, 7 hdc in end ch, working on opposite side of foundation ch, hdc in next 21 chs, 2 hdc in next ch, join in top of beg ch-2. (56 hdc)

Rnd 2: Working in back lps for this rnd only, ch 2, 2 hdc in each of next 3 sts, hdc in each of next 25 sts, 2 hdc in each of next 3 sts, hdc in each of next 24 sts, join in top of beg ch-2. (62 hdc)

Rnd 3: Ch 2, 2 hdc in each of next 4 hdc, hdc in each of next 27 hdc, 2 hdc in each of next 4 hdc, hdc in each of next 26 hdc, join in top of beg ch-2. (70 hdc)

Rnd 4: Ch 3, sc in next hdc, [ch 3, sk next hdc, sc in next hdc] rep around, ending with ch 3, sl st in base of beg ch-3. (36 ch-3 sps)

Rnd 5: Sl st into next ch-3 sp, beg cl in same sp, ch 2, [cl in next ch sp, ch 2] rep around, join in top of beg cl. (36 cls)

Rnd 6: Sl st into next ch-2 sp, ch 4, [sc in next ch sp, ch 4] rep around, join in base of beg ch-4, fasten off lilac, attach mauve. (36 ch-4 sps)

Rnd 7: Sl st into ch-4 sp, ch 3 (counts as first dc throughout), 4 dc in same ch sp, [5 dc in next ch-4 sp] 3 times, [3 dc in next ch-4 sp] 12 times, [5 dc in next ch-4 sp] 6 times, [3 dc in next ch-4 sp] 12 times, [5 dc in next ch-4 sp] twice, join in top of beg ch-3. (132 dc)

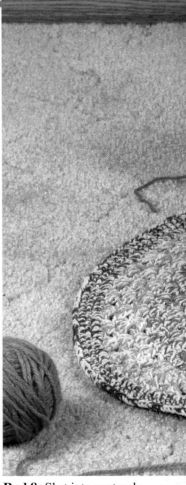

Rnd 8: Sl st into center dc of 5-dc group, ch 3, 5 dc in same dc, 6 dc in center dc of next 5-dc group, *[5 dc in center dc of next 5-dc group] twice, [3 dc in center dc of next 3-dc group] 12 times, [5 dc in center dc of next 5-dc group] twice *, [6 dc in center dc of next 5-dc group] twice, rep from * to *, join in top of beg ch-3.

Rnd 9: [Ch 3, sk next 2 dc, sc in next dc] rep around, ch 3, sl st in base of first ch-3. (46 ch-3 sps)

Rnd 10: Sl st into ch-3 sp, beg cl in same sp, ch 2, [cl in next ch-3 sp, ch 2] rep around, join in top of beg cl.

Rnd 11: Sl st into ch-2 sp, ch 4, [sc in next ch-2 sp, ch 4] rep around, join in base of beg ch-4, fasten off mauve, attach yellow. (46 ch-3 sps)

Rnd 12: Sl st into ch-4 sp, ch 3, 5 dc in same ch sp, 6 dc in next ch sp, * [4 dc in next ch sp] 3 times, [3 dc in next ch sp] 14 times, [4 dc in next ch sp] 3 times *, [6 dc in next ch sp] 3 times, rep from * to *, 6 dc in last ch sp, join in top of beg ch-3. (168 dc)

Rnd 13: Ch 4, [sk next 2 dc, sc in next dc, ch 4] rep around, sl st in base of beg ch-4. (56 ch-4 sps)

Rnd 14: Sl st into ch-4 sp, ch 3, 5 dc in same sp, *[4 dc in next ch sp] 4 times, [3 dc in next ch sp] 19 times, [4 dc in next ch sp] 4 times *, 6 dc in next ch sp, rep from * to *, join in top of beg ch-3. (190 dc)

Rnd 15: Sl st in next 2 dc, ch 3, 5 dc in same dc, *[4 dc in 3rd dc of next 4-dc group] 4 times, [3 dc in

2nd dc of next 3-dc group] 19 times, [4 dc in 3rd dc of next 4-dc group] 4 times *, 6 dc in 4th dc of next 6-dc group, rep from * to *, join in top of beg ch-3.

Rnd 16: [Ch 3, sk next 2 dc, sc in next dc] rep around, ch 3, sl st in base of beg ch-3, fasten off yellow, attach green. (64 ch-3 sps)

Rnd 17: Sl st into ch-3 sp, ch 3, 4 dc in same sp, [4 dc in next ch sp] 31 times, 5 dc in next ch sp, [4 dc in next ch sp] 31 times, join in top of beg ch-3. (258 dc)

Rnd 18: Ch 3, dc in next dc, 3 dc in next dc, dc in each of next 2 dc, [4 dc in 3rd dc of next dc group] 31 times, [dc in next 2 dc, 3 dc in next dc, dc in each of next 2 dc] across next 5-dc group, [4 dc in 3rd dc of next dc group] 31

times, join in top of beg ch-3. (262 dc)

Rnds 19 & 20: Ch 3, dc in each of next 6 dc, [4 dc in 3rd dc of next 4-dc group] 31 times, dc in each of next 7 dc, [4 dc in 3rd dc of next 4-dc group] 31 times, join in top of beg ch-3, fasten off green, attach tan.

Rnd 21: Ch 3, dc in each of next 2 dc, 3 dc in next dc, dc in each of next 3 dc, [4 dc in 3rd dc of next 4-dc group] 31 times, [dc in next 3 dc, 3 dc in next dc, dc in each of next 3 dc] across 7-dc group, [4 dc in 3rd dc of next 4-dc group] 31 times, join in top of beg ch-3. (266 dc)

Rnd 22: Ch 3, dc in each of next 3 dc, 3 dc in next dc, dc in each of next 4 dc, [4 dc in 3rd dc of next 4-dc group] 31 times, [dc in

each of next 4 dc, 3 dc in next dc, dc in each of next 4 dc] across 9-dc group, [4 dc in 3rd dc of next 4-dc group] 31 times, join in top of beg ch-3. (270 dc)

Rnd 23: Sl st into next 2 dc, ch 3, 3 dc in same dc, *sk next 2 dc, 5 dc in next dc, sk next 2 dc, 4 dc in next dc, [4 dc in 3rd dc of next 4-dc group] 31 times *, sk next 2 dc of end 11-dc group, 4 dc in next dc, rep from * to *, sl st to join in top of beg ch-3, fasten off tan, attach burgundy.

Rnd 24: Ch 2, hdc in each dc around, join in top of beg ch-2.

Rnds 25 & 26: Ch 1, sc in each st around, join in beg sc.

At the end of Rnd 26, fasten off. For best results, wet-block rug. ✂

Scallops & Shells Edgings

Scallop Edging

Design by Sharon Valiant

Skill Level: Beginner

Size: 2½ inches wide

Materials

- ▶ DMC Cebelia crochet cotton size 10: 1 ball very light sky blue #747
- ▶ Size 7 steel crochet hook or size needed to obtain gauge
- ▶ 21-inch-wide linen towel
- ▶ Sewing needle and thread
- ▶ Starch

Gauge

2 shells = 1 inch

Check gauge to save time.

Pattern Notes

Weave in loose ends as work progresses.

Edging may be crocheted to length desired.

Pattern Stitch

Shell: [2 dc, ch 1, 2 dc] in indicated st.

Edging

Row 1: Ch 12, 2 dc in 7th ch from hook, ch 1, 2 dc in next ch, ch 1, sk next 2 chs, 2 dc in next ch, ch 1, 2 dc in last ch, turn.

Row 2: Ch 3 (counts as first dc throughout), shell in next ch-1 sp, ch 1, sk next ch-1 sp, shell in next ch-1 sp, ch 1, dc in last lp, turn.

Row 3: Ch 4, shell in next ch-1 sp of shell, ch 1, shell in next ch-1 sp of shell, ch 6, sl st in ch-3 sp, turn.

Row 4: Ch 2, 8 hdc in ch-6 sp, ch 1, [shell in next ch-1 sp of next shell, ch 1] twice, dc in 3rd ch of ch-4, turn.

Row 5: Ch 4, shell in ch-1 sp of shell, ch 1, shell in next ch-1 sp of shell, ch 6, sl st in ch-1 sp immediately before hdc scallop, turn.

Row 6: Ch 2, 4 hdc in ch-6 sp, ch 6, draw up a lp, remove hook and insert hook in center of previous hdc scallop, pick up dropped lp, draw through and tighten, ch 2, 4 hdc in lp just made, ch 3, sl st in top of last hdc (for p), 4 hdc in same lp, 4 hdc in rem of previous lp, [ch 1, shell in next ch-1 sp of shell] twice, ch 1, dc in 3rd ch of ch-4, turn.

Row 7: Ch 4, shell in next ch-1 sp of shell, ch 1, shell in next ch-1 sp of shell, ch 6, sl st in ch-1 sp immediately before hdc, turn.

Row 8: Ch 3, 8 hdc in lp just made, ch 1, [shell in next ch-1 sp of shell, ch 1] twice, dc in 3rd ch of ch-4, turn.

Row 9: Ch 4, [shell in next ch-1 sp of shell, ch 1] twice, sk last 2 dc of shell, working across dc scallop, *[dc, ch 1, dc] in next dc, sk next dc, rep from * 3 times, in top of starting ch work [dc, ch 1, dc], sl st in hdc where previous scallop was joined, turn.

Row 10: [{Sc, ch 3, sc} in next ch-1 sp] 5 times, ch 3, [shell in next ch-1 sp of shell, ch 1] twice, dc in 3rd ch of ch-4, turn.

Rep Rows 3–10 until same width as towel or desired length, ending last rep at Row 6. At the end of last row, turn.

Top Border

Working across long top edge, ch 1, 2 sc in ch lp, [ch 2, 2 sc in next ch lp] rep across, fasten off.

Finishing

Starch lightly. Pin to measurements and allow drying completely. Sew in place on towel.

This enchanting set of three edgings demonstrates the lovely effects achieved by color. Achieve a crisp, clean look with white on white, or add a splash of lively color with mixing edging and fabric shades. You're sure to find a look that pleases you while suiting your decor!

Pointing the Way

Design by Ruth Shepherd

Skill Level: Beginner

Size: 1¾ inches wide

Materials

- ▶ DMC Baroque crochet cotton: white
- ▶ Size 8 steel crochet hook or size needed to obtain gauge
- ▶ Sewing needle and thread

Gauge

4 rows = 1¼ inches

Check gauge to save time.

Pattern Notes

Weave in loose ends as work progresses.

Amount of crochet cotton depends on length of edging desired.

Pattern Stitch

Shell: [3 dc, ch 2, 3 dc] in indicated st.

Edging

Row 1: Ch 15, dc in 9th ch from hook, [ch 2, sk next 2 chs, dc in next ch] twice, turn.

Row 2: Ch 5 (counts as first dc, ch 2 throughout), dc in next dc, ch 2, sk next ch-2 sp and next dc, shell in next ch sp, turn.

Row 3: Ch 3, shell in ch-2 sp of shell, ch 2, sk next 2

dc of previous shell, dc in next dc, ch 2, sk next ch-2 sp, dc in next dc, ch 2, dc in 3rd ch of ch-5, turn.

Row 4: Ch 5, dc in next dc, [ch 2, sk next ch-2 sp, dc in next dc] twice, turn.

Row 5: Ch 5, dc in next dc, ch 2, sk next ch-2 sp, dc in next dc, ch 2, dc in 3rd ch of ch-5, turn.

Rep Rows 2–5 for desired length. At the end of last rep, fasten off.

Outer Edging

Row 1: With RS facing, attach cotton in ch-5 sp at beg of Row 1, ch 1, sc in same ch sp, [ch 3, sc in next ch-3 sp, ch 3, sc in next ch-2 sp of shell, ch 3, sc in end of next row] rep across, fasten off.

Row 2: With RS facing, attach cotton in ch-2 sp at

beg of Row 1 (next to foundation ch), ch 1, 3 sc in same ch-2 sp, 3 sc in each of next 2 ch-2 sps, [5 sc in next ch sp, {5 sc, ch 3, 5 sc} in next ch sp, 5 sc in each of next 2 ch sps] rep across to opposite end,

working across end of last row of edging, work 3 sc in each ch-2 sp across, end, fasten off.

Finishing

Press edging lightly. Sew edging to piece.

Imagination

Design by Ruth Shepherd

Skill Level: Beginner

Size: 2½ inches wide

Materials

► DMC Baroque crochet cotton: white

► Size 8 steel crochet hook or size needed to obtain gauge

► Sewing needle and thread

► Starch

Continued on page 73

Blushing Rose Valance

Design by Carol Alexander for Crochet Trends & Traditions

Skill Level: Intermediate

Size: 16 x 38 inches

Materials

▶ J. & P. Coats Knit-Cro-Sheen crochet cotton size 10: 950 yds cream #42, 100 yds almond pink #35, 12 yds spruce #179

▶ Size 7 steel crochet hook or size needed to obtain gauge

▶ 9 (5mm) cream pearl beads

▶ Tapestry needle

Dress up any window and room with this beautiful valance trimmed with tiny roses!

Gauge

Row 1 bottom border, 8 dc = 1 inch; Rows 2–17 pattern rep = 4¼ inches; valance body, 8 dc = 1 inch; Rows 2–5 pattern rep = 1 inch

Check gauge to save time.

Pattern Notes

Weave in loose ends as work progresses.

Join rnds with a sl st unless otherwise stated.

Pattern Stitches

Dc dec: [Yo hook, insert hook in indicated st, yo, draw up a lp, yo, draw through 2 lps on hook] twice, yo, draw through all 3 lps on hook.

Popcorn (pc): 5 dc in indicated st, drop lp from hook, insert hook back to front in top of first dc of 5-dc group, pick up dropped lp, draw lp through st on hook (this pushes the pc to RS of work).

Shell: 5 dc in indicated st.

P: [Sc, ch 3, sc] in indicated st.

V-st: [Dc, ch 2, dc] in indicated st.

Sc picot (scp): Ch 2, sc around top of post of last tr made.

Bottom Border

Row 1 (RS): With cream, ch 56, sk 7 chs (counts as first dc, ch 2 and 2 skipped chs), [dc in each of next 10 chs, ch 2, sk next 2 chs] 4 times, dc in last ch, turn.

Row 2: Ch 5, sk first dc and next 2 chs, [dc in next st, ch 2, sk next 2 sts] 16 times, dc in 3rd ch of beg ch-3 of previous row.

Row 3: Ch 5, sk first dc and next 2 chs, dc in next dc, [ch 5, dc dec in next 2 dc] 5 times, ch 5, dc in next dc, ch 2, sk next 2 chs, dc in each of next 10 sts, ch 2, sk next 2 chs, dc in 3rd ch of beg ch-5 of previous row, turn.

Row 4: Ch 5, sk first dc and next 2 chs, dc in each of next 4 dc, pc in next dc, dc in each of next 5 dc, ch 2, sk next 2 chs, dc in next dc, ch 2, sc in next ch-5 sp, ch 1, shell in next dc dec, sc in next ch-5 sp, [ch 5 p in 3rd ch of next ch-5 sp] twice, ch 5, sc in next ch-5 sp, shell in next dc dec, sc in next ch-5 sp, shell in next dc, turn.

Row 5: Ch 5, shell in first dc of first shell, sc in 3rd dc of same shell, ch 5, sc in 3rd dc of next shell, shell in next sc, sc in next ch-5 sp, ch 5, p in 3rd ch of next ch-5 sp, ch 5, sc in next ch-5 sp, shell in next sc, sc in 3rd dc of next shell, ch 5, dc in next dc, ch 2, sk next 2 chs, dc in each of next 10 sts, ch 2, dc in 3rd ch of beg ch-5 of previous row, turn.

Row 6: Ch 5, sk first dc and next 2 chs, [dc in next dc, ch 2, sk next 2 dc] 3 times, [dc in next dc, ch 2, sk next 2 chs] twice, sc in next ch-5 sp, ch 5, sc in 3rd dc of next shell, shell in next sc, sc in next ch-5 sp, ch 5, sc in next ch-5 sp, shell in next sc, sc in 3rd dc of next shell, ch 5, p in 3rd ch of next ch-5 sp, ch 5, sc in 3rd dc of last shell, shell in next ch-5 sp at beg of previous row, turn.

Row 7: Ch 5, shell in first dc of first shell, sc in 3rd dc of same shell, [ch 5, p in 3rd ch of next ch-5 sp] twice, ch 5, sc in 3rd dc of next shell, shell in next sc, sc in next ch-5 sp, shell in next sc, sc in 3rd dc of next shell, ch 5, p in 3rd ch of next ch-5 sp, ch 5, dc in next dc, ch 2, sk next 2 chs, dc in each of next 10 sts, ch 2, sk next 2 chs, dc in 3rd ch of beg ch-5 of previous row, turn.

Row 8: Ch 5, sk first dc and next 2 chs, dc in each of next 4 dc, pc in next dc, dc in each of next 5 dc, ch 2, sk next 2 chs, dc in next dc, ch 2, sc in next ch-5 sp, ch 5, p in 3rd ch of next ch-5 sp, ch 5, sc in 3rd dc of next shell, shell in next sc, sc in 3rd dc of next shell, [ch 5, p in 3rd ch of next ch-5 sp] 3 times, ch 5, sc in 3rd dc of next shell, shell in ch-5 sp at beg of previous row, turn.

Row 9: Sl st in each dc of first shell, shell in next sc, sc in next ch-5 sp, [ch 5, p in 3rd ch of next ch-5 sp] twice, ch 5, sc in next ch-5 sp, shell in next sc, sc in 3rd dc of next shell, shell in next sc, sc in next ch-5 sp, ch 5, p in next 3rd ch of next ch-5 sp, ch 5, dc in next dc, ch 2, sk next 2 chs, dc in each of next 10

sts, ch 2, sk next 2 chs, dc in 3rd ch of beg ch-5 of previous row, turn.

Row 10: Ch 5, sk first dc and next 2 chs, [dc in next dc, ch 2, sk next 2 dc] 3 times, [dc in next dc, ch 2, sk next 2 chs] twice, sc in next ch-5 sp, ch 5, sc in next ch-5 sp, shell in next sc, sc in 3rd dc of next shell, ch 5, sc in 3rd dc of next shell, shell in next sc, sc in next ch-5 sp, ch 5, p in 3rd ch of next ch-5 sp, ch 5, sc in next ch-5 sp, shell in next sc, sc in 3rd dc of last shell, turn.

Row 11: Sl st in each dc of first shell, shell in next sc, sc in next ch-5 sp, ch 5, sc in next ch-5 sp, shell in next sc, sc in 3rd dc of next shell, ch 5, p in 3rd ch of next ch-5 sp, ch 5, sc

in 3rd dc of next shell, shell in next sc, sc in next ch-5 sp, ch 5, dc in next dc, ch 2, sk next 2 chs, dc in each of next 10 sts, ch 2, sk next 2 chs, dc in 3rd ch of beg ch-5 of previous row, turn.

Row 12: Ch 5, sk first dc and next 2 chs, dc in each of next 4 dc, pc in next dc, dc in each of next 5 dc, ch 2, sk next 2 chs, dc in next dc, ch 2, sc in next ch-5 sp, shell in next sc, sc in 3rd dc of next shell, [ch 5, p in 3rd ch of next ch-5 sp] twice, ch 5, sc in 3rd dc of next shell, shell in next sc, sc in next ch-5 sp, shell in next sc, sc in 3rd dc of last shell, turn.

Row 13: Sl st in each of first 3 dc of first shell, ch 5, V-st in 3rd dc of next

shell, [ch 2, V-st in 3rd ch of next ch-5 sp] 3 times, ch 2, V-st in 3rd dc of next shell, ch 2, dc in next dc, ch 2, sk next 2 chs, dc in each of next 10 sts, ch 2, sk next 2 chs, dc in 3rd ch of beg ch-5 of previous row, turn.

Row 14: Ch 5, sk first dc and next 2 chs, [dc in next dc, ch 2, sk next 2 sts] 15 times, dc in 3rd ch of beg ch-5 of previous row, ch 2, sk 2 chs, dc in base of ch-5, turn.

Row 15: Ch 5, sk first dc and next 2 chs, [dc in each of next 10 sts, ch 2, sk 2 chs] 4 times, dc in 3rd ch of beg ch-5 of previous row, turn.

Row 16: Ch 5, sk first dc and next 2 chs, [dc in each of next 4 dc, pc in next dc,

dc in each of next 5 dc, ch 2, sk 2 chs] 4 times, dc in 3rd ch of beg ch-5 of previous row, turn.

Row 17: Ch 5, sk first dc and next 2 chs, [dc in each of next 10 dc, ch 2, sk next 2 chs] 4 times, dc in 3rd ch of beg ch-5 of previous row, turn.

[Rep Rows 2–17] 7 times, then rep Rows 2–15, fasten off.

Body

Row 1: With WS of bottom border facing, attach cream in corner at right end of top edge, working in the 143-ch sps across top edge of border, sc in first ch sp, work 2 sc in each rem ch sp across top edge, turn. (285 sc)

Continued on page 75

Nawina Pillow

Design by Belinda Carter

Skill Level: Intermediate

Size: Approximately 16 inches square

Materials

▶ J. & P. Coats Lustersheen sport weight yarn (1.75 oz per ball): 4 balls black #2, 1 ball each tea leaf #615, bluette #425, rally red #910, vanilla #7, natural #805 and small amount white #1

▶ Size D/3 crochet hook or size needed to obtain gauge

▶ Size B/1 crochet hook

▶ 14-inch-square pillow form

▶ Yarn needle

Gauge

9 sts = 2 inches; 7 rows = 1 inch

Check gauge to save time.

Pattern Notes

Weave in loose ends as work progresses.

Join rnds with a sl st unless otherwise stated.

Use crochet hook size D to work pillow cover; use crochet hook size B to work Indian girl.

Pattern Stitches

Long sc (Lsc): Insert hook in next st in indicated row below working row, yo, draw up a lp level with working row, yo, draw through 2 lps on hook.

2-dc cl: [Yo hook, insert hook in indicated st, yo, draw up a lp, yo, draw through 2 lps on hook] twice, yo, draw through all 3 lps on hook.

Pillow Front

Row 1 (RS): With bluette, ch 50, sc in 2nd ch from hook, sc in each rem ch across, turn. (49 sc)

Row 2: Ch 1, sc in each st across, turn.

Rows 3 & 4: Rep Row 2.

Row 5: Ch 1, sc in next sc, [Lsc 1 row below, Lsc 2 rows below, Lsc 3 rows below, Lsc 2 rows below, Lsc 1 row below, sc in next sc] rep across, turn.

Rows 6–8: Rep Row 2.

Row 9: Ch 1, Lsc 3 rows below, [Lsc 2 rows below, Lsc 1 row below, sc in next st, Lsc 1 row below, Lsc 2 rows below, Lsc 3 rows below] rep across, turn.

Rows 10–35: Rep Rows 2–9, ending after a Row 3.

Row 36: Ch 1, sc in each st across, changing to tea leaf in last sc, turn.

Rows 37–41: Rep Rows 5–9.

Rows 42–78: Rep Rows 2–9, ending with a Row 6, at the end of Row 78, fasten off.

Border

Rnd 1 (RS): Attach black with a sl st in top corner st of pillow front, ch 1, working in rem lps across opposite side of foundation ch, sc in same st as joining, sc in each rem st across, ch 2, working over ends of rows down side, 49 sc evenly sp across to bottom, ch 2, sc in each sc across bottom, ch 2, working over ends of rows up opposite side, 49 sc evenly sp across, ch 2, join in beg sc, fasten off.

Rnd 2 (RS): Attach rally red with a sl st in top corner ch-2 sp, ch 1, [sc, ch 2, sc] in same ch-2 sp, sc in each st around, working [sc, ch 2, sc] in each corner ch-2 sp, join in beg sc, fasten off.

Rnd 3: With black, rep Rnd 2.

Rnd 4 (RS): Attach tea leaf in top corner ch-2 sp, ch 2 (counts as first hdc throughout), [sc in next sc, hdc in next sc, 2-dc cl in next sc, tr in next sc, 2-dc cl in next sc, hdc in next sc] 9 times, working last hdc of last rep in corner ch-2 sp, ch 2, *hdc in same sp, rep between [ ] 9 times, working last hdc of last rep in corner ch-2 sp, ch 2, rep from * around, join in top of beg ch-2, fasten off.

Rnd 5 (RS): Attach bluette with a sl st in top corner ch-2 sp, ch 2, *[2-dc cl in next st, tr in next st, 2-dc cl in next st, hdc in next st, sc in next st, hdc in next st] 9 times, 2-dc cl in next st, hdc in corner ch-2 sp, ch 2, *hdc in same sp, rep between [ ] 9 times, 2-dc cl in next st, hdc in corner ch-2 sp, ch 2, rep from * around, join in top of beg ch-2, fasten off.

Rnd 6: With black, rep Rnd 2.

Rnds 7 & 8: With rally red, rep Rnd 2, at the end of Rnd 8, fasten off.

Lightning

With white, ch 50, leaving a length of yarn, fasten off.

With white, ch 45, leaving a length of yarn, fasten off.

With yarn needle and rem length, referring to photo for placement, sew to pillow front.

Water Jars

No. 1

Row 1: With rally red, ch 6, sc in 2nd ch from hook,

sc in each rem ch across, turn. (5 sc)

Row 2: Ch 1, 2 sc in first sc, sc in each sc across to last sc, 2 sc in last sc, turn. (7 sc)

Row 3: Ch 1, sc in each sc across, turn.

Row 4: Rep Row 2. (9 sc)

Fig. 1
Horse Symbol

Row 5: Rep Row 3, leaving a length of yarn, fasten off. With yarn needle and 1

strand black, use straight sts to embroider horse symbol (Fig. 1).

With yarn needle and rem length, referring to photo for placement, sew to pillow front.

No. 2

Row 1: With black, ch 4, sc in 2nd ch from hook, sc in each rem ch across, turn. (3 sc)

Row 2: Ch 1, 2 sc in first sc, sc in next sc, 2 sc in last sc, turn. (5 sc)

Row 3: Ch 1, sc in each sc across, turn.

Row 4: Ch 1, 2 sc in first sc, sc in each of next 3 sc, 2 sc in last sc, turn. (7 sc)

Row 5: Rep Row 3.

Row 6: Ch 1, sc dec over next 2 sc, sc in each of next 3 sc, sc dec over next 2 sc, turn. (5 sc)

Row 7: Ch 1, sc dec over next 2 sc, sc in next sc, sc dec over next 2 sc, turn. (3 sc)

Rows 8 & 9: Rep Row 3.

Row 10: Ch 1, 2 sc in each

Fig. 2
Water Symbol

sc across, leaving a length of yarn, fasten off. (6 sc)

With yarn needle and 1 strand each rally red and natural held tog, use straight sts to embroider water symbols (Fig. 2).

With yarn needle and rem length, referring to photo for placement, sew to pillow front.

No. 3

Row 1: With natural, ch 6, sc in 2nd ch from hook, [hdc in next ch, sc in next ch] twice, turn. (5 sts)

Row 2: Ch 1, sc in each of next 2 sc, 3 hdc in next sc, sk next hdc, sc in last sc, turn.

Row 3: Ch 1, sc in each of

next 3 sts, sk next hdc, 3 hdc in next sc, sc in next sc, turn.

Row 4: Ch 1, sc in each of next 3 sts, sk next hdc, 3 hdc in next sc, sk next sc, sc in last sc, turn.

Row 5: Ch 1, sc dec over first 2 sts, hdc in next st, sc in next st, hdc in next st, sc dec over next 2 sts, turn.

Row 6: Ch 1, sc dec over next 2 sts, sc in next st, sc dec over next 2 sts, turn. (3 sts)

Row 7: Sl st in first 2 sts, ch 3, sc in 2nd ch from hook, sc in next ch of ch-3, sl st in same sc as last sl st on row, leaving a length of yarn, fasten off.

With yarn needle and rally red, use straight sts to embroider mountain symbols (Fig. 3).

Fig. 3
Mountains Symbol

With yarn needle and rem length, referring to photo for placement, sew to pillow front.

Drum
Side

Row 1: Beg at bottom with rally red, ch 9, sc in 2nd ch from hook, sc in each rem ch across, turn. (8 sc)

Rows 2–8: Ch 1, sc in each sc across, turn, at the end of Row 8, fasten off.

With yarn needle and 2

strands of black held tog, use straight sts to embroider zigzag pattern (Fig. 4).

Fig. 4
Drum

Top & Bottom
Make 2

Row 1: With vanilla, ch 9, sc in 2nd ch from hook, [ch 2, sc in each of next 2 chs] 3 times, ch 2, sc in last ch, leaving a length of yarn, fasten off.

Position drum top and bottom on drum side; with yarn needle and rem length, referring to photo for placement, sew drum to pillow front through all thicknesses.

Indian Girl
Moccasins
Make 2

Row 1: With vanilla, ch 5, sc in 2nd ch from hook, sc in each rem ch across, turn. (4 sc)

Row 2: Ch 1, sc in each sc across, turn.

Row 3: Sl st in first sc, ch 3, sl st in 2nd ch of ch-3, sl st in next ch of ch-3, sl st in same sc as first sl st of row, [sl st in next sc, ch 3, sl st in 2nd ch of ch-3, sl st in next ch of ch-3, sl st in same sc as last sl st on row] rep across, leaving a length of yarn, fasten off.

Leggins (right pant leg)
Row 1: With natural, ch 4, insert hook in 2nd ch from

hook, yo, draw up a lp, [insert hook in next ch, yo, draw up a lp] twice, yo, draw through 1 lp on hook, [yo, draw through 2 lps on hook] 3 times.

Rows 2–9: Sk first vertical bar, [insert hook directly through center of next vertical bar, draw up a lp] 3 times (4 lps on hook), yo, draw through 1 lp on hook, [yo, draw through 2 lps on hook] 3 times.

Row 10: Ch 1, turn to work down side of pant leg, sl st in end of first row, ch 3, sl st in 2nd ch of ch-3, sl st in next ch of ch-3, sl st in same st as last sl st on pant leg, *sl st in end of next row, ch 3, sl st in 2nd ch of ch-3, sl st in next ch of ch-3, sl st in same st as last sl st on pant leg, rep from * across to bottom edge of pant leg, ch 1, working in rem lps across opposite side of foundation ch, sc in each st across, ch 1, turn to work up opposite side of pant leg, sl st in end of first row, ch 3, sl st in 2nd ch of ch-3, sl st in next ch of ch-3, sl st in same st as last sl st on pant leg, †sl st in end of next row, ch 3, sl st in 2nd ch of ch-3, sl st in next ch of ch-3, sl st in same st as last sl st on pant leg, rep from † across to top edge of pant leg, leaving a length of yarn, fasten off.

Leggins (left pant leg)
Rows 1–4: Rep Rows 1–4 of right pant leg.

Row 5: Rep Row 10 of right pant leg.

Sleeve
Make 2

Row 1: With vanilla, ch 8,

[sc, 2 dc] in 2nd ch from hook, sk next 2 chs, [sc, 2 dc] in next ch, sk next 2 chs, sc in last ch, turn. (7 sts)

Rnd 2: Ch 1, 2 sc in end of row, ch 1, working in rem lps across opposite side of foundation ch, sc in each st across, ch 1, 2 sc in other end of row, ch 1, working across Row 1, sl st in first st, ch 3, sl st in 2nd ch of ch-3, sl st in next ch of ch-3, sl st in same st as first sl st on sleeve, [sl st in next st, ch 3, sl st in 2nd ch of ch-3, sl st in same st as last sl st on sleeve] 4 times, sc in each of last 2 sts, working over first 2 sc of rnd, hdc in next sc, dc in next sc, leaving a length of yarn, fasten off.

Dress

Row 1 (WS): Beg at bottom with vanilla, ch 14, [sc, 2 dc] in 2nd ch from hook, [sk next 2 chs, {sc, 2 dc} in next ch] 3 times, sk next 2 chs, sc in last ch, turn. (13 sts)

Rows 2–8: Ch 1, [sc, 2 dc] in first sc, [sk next 2 dc, {sc, 2 dc} in next sc] 3 times, sk next 2 dc, sc in last sc, turn.

Row 9: Ch 1, [sc dec over next 2 sts] 3 times, sc in next st, [sc dec over next 2 sts] 3 times, turn. (7 sc)

Row 10: Ch 1, sc in first st, [2 sc in next st, sc in next st] 3 times, turn. (10 sc)

Row 11: Ch 1, [sc 2 dc] in first sc, [sk next 2 sc, {sc, 2 dc} in next sc] twice, sk next 2 sts, sc in last sc, turn.

Rows 12–17: Ch 1, [sc, 2 dc] in first sc, [sk next 2 dc, {sc, 2 dc} in next sc] twice, sk next 2 dc, sc in last sc, turn.

Row 18: Ch 1, sc dec over next 2 sts, sc in each of next 6 sts, sc dec over last 2 sts, turn.

Row 19: Ch 1, working over ends of rows down side, 18 sc evenly sp across to bottom, ch 1, working in rem lps across opposite side of foundation ch, sc in each of next 13 chs, ch 1, working over ends of rows up opposite side, 18 sc evenly sp across to top, fasten off.

Dress fringe

Row 1 (RS): Attach vanilla with a sl st in beg sc at bottom of dress, ch 3, sl st in 2nd ch of ch-3, sl st in next ch of ch-3, sl st in same st as joining on dress, [sl st in next st on dress, ch 3, sl st in 2nd ch of ch-3, sl st in next ch of ch-3, sl st in same st as last st on dress] rep across bottom of dress, leaving a length of yarn, fasten off.

Belt

Row 1: With natural, ch 2, 2 sc in 2nd ch from hook, ch 1, turn.

Rows 2–14: Sc in side of turning ch-1, sc in first sc, ch 1, turn, at the end of Row 14, leaving a length of yarn, fasten off.

Hair

With black, ch 34, sl st to join to form a ring, ch 12, sl st in 17th ch of beg ch-34 to form a circle with a line running vertically through the center, leaving a length of yarn, fasten off.

Cut 54 (20-inch) lengths of black; pull strand through ch at side of circle, ch of ch-12 and corresponding ch on other side of circle, having ends even. Rep, using all chs of circle and ch-12 until all strands are used.

Hair Bow

Make 2

With rally red, ch 65, fasten off.

Attaching to pillow front

Referring to photo for placement, position moccasins, leggins, dress, sleeves, hair and belt on pillow front; sew in place using yarn needle and rem lengths.

Braid hair and tie with bows. Trim ends of braids evenly.

Pillow Back

Make 2

Row 1 (RS): With black, ch 64, sc in 2nd ch from hook, sc in each rem ch across, turn. (63 sc)

Rows 2–54: Rep Rows 2–9 of pillow front, working 1 additional sc at beg and end of each row on Row 5 and Row 9.

Row 55: Ch 1, sc in each st across, turn to work over ends of rows across side.

Edging

Rnd 1: Ch 2, 34 sc evenly sp down side, ch 2, working on opposite side of foundation ch, sc in each ch across, ch 2, 34 sc evenly sp across opposite side, ch 2, join in beg sc, fasten off.

Place back pieces tog so sides are overlapping by 5 sts on sides. With yarn needle and black, sew tog across 5 sts on each side.

Note: Back should be square with 63 sts across each side.

Joining Front & Back

Rnd 1: Holding front and back with WS tog, working through both thicknesses, attach black with sl st in top corner ch-2 sp, ch 1, [sc, ch 2, sc] in same sp as joining, sc in each rem st around entire outer edge, working [sc, ch 2, sc] in each corner ch-2 sp, join in beg sc, fasten off.

Rnd 2: Rep Rnd 4 of pillow front border, working 11 reps instead of 9.

Rnd 3: Rep Rnd 5 of pillow front border, working 11 reps on each side instead of 9.

Insert pillow form through opening in back. ✄

Scallops & Shells Edgings

Continued from page 67

Gauge

3 rows = 1 inch

Check gauge to save time.

Pattern Notes

Weave in loose ends as work progresses.

Amount of crochet cotton will depend on length of edging desired.

Edging

Row 1 (WS): Ch length desired with a multiple of 3 plus 2, dc in 8th ch from hook, [ch 2, sk next 2 chs, dc in next ch] rep across, turn.

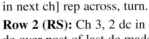

Row 2 (RS): Ch 3, 2 dc in ch sp, [dc in next dc, ch 4, 3 dc over post of last dc made] rep across to last dc before last ch sp, dc in next dc, 2 dc in ch sp, dc in 3rd ch of turning ch, turn.

Row 3: Ch 3, dc in each of next 3 dc, [ch 3, sc in next ch-4 sp, ch 3, dc in next dc] rep across, ending with dc in each of last 3 dc, turn.

Rows 4–7: Rep Rows 2 and 3.

Row 8: [Ch 6, sc in next ch sp] rep across, ending with ch 6, sl st in last dc, turn.

Row 9: Ch 1, [{4 sc, ch 3, 4 sc} in next ch-6 sp] rep in each ch-6 sp across, fasten off.

Finishing

Press and starch lightly. Sew Row 1 of edging to piece. ✄

Tabletop Ecru Doily

Continued from page 54

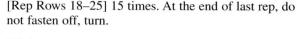

of next 12 tr, sk next 4 tr, tr in each of next 13 tr, turn.

Row 21: Ch 4, tr in each of next 10 tr, sk next 4 tr, tr in each of next 11 tr, turn.

Row 22: Ch 4, tr in each of next 8 tr, sk next 4 tr, tr in each of next 9 tr, turn.

Row 23: Ch 4, tr in each of next 6 tr, sk next 4 tr, tr in each of next 7 tr, turn.

Row 24: Ch 4, tr in each of next 4 tr, sk next 4 tr, tr in each of next 5 tr, turn.

Row 25: Ch 4, holding back last lp of each st, tr in next 3 tr, sk next 2 sts, tr in each of next 3 tr, yo, draw through all 7 lps on hook, tr in next tr, fasten off.

[Rep Rows 18–25] 15 times. At the end of last rep, do not fasten off, turn.

Edging

Rnd 26: *Ch 7, working along ends of rows, 2 dtr in same sp, sl st in same sp, [ch 7, 2 dtr in same sp, sk next row, sl st in next row, ch 7, 2 dtr in same sp, sl st in same sp] 3 times, ch 7, 2 dtr in same sp, sk next row, 5 sc in next row, 5 sc in first tr of next section, [ch 7, 2 dtr in same sp, sk next row, sl st in next row, ch 7, 2 dtr in same sp, sl st in same sp] 3 times, ch 7, 2 dc in same sp, sl st in top point of cl, rep from * around, fasten off.

Inner Trim

Rnd 1: Working in top of cls and skipped 2-tr groups of Rnd 9, attach cotton with sl st in top of any cl, *[ch 7, 2 dtr in same sp, sl st in next 2 tr] 4 times, ch 7, 2 dtr in same sp, sl st in top of cl, rep from * around, join, sl st into 4th ch of next ch-7 sp.

Rnd 2: [Ch 9, 2 trtr in same sp, sl st in 4th ch of next ch-7 sp] rep around, join in same st as beg ch-9, fasten off. ✂

Kitchen Dress-Ups

Continued from page 59

Rnd 19: Attach CC in first ch-3 sp of previous rnd, ch 1, [sc, ch 3, sc] in same ch-3 sp, ch 1, [{sc, ch 3, sc} in next ch-3 sp, ch 1] rep around, join in beg sc.

Rnd 20: Sl st into ch-3 sp, ch 1, [sc, ch 3, sc] in same ch-3 sp, ch 1, [{sc, ch 3, sc} in next ch-3 sp, ch 1] rep around, join in beg sc, fasten off.

Rnd 21: With MC, rep Rnd 19.

Rnds 22 & 23: Sl st into ch-3 sp, ch 1, [sc, ch 3, sc] in same ch-3 sp, ch 1, [{sc, ch 3, sc} in next ch-3 sp, ch 1] rep around, join in beg sc. At the end of Rnd 23, fasten off.

Rnd 24: Rep Rnd 19, fasten off.

Neck Trim

With CC, rep Rnd 1 of neck trim of hot pad.

Magnet

Rnd 1: With MC, ch 16, sl st to join to form a ring, ch 1, sc in each ch around, join in beg sc. (16 sc)

Rnd 2: Ch 1, sc in same sc as beg ch, ch 2, [sc in next sc, ch 2] rep around, join in beg sc. (16 ch-2 sps)

Rnd 3: Sl st into ch-2 sp, ch 1, [sc, ch 3, sc] in same ch-2 sp, [sc, ch 3, sc] in each rem ch-2 sp around, join in beg sc.

Rnd 4: Sl st into ch-3 sp, ch 1, [sc, ch 3, sc] in same ch-3 sp, [{sc, ch 3, sc} in next ch-3 sp] twice, sk next 5 ch-3 sps, [{sc, ch 3, sc} in next ch-3 sp] 3 times, sk next 5 ch-3 sps, join in beg sc. (6 ch-3 sps)

Rnd 5: Sl st into ch-3 sp, ch 3, 3 dc in same ch-3 sp, 4 dc in each rem ch-3 sp around, join in top of beg ch-3. (24 dc)

Rnd 6: Ch 1, sc in same st as beg ch, ch 3, sk next st, [sc in next st, ch 3, sk next st] rep around, join in beg sc, fasten off. (12 ch-3 sps)

Rnd 7: Attach CC in first ch-3 sp of previous rnd, ch 1, [sc, ch 3, sc] in same ch-3 sp, [sc, ch 3, sc] in each ch-3 sp around, join in beg sc, fasten off.

Rnd 8: Attach MC in first ch-3 sp of previous rnd, ch 1, [sc, ch 3, sc] in same ch-3 sp, [sc, ch 3, sc] in each rem ch-3 sp around, join in beg sc.

Rnd 9: Sl st into ch-3 sp, ch 1, [sc, ch 3, sc] in same ch-3 sp, [sc, ch 3, sc] in each rem ch-3 sp around, join in beg sc, fasten off.

Rnd 10: Rep Rnd 7.

Finishing

Glue magnet strip to back of dress. ✂

Blushing Rose Valance

Continued from page 69

Note: Number of sc sts must be a multiple of 4 plus 1.

Row 2: Ch 3 (counts as first dc throughout), sk first st, dc in each rem st across, turn.

Row 3: Ch 1, sc in each of first 2 dc, p in next dc, *sc in each of next 3 dc, p in next dc, rep from * across, ending with sc in last dc, sc in 3rd ch of turning ch, turn.

Row 4: Ch 3, work [2 dc, ch 3, 2 dc] in each p across, ending with dc in last sc, turn.

Row 5: Ch 3, 3 sc in next ch-3 sp, *dc in sp between next 2 dc groups, 3 sc in next ch-3 sp, rep from * across, dc in 3rd ch of turning ch, turn.

[Rep Rows 2–5] 8 times, then rep Row 2, ending Row 38, do not fasten off.

Side edging

Continuing from end of Row 38, work 2 sc in each of next 28 turning ch-3 lp across side edge of body, now working across foundation edge of bottom border, 2 sc in next ch sp, [sk next dc, sc in bottom of each of next 8 dc, sk next dc, 2 sc in next ch sp] 4 times, sl st in end, fasten off.

Attach cream at bottom corner on opposite side of bottom border, rep edging in reverse across other side edge of bottom border and body to top corner, fasten off.

Top Border

Row 1: With RS facing, attach cream in corner at right end of top edge, ch 1, sc in same place, [ch 8, sk next 3 sts, sc in next st] rep across, ending in left corner, fasten off.

Row 2: Attach almond pink in first ch-8 sp, ch 1, work [sc, 2 p, sc] in same sp and each rem ch-8 sp across, fasten off.

Bottom Border Edging

Row 1: Holding piece upside down with RS facing and working around bottom edge, attach cream in right bottom corner, 3 sc in next ch sp (end of Row 1), *3 sc in next sp [end of Row 2), ch 6, sk next row, sl st in top end of Row 4, ch 8, sk next row, sl st in top end of Row 6, ch 6, sk next row, work [sl st, ch 6, sl st] in end of Row 8 (tip of diamond point), ch 6, sl st in top end of Row 9, ch 8, sl st in center of end of Row 11, ch 8, sl st in beg of Row 13, 3 sc in each of next 2 ch sps **, 3 sc in each of next 2 ch sps, rep from * 8 times, ending last rep at **, turn.

Row 2: Ch 1, sc in each of next 5 sc, *ch 2, sk next sc, V-st in next ch sp, ch 2, [sl st in next sl st, ch 2, {2 dc, ch 3, 2 dc} in next ch sp, ch 2] twice, sl st in next sl st, sl st in ch-6 lp at diamond point, ch 3, [dc, ch 3, dc, ch 3, sl st] in same lp, rep between [ ] twice, sl st in next sl st, ch 2, V-st in next ch sp, ch 2, sk next sc, sc in each of next 3 sc **, [sc dec in next 2 sc, sc in each of next 3 sc] twice, rep from * 8 times, ending last rep at **, sc in each of last 2 sc, pulling almond pink through on last lp of last sc, turn.

Row 3: Ch 1, sc in first sc, sk next sc, p in next sc, sk next sc, sc in next sc, *ch 3, p in next V-st, ch 3, [sl st in next sl st, ch 3, 3 p in next ch-3 sp, ch 3] twice, sl st in next sl st, ch 5, 4 p in ch-3 sp at tip, ch 5, rep between [ ] twice, sl st in next sl st, ch 3, p in next V-st, ch 3 **, sk next 3 sc, sl st in next sc, ch 7, sk next 3 sc, sl st in next sc, turn, work 9 sc in lp just made, sl st in same sc as first sl st of lp, turn, working in the 9 sc just made, [p in next sc, sk next sc] 4 times, p in last sc, sl st in same sc as last sl st of lp, sk next 3 sc, rep from * 8 times, ending last rep at **, sc in next sc, sk next sc, p in next sc, sk next sc, sc in last sc, fasten off.

Rose Motif

Make 9

Rnd 1: With almond pink, ch 5, sl st to join to form a ring, ch 1, 16 sc in ring, join in beg sc. (16 sc)

Rnd 2: Ch 1, sc in same st as beg ch, ch 3, sk 1 sc, [sc in next sc, ch 3, sk 1 sc] 7 times, join in beg sc. (8 ch-3 sps)

Rnd 3: Sl st into ch-3 sp, [sl st, ch 2, 3 dc, ch 2, sl st] in each ch-3 sp around, sl st to front of first sc of Rnd 2, do not fasten off. (8 petals)

Rnd 4: For inner petals, beg in next sk sc of Rnd 1, work [sl st, ch 2, 2 dc, ch 2, sl st] in each sk sc of Rnd 1, fasten off. (8 petals)

Flatten and smooth petals. Sew bead to center of rose.

Leaf

Note: Make 3 leaves on each rose motif.

With front of rose motif facing, attach spruce to back between any 2 outside petals, [ch 3, 2 tr, sc p, tr, ch 3, sl st] in same place for leaf, fasten off, [sk 2 petals, work leaf as before between 2 petals on back of rose, fasten off] twice. (3 leaves)

Using photo as a guide, sew rose motifs to bottom border of valance as shown.

Weave small curtain rod through ch sps of top border or attach decorative curtain rings spaced as desired across top and insert rod through rings. ✀

Baby Boutique

Soft and cuddly
treasures abound
here for little ones—
one of life's most
precious treasures of all.
From delightful layettes
to warm, snuggly
afghans, celebrate the
blessing of children
with a gift that's certain
to become a cherished
keepsake!

Red & White Layette

Designs by Ann E. Smith

Skill Level: Beginner

Size:

Sleeper: 6, 12 and 18 months
Chest: 23 (25, 27) inches
Length: 24 (26, 28) inches

Cap: One size fits all

Sock: 6, 12 and 18 months

Afghan: 42 inches square

Materials

► Spinrite Patons Astra yarn (178 yds per skein) Layette set: 5 (5, 6) skeins white #2751, 2 skeins crayon red #2225 Afghan: 5 skeins white #2751, 6 skeins crayon red #2225

► Size F/5 crochet hook or size needed to obtain gauge

► 3 (½-inch) red buttons

► Tapestry needle

Gauge

Layette set in body pattern, 16 sts = 4 inches; 16 rows = 6 inches

Afghan, 7 V-sts and 10 rows = 4 inches

Check gauge to save time.

Pattern Notes

Weave in loose ends as work progresses.

Join rnds with a sl st unless otherwise stated.

Ch 3 counts as first dc throughout.

To change color at the end of a sc row, with present color draw up a lp in last st, then with next color complete the sc. Cut and join colors as necessary.

When crocheting the afghan, change color in the last hdc as follows, with present color, yo and draw up a lp in last hdc, with new color draw through all 3 lps on hook.

Pattern Stitch

V-st: [Hdc, ch 1, hdc] in next ch-1 sp.

Garment Pattern

Row 1 (RS): With crayon red, ch 1, sc in each sc across, turn.

Row 2: Rep Row 1, changing to white in last st, turn.

Row 3: With white, ch 3, dc in each sc across, turn.

Row 4: With white, ch 1, sc in each dc across, turn.

Rows 5–8: Rep Rows 3 and 4. At the end of Row 8, change to crayon red, turn.

Rep Rows 1–8 for garment patterns.

Sleeper

Back

Row 1 (RS): Beg at lower edge with white, ch 48 (52, 56), dc in 4th ch from hook, dc in each rem ch across, turn. (46, 50, 54 sts)

Row 2: Ch 1, sc in each dc across, turn.

Row 3: Ch 3, dc in each sc across, turn.

Rows 4 & 5: Rep Rows 2 and 3.

Row 6: Rep Row 2, changing to crayon red in last st, turn.

Rep Rows 1–8 of garment pattern until piece measures 19¾ (21½, 23¼) inches from beg, ending with a WS row, fasten off.

Armhole shaping

With RS facing, sk first 4 sts, attach correct color in next st with a sl st, continue in pattern across to last 4 sts, turn. Work even on 38 (42, 46) sts to approximately 24 (26, 28) inches from beg, fasten off.

Front

Work as for back until piece measures 18 (20, 22) inches from beg ending with a RS row.

Neck placket

Work in established pattern across first 21 (23, 25) sts, sk next 4 sts, join new strand in next st with a sl st, ch 1, sc in same st as joining, sc in each rem st across. Working sides separately and at the same time, continue in pattern shaping armholes as for back. Work even on 17 (19, 21) sts for each shoulder to approximately 22 (24, 26) inches from beg ending with a WS row.

Left front neck shaping

Work in pattern across leaving last 4 (5, 6) sts unworked. Dec 1 st at neck edge every row 4 times. Continue in pattern on rem 9 (10, 11) sts until piece measures same length as back, fasten off.

Right front neck shaping

With RS facing, attach correct color in 5th (6th, 7th) st from right edge. Working [ch 1, sc] or [ch 3 for dc) in same st, continue in pattern across. Complete as for left neck.

Sleeve

Make 2

Row 1: Beg at lower edge and above cuff, with white, ch 20 (22, 24), dc in 4th ch from hook, dc in each rem ch across, turn.

Rows 2–6: Rep Rows 2–6 the same as back; inc 1 st each edge every row.

Then beg garment pattern, continue to inc until there are 34 (36, 38) sts. Work even in pattern to approximately 5½ (5¾, 6) inches, fasten off.

Joining

Join shoulder seams. Set in sleeve joining side edges to skipped armhole sts. Join underarm and side seams.

Sleeve Trim

Rnd 1: With RS facing, attach crayon red, ch 1, sc evenly sp around, join in beg sc.

Rnds 2–6: Ch 1, sc in each sc around, join in beg sc. At the end of Rnd 6, fasten off.

Tie

With crayon red, ch 145 (150, 160), sl st in 2nd ch from hook, sl st in each rem ch across, fasten off.

Lower Trim

With RS facing, attach crayon red with a sl st near seam, working along rem lps from foundation ch, ch 4 (counts as first dc, ch 1), *sk next lp, dc in next lp, ch 1, rep from * around, join in 3rd ch of beg ch-4, fasten off. Weave tie through ch-1 sps, tie in a bow.

Neck Trim

Row 1: With RS facing, attach white with sl st on right front near placket opening, ch 1, work 14 (15, 16) sc evenly sp to corner, 3 sc in corner, work 13 (14, 15) sc evenly sp to shoulder, dec 1 sc over next 2 sts, 19 (21, 23) sc evenly sp along back neck, dec 1 sc over next 2 sts, 13 (14, 15) sc evenly sp to corner, 3 sc in corner, 14 (15, 16) sc evenly sp to lower edge of placket, turn.

Row 2: Ch 1, sc in each sc, dec 1 sc at each shoulder edge, turn.

Row 3: Ch 1, sc in first 4 (5, 6) sc, [ch 1, sk 1 sc, sc in each of next 4 sc] twice, ch 1, sk 1 sc, 3 sc in corner sc, sc in each rem sc around working 3 sc in next corner, turn.

Row 4: Ch 1, sc in each sc around working sc in each ch-1 sp, turn.

Row 5: Ch 1, sc in each sc around working 3 sc in each corner, fasten off.

Sew buttons opposite buttonholes.

Cap

With white, ch 82, dc in 4th ch from hook, dc in each rem ch across, sl st to join in top of first dc.

Rnd 1: Ch 1, sc in each dc around, join in beg sc.

Rnd 2: Ch 3, dc in each sc around, join in top of beg ch-3.

Rnds 3 & 4: Rep Rnds 1 and 2.

Rnd 5: Rep Rnd 1.

Body Pattern

Rnds 1 & 2: With crayon red, sc in each st around.

Rnd 3: With white, dc in each st around.

Rnd 4: With white, sc in each st around.

Rnd 5: With white, dc in each st around.

Rep Rnds 1 and 2. Continue in established color and stitch patterns, dec on each dc rnd as follows:

Rnd 1: [Dc in next 14 sts, dec] 5 times. (75 sts)

Rnd 3: [Dc in next 13 sts, dec] 5 times. (70 sts)

Rnd 5: [Dc in 12 sts, dec 5] 5 times. (65 sts)

Continue as established until 10 sts rem. Work 2 sc rnds with crayon red. With white, [dec 1 dc over next 2 dc] 5 times. (5 sts)

Sc in each rem st around, sl st in each st around, fasten off.

Pompom

Wrap crayon red yarn around your hand 30 times. Remove lps; tie a separate strand tightly around center. Cut lps at each end, trim pompom. Attach to tip of cap.

Tie

With white, ch 200, fasten off. Fold in half and weave through 3rd rnd of dc sts at lower edge. Try on child then tie for a comfortable fit.

Sock

Make 2

Rnd 1 (RS): With white, ch 24, sc in 2nd ch from hook, sc in each rem ch across, sl st to join in beg sc, ch 1, sc in each sc around.

Rnd 2: With crayon red, sc in each sc around.

Rnds 3 & 4: With white, sc in each sc around.

Rnds 5–7: Rep Rnds 2–4.

Rnd 8: Rep Rnd 2, sl st to join in first sc, fasten off.

Heel

Row 1 (RS): Attach white with sl st in 5th sc to the right of joining, ch 1, sc in same st as beg ch, sc in next 9 sc, turn. (10 sc)

Row 2: Ch 1, sc in next 7 sc, turn.

Row 3: Ch 1, sc in next 4 sc, turn.

Row 4: Ch 1, sc in next 5 sc, turn.

Row 5: Ch 1, sc in next 6 sc, turn.

Row 6: Ch 1, sc in next 7 sc, turn.

Row 7: Ch 1, sc in next 8 sc, turn.

Row 8: Ch 1, sc in next 9 sc, turn.

Row 9: Ch 1, sc in next 10 sc, fasten off.

Instep

Rnd 1: With RS facing, attach white with sl st in 6th heel st from right edge, ch 1, sc in same st, sc in next 4 sc dec 1 sc over next 2 sts on foot, sc in each of next 9 sc, dec 1 sc over next 2 sts, sc in last 5 heel sts. (21 sc)

Rnd 2: Ch 1, sc in each sc around.

Rnd 3: With crayon red, sc in each sc around.

For size 6 months only stop here. Continue in rnds working 2 white and 1 crayon red for 0, (1, 2) times.

Toe shaping

Note: Maintain stripe pattern for rem of sock.

Rnd 1: [Sc in each of next 3 sts, dec 1 sc over next 2 sts] 4 times, sc in last sc. (17 sc)

Rnd 2: Sc in each sc around.

Rnd 3: [Sc in each of next

2 sc, dec 1 sc over next 2 sc] 4 times, sc in last sc. (13 sc)

Rnd 4: Rep Rnd 2.

Rnd 5: [Sc in next sc, dec 1 sc over next 2 sts] 4 times, sc in last sc. (9 sc)

Rnd 6: With white, rep Rnd 2.

Rnd 7: With white, [dec 1 sc over next 2 sc] 4 times, sc in last sc, leaving a length of yarn, fasten off. (5 sc)

Weave yarn through rem sts, pull to close opening, secure, fasten off.

Rnd 8: Attach white in opposite side of foundation ch, sl st in each st around, fasten off.

Pompom

Make 2

Wrap crayon red around your hand 20 times. Complete as for pompom for cap. Attach to toe.

Afghan

Row 1 (RS): Beg at lower edge with crayon red, ch 193, hdc in 2nd ch from hook, [sk next 2 chs, V-st in next ch] rep across ending with, sk next ch, hdc in last ch, change to white, turn. (63 V-sts; 2 dc)

Row 2: With white, ch 1, hdc in first hdc, [V-st in next ch-1 sp of next V-st] rep across, ending with hdc in last hdc, turn.

Row 3: Rep Row 2, changing to crayon red in last hdc, turn.

Rnds 4 & 5: With crayon red, rep Rows 2 and 3. In last hdc of Row 5, change to white.

[Rep Rows 2–5] 23 times, then rep Rows 2-4.

Border

Note: Rnd 1 of border must be a multiple of 3 sts.

Rnd 1: Continuing with crayon red, ch 1, 3 sc in first hdc (for corner), sk ch-1 sps, work 132 sc across top, 3 sc in last hdc (for corner), 147 sc evenly sp along side, 3 sc in foundation ch (for corner), [sk 1 ch, sc in each of next 2 chs] rep across, ending with 3 sc in last ch. (132 sts)

Work 147 sc evenly sp along side, join in beg sc.

Rnd 2: Ch 1, sc in same st as beg ch, ch 3, sk next 2 sc, [sc in next sc, ch 3, sk next 2 sc] rep around, join in beg sc, fasten off.

Rnd 3: With RS facing, attach white with a sl st in joining st from Rnd 2, [ch 4, remove hook from lp, take ch from back to front and into the ch-3 sp, sl st in next sc] rep around, join in beg sl st, fasten off. ✁

A true heirloom, this tiny bonnet fits the shape and the beauty of Baby's little head. Crochet this delicate bonnet for the newborn child, and then pass it down to future generations.

Christening Bonnet

Design by Sharon Valiant

Skill Level: Beginner

Size: Newborn

Materials

▶ DMC Cebelia crochet cotton size 10: 1 ball ecru

▶ Size 7 steel crochet hook or size needed to obtain gauge

▶ 1 yd ⅜-inch-wide ivory satin ribbon

▶ Sewing needle and ivory thread

▶ Tapestry needle

Gauge

Rnds 1 and 2 = 1 inch
Check gauge to save time.

Pattern Notes

Weave in loose ends as work progresses.

Join rnds with a sl st unless otherwise stated.

Bonnet

Rnd 1: Ch 8, sl st to join to form a ring, ch 1, 12 sc in ring, join in beg sc. (12 sc)

Rnd 2: Ch 6 (counts as first dc, ch 3 throughout), dc in same sc, [sk next sc, {dc, ch 3, dc} in next sc] 5 times, join in 3rd ch of beg ch-6.

Rnd 3: Sl st into ch-3 sp, ch 3 (counts as first dc throughout), 4 dc in same ch-3 sp, ch 1, [5 dc in next ch-3 sp, ch 1] rep around, join in top of beg ch-3.

Rnd 4: Sl st into 3rd dc of 5-dc group, ch 6, dc in same st, 5 dc in next ch-1 sp, [{dc, ch 3, dc} in 3rd dc of 5-dc group, 5 dc in next ch-1 sp] rep around, join in 3rd ch of beg ch-6.

Rnd 5: Sl st into ch-3 sp, ch 3, 6 dc in same ch-3 sp, *ch 1, sc in center dc of next 5-dc group, ch 1 **, 7 dc in next ch-3 sp, rep from * around, ending last rep at **, join in top of beg ch-3.

Rnd 6: Sl st into center dc of 7-dc group, ch 1, sc in center dc of 7-dc group, *[ch 2, 5 dc in next ch-1 sp] twice, ch 2 **, sc in center dc of next 7-dc group, rep from * around, ending last rep at **, join in beg sc.

Rnd 7: Sl st into ch-2 sp, ch 6, dc in same ch-2 sp, ch 3, [{dc, ch 3, dc} in next ch-2 sp, ch 3] rep around, join in 3rd ch of beg ch-6.

Rnd 8: Sl st into ch-3 sp, ch 3, 4 dc in same ch-3 sp, sc in next ch-3 sp, [5 dc in next ch-3 sp, sc in next ch-3 sp] rep around, join in top of beg ch-3. (18 groups 5-dc)

Rnd 9: Sl st to center dc of 5-dc group, ch 1, sc in same center dc, ch 1, *5 dc in next sc, ch 1 **, sc in center dc of next 5-dc group, ch 1, rep from * around, ending last rep at **, join in top of beg ch.

Note: Mark 4 groups of 5-dc just prior to joining for back of bonnet.

Row 10: Ch 3, 2 dc in same sc, [sc in center dc of next 5-dc group, 5 dc in next sc] 13 times, sc in center dc of next 5-dc group, 3 dc in next sc, do not work on rem sts between markers, turn.

Row 11: Ch 1, sc in first dc, [5 dc in next sc, sc in center dc of next 5-dc group] 13 times, 5 dc in next sc, sc in last st, turn.

Rows 12–17: Rep Rows 10 and 11.

Row 18: Rep Row 10.

Row 19: Ch 1, sc in first dc, *[dc, ch 3, dc] in next sc, sc in center dc of next 5-dc group, rep from * across, ending with sc in last st, turn.

Row 20: Ch 3, dc in same st, *[2 dc, ch 3, 2 dc] in next ch-3 sp, rep from * across, ending with 2 dc in last st, turn.

Continued on page 84

Playpen Pad Cover

Design by Margaret Dick

Skill Level: Intermediate

Size: 26 x 36 inches

Materials

- ► Sugar 'n Cream 4-ply crochet cotton (840 yds per cone): 2 cones fairy tales #151
- ► Size F/5 crochet hook or size needed to obtain gauge
- ► 1½ yds ½-inch-wide elastic
- ► Tapestry needle

Gauge

8 sts = 1½ inches; 4 rows = 1 inch

Check gauge to save time.

Pattern Notes

Weave in loose ends as work progresses.

Join rnds with a sl st unless otherwise stated.

Pad Cover

Row 1: Ch 132, sc in 2nd ch from hook, [ch 1, sk 1 ch, sc in next ch] rep across, turn. (66 sc; 65 ch-1 sps)

Row 2: Ch 1, sc in first st, sc in next ch-1 sp, [ch 1, sc in next ch-1 sp] rep across, ending with sc in last 2 sts, turn. (67 sc; 64 ch-1 sps)

Row 3: Ch 1, sc in first sc, ch 1, [sc in next ch-1 sp, ch 1] rep across, ending with sc in last st, turn. (66 sc; 65 ch-1 sps)

Rep Rows 2 and 3 until piece measures 36 inches.

Add comfort to your baby's playpen with this quick and easy pad cover. Pattern fits standard size playpen pads!

sc in corner] twice, join in back lp only of first sc.

Rnd 2: Working in back lps only, ch 3 (counts as first dc throughout), dc in each st around, join in top of beg ch-3.

Rnd 3: Ch 3, [dc in each st across to corner, {sk 1 st, dc in next st} twice] rep around, join in top of beg ch-3.

Rnd 4: Sl st in next st, ch 3, [dc in each st across edge, sk 3 dc at corner] rep around, join in top of beg ch-3.

Rnd 5: Ch 4 (counts as first dc, ch 1), *[sk 1 st, dc in next st, ch 1] rep across to last 9 sts before corner,

[dc in next st, sk 1 st] 5 times, dc in next st, [sk 1 st, dc in next st] 4 times, ch 1, rep from * around, join in 3rd ch of beg ch-4.

Rnd 6: Ch 1, sc in same st as beg ch-1, sc in each ch-1 sp and each dc around, join in beg sc, fasten off.

Rnd 7: Attach yarn in rem free lp of Rnd 1, working in rem front lps, ch 1, sc in each st around, working 3 sc in each corner st, sl st to join in beg sc, fasten off.

Finishing

Weave elastic through Rnd 5 of edging and secure ends tog. ✂

Edging

Rnd 1: Ch 1, sc in same st as beg ch-1, [sc evenly sp along length, 3 sc in corner, sc in each st and each ch-1 sp across next edge, 3

This simple afghan is not only fun to make, but the knotted ends and beautiful colors will delight and amuse your baby!

Rainbow Knots Baby Afghan

Design by Shirley Patterson

Skill Level: Beginner

Size: 42 inches square

Materials

▶ Baby weight yarn: 2 oz each peach, lavender, light blue, light pink, light yellow and light green

▶ Size K/10½ crochet hook or size needed to obtain gauge

▶ Tapestry needle

Gauge

8 hdc = 2 inches; 8 rows = 3½ inches

Check gauge to save time.

Pattern Note

Weave in loose ends as work progresses.

Strip

Note: Make 2 each peach, light green, light yellow, lavender, light blue and light pink.

Row 1: Ch 193, sl st in 2nd ch from hook, sl st in each of next 29 chs, hdc in each of next 132 chs, sl st in each of next 30 chs, turn. (60 sl sts; 132 hdc)

Rows 2–8: Ch 1, sl st in each of next 30 sl sts, working in back lps only, hdc in each of next 132 sts, sl st in each of next 30 sl sts, turn.

At the end of Row 8, leaving a length 6 times as long as strip, fasten off.

Joining Strips

With rem yarn length on a peach strip, sl st across 30 sl sts of peach strip only. Working in back lps only of Row 8 of peach strip and rem lps of foundation ch of light green strip, sl st strips tog across next 132 sts; sl st across rem 30 sts of peach strip only, fasten off.

Continue joining light yellow, lavender, light blue and light pink strips in same manner, then rep color sequence. On last edge of last strip, sl st in each st across, fasten off.

Finishing

Wrap each sl-st end around itself to form a knot; using tapestry needle and matching yarn, tack in place to secure. ✄

Christening Bonnet

Continued from page 82

Row 21: Ch 3, dc in next dc, *[2 dc, ch 3, 2 dc] in next ch-3 sp, rep from * across, ending with dc in each of last 2 sts, turn bonnet to work across neck edge.

Neck Border

Row 1: Ch 3, 2 dc in each dc (or ch-3) post to marker (marker for center circle), sc evenly sp across circle, 2 dc in each dc post across rem side, turn.

Row 2: Ch 1, sc in each st across, fasten off.

Finishing

Steam-press bonnet lightly. Cut ribbon in half. On each length, fold 3 lps at edge; sew lps to secure. Sew lp end to side of bonnet. ✄

Hooded Cardigan

Design by Ann E. Smith

Skill Level: Intermediate

Size: 2, 4 and 6

Chest: 25½ (28, 30½) inches

Length: 12¾ (14¾, 15¾) inches

Materials

▶ Patons Look At Me yarn (1.75 oz per skein): 2 (3, 3) skeins hot pink #6357 (MC), 1 (2, 2) skeins each lilac #6358, mango #6356, lagoon #6361 and apple green #6362

▶ Size F/5 crochet hook or size needed to obtain gauge

▶ 5 (20mm) pansy buttons

▶ Tapestry needle

Gauge

In body pattern, 16 sts and 13 rows = 4 inches

Check gauge to save time.

Pattern Notes

Weave in loose ends as work progresses.

Join rnds with a sl st unless otherwise stated.

Pattern Stitch

Ringlet: [Sl st, ch 5, sc] in next st.

Body Pattern

Row 1: Ch 1, sc in first 4 (3, 2) sc, *keeping ringlet to RS of fabric, sc in sc from ringlet, sk sl st **, sc in each of next 5 sc, rep from * across, ending last rep at **, sc in each of last 4 (3, 2) sc, turn.

Row 2: Ch 3 (counts as first dc throughout), dc in each sc across, turn.

Row 3: Ch 1, sc in each of first 4 (3, 2) dc, *make ringlet in next st **, sc in each of next 5 dc, rep from * across, ending last rep at **, sc in each of last 4 (3. 2) dc, turn.

Rep Rows 1–3 for pattern note that the ringlet rows alternate between right and wrong side rows.

Back

Beg at lower edge and above border, with apple green, ch 53 (57, 61).

Foundation Row: Dc in 4th ch from hook, dc in each rem ch across, turn. (51, 55, 59 sts)

Next row: With apple green, work Row 3 of body pattern, fasten off.

Dress your child in style with this beautiful cardigan. Use colors from your scrap yarn basket or allow him or her to pick the colors to really make it their own!

For body, rep Rows 1–3 in the following color sequence: hot pink, mango, lagoon, lilac and apple green. Work even to about 11½ (13½, 14½) inches from beg, ending with a dc row, fasten off.

Right Front

Beg at lower edge and above border with apple green, ch 25 (28, 31), work foundation row and next row as for back. (23, 26, 29 sts).

Work color sequence as for back to about 9 (11, 12) inches from beg, ending ready to work a dc row, fasten off.

Neck shaping

Row 1: Keeping to established color and st pattern, sk first 2 (3, 4) sts, attach yarn with sl st in next st, sc in next st, hdc in next st, dc in rem 18 (20, 22) sts, turn.

Row 2: Work in established pattern on 18 (20, 22) sts, turn.

Row 3: Ch 1, dec 1 sc over next 2 sts, work in pattern across rem sts, turn.

Row 4: Rep Row 2 across to last 3 sts, hdc in next st, sc in next st, sl st in next st, turn.

Row 5: Ch 1, sk sl st, sl st in sc, sc in hdc, work in established pattern on 14, (16, 18) sts, turn.

Continue in established pattern on 14 (16, 18) sts until front measures the same as back, ending with a dc row, fasten off.

Left Front

Work as for right front to neck shaping, ending ready to work a dc row.

Row 1: Rep Row 2 across first 18 (20, 22) sts, hdc in next st, sc in next st, sl st in next st, sk last 2 (3, 4) sts, turn.

Row 2: Ch 1, sk sl st, sl st in sc, sc in hdc, pattern on 18 (20, 22) sts, turn.

Row 3: Work in established pattern on 16 (18, 20) sts, dec 1 sc over next 2 sts, turn.

Row 4: Ch 1, sk 1 st, sc in next st, hdc in next st, pattern across rem sts, turn.

Row 5: Work in established pattern on 14 (16, 18) sts.

Complete as for right front.

Sleeve

Make 2

Beg at lower edge and above the cuff, with apple green, ch 23 (27, 31), work foundation row and next row as for back. (21, 25, 29 sts)

Keeping to color and st pattern, and including new sts into pattern as they accumulate, inc 1 st each edge every other row until there are 45 (49, 53) sts. Work even to 9 (10, 11½) inches from beg, ending with a dc row, fasten off.

Cuff

Rnd 1: With RS facing and working along opposite side of foundation ch, attach MC with a sl st in first ch at right edge, ch 1, sc in same st as joining and in each ch across, join in beg sc.

Rnd 2: Ch 1, sc in each sc around, join in beg sc.

Rep Rnd 2 until cuff measures 1½ inches. At the end of last rep, turn. Sl st in each sc around, join in beg st, fasten off.

Finishing

Join shoulder seams. Place markers 5½ (6, 6½) inches from shoulder seam along each edge. Set in sleeve between markers. Join underarm and side seams.

Hood Preparation

Rnd 1: With RS facing, attach MC at lower edge of right front, ch 1, work 40 (48, 52) sc evenly sp to neck, 3 sc in corner, 12 (13, 14) sc evenly sp to shoulder, 25 sc along back neck, 12 (13, 14) sc evenly sp to neck shaping, 3 sc in corner, 40 (48, 52) sc evenly sp along left edge, 3 sc in corner, working along opposite side of foundation ch, sc in each ch across, ending with 3 sc in last ch, sl st to join in beg sc, fasten off.

Hood

With RS facing, attach MC with sl st in center sc at right neck edge, ch 1, sc in same sc, sc in each of next 52 (54, 56) sc ending with last sc in center sc at opposite neck edge, turn.

With MC, rep Rows 2 and 3. In color sequence as established on back, work body pattern to 8½, (9½, 9½) inches from beg, ending with Row 3.

For top of hood: With RS facing, sk next 18 (18, 19) sts, attach next color with sl st in next st, work Row 1 across 17 (19, 19) sts, turn, leaving rem 18 (18, 19) sts unworked. Work in established pattern for 4½ inches, ending with a dc row, fasten off.

Row 1: To join sides of hood to top, with WS facing, attach MC with sl st in lower edge of hook at right neck edge, ch 1, work 28 (34, 34) sc evenly sp on top, 18 sc along top, then work 28, (34, 34) sc evenly sp along opposite edge of hook, turn.

Row 2: Working in front lps for this row only, ch 1, sc in each of next 10 sts, hdc in next 10 sts, dc in next 34 (46, 46) sts, hdc in next 10 sts, sc in next 10 sts, turn.

Row 3: Working through both lps, rep Row 2.

Row 4: Ch 3, dc in each st across, turn.

Row 5: Ch 1, sl st in each dc across, do not turn.

Row 6: Working from left to right for reverse sc, ch 1, reverse sc over last skipped st row (not into the sl sts), reverse sc in each st across, fasten off.

Body Border

Row 1: With RS facing, attach MC with sl st in same st as hood joining at left neck edge, ch 3, dc in each sc around, working 3 sc in each lower corner st, turn.

Rows 2 & 3: Rep Rows 5 and 6 of hood.

With RS facing, attach MC with sl st in first rem ch on hood from Row 2, sl st in each rem ch around, sl st across top of body border (button band), do not turn. Work Row 6 as for hood, ending with working reverse sc across 2nd button band, fasten off.

Sew first button onto left front 2½ inches above lower edge of band. Sew 2nd button ½ inch from neck edge. Space the rem 3 buttons between the first 2 and sew in place. For buttonholes, use natural sps between dc sts on right front.✂

Baby's Hat & Mitten Set

Designs by Beverly Mewhorter

Skill Level: Beginner

Size: Newborn–3 months

Materials

- ▶ Coats & Clark Red Heart Baby pompadour weight yarn: 2 oz light pink #722, small amount white #1
- ▶ Size F/5 crochet hook or size needed to obtain gauge
- ▶ 6 (5mm) yellow pompoms
- ▶ 66 inches ³⁄₁₆-inch-wide white picot edged ribbon
- ▶ Hot-glue gun
- ▶ Tapestry needle

Gauge

7 dc = 1½ inches; 4 dc rnds = 1½ inches

Check gauge to save time.

Pattern Notes

Weave in loose ends as work progresses.

Join rnds with a sl st unless otherwise stated.

Mitten

Make 2

Rnd 1: With pink, ch 2, 10 sc in 2nd ch from hook, join in beg sc. (10 sc)

Rnd 2: Ch 1, 2 sc in each sc around, join in beg sc. (20 sc)

Rnd 3: Ch 1, 2 sc in first sc, [sc in each of next 2 sc, 2 sc in next sc] 6 times, 2 sc in last sc, join in beg sc. (28 sc)

Rnds 4–12: Ch 1, sc in each sc around, join in beg sc.

Rnd 13: Ch 1, sc in same sc as beg ch, ch 2, sk 1 sc, [sc in next sc, ch 2, sk 1 sc] rep around, join in beg sc. (14 ch-2 sps)

Rnd 14: Sl st into ch-2 sp, 6 dc in next ch-2 sp, [sl st in next ch-2 sp, 6 dc in next ch-2 sp] rep around, join in beg st, fasten off.

Flower

Make 2

Rnd 1: With white, ch 7, sl st in 7th ch from hook, [ch 6, sl st in same ch as previous sl st] 4 times, fasten off.

Sew flower to center top of mitten. Glue a yellow pompom to center of flower.

Cut an 18-inch length of ribbon, weave through ch-2 sps of Rnd 13, and tie ends in a bow.

Hat

Rnd 1: With pink, ch 4, 13 dc in 4th ch from hook, join in top of beg ch-4. (14 dc)

Rnds 2 & 3: Ch 3 (counts as first dc throughout), dc in same st as beg ch, 2 dc in each dc around, join in top of beg ch-3. (56 dc)

Rnds 4–12: Ch 3, dc in each dc around, join in top of beg ch-3.

Rnd 13: Ch 1, sc in same st as beg ch, ch 2, sk 1 st, [sc in next st, ch 2, sk next st] rep around, join in beg sc. (28 ch-2 sps)

Rnd 14: Sl st into ch-2 sp, 6 dc in next ch-2 sp, [sl st in next ch-2 sp, 6 dc in next ch-2 sp] rep around, join, fasten off.

Flower

Make 4

Make 4 flowers the same as for mitten. Attach flowers between Rnds 9–11 spacing ¼ inch apart. Glue a yellow pompom to center of each flower.

Weave rem 30-inch length of ribbon through ch-2 sps of Rnd 13; tie ends in a bow. ✄

Plan now for those cold winter months with this quick and easy hat and mitten set. Decorate with cheery flowers for a finishing touch!

Reversible Baby Bib

Design by Darla Fanton

This cool cotton baby bib offers more than good looks—it's reversible, so you can use it twice as often!

Skill Level: Beginner

Size: 6 x 10 inches

Materials

► Peaches & Creme cotton worsted weight yarn: ½ oz each peacock #19 and fairy tales #151 and ¼ oz white #1

► Size J/10 double ended crochet hook or size needed to obtain gauge

► Size I/9 crochet hook

► Yarn needle

Gauge

9 sts and 10 rows = 2 inches
Check gauge to save time.

Pattern Notes

Weave in loose ends as work progresses.

Bib is crocheted from neck downward.

To pick up a lp in horizontal st; insert hook under top lp only of indicated horizontal st, yo and draw through.

Bib

Row 1 (WS): With peacock and double ended hook, ch 25, working through back lps only, insert hook in 2nd ch from hook, yo, draw through, [insert hook in back lp of next ch, yo, draw through rep across foundation ch retaining all lps on hook; slide all sts to opposite end of hook, turn. (25 lps)

Row 2: To work lps off hook, place variegated on hook with a sl knot, working from left to right draw through first lp, [yo, draw through 2 lps] rep across until 1 lp remains on hook, do not turn.

Row 3: With variegated and working right to left, ch 1, sk first vertical bar, [draw up a lp in next horizontal st] 11 times, draw up lp under next vertical bar, draw up lp in next horizontal st, draw up lp under next vertical bar, [draw up lp in next horizontal st] 12 times; slide all sts to opposite end of hook, turn. (27 lps)

Row 4: Pick up peacock, working from left to right, yo, draw through first lp, [yo, draw through 2 lps] rep across until 1 lp remains on hook, do not turn.

Row 5: With peacock, working right to left, ch 1, sk first vertical bar, [draw up a lp in next horizontal st] 12 times, draw up a lp under next vertical bar, draw up a lp in next horizontal st, draw up a lp under next vertical bar, [draw up a lp in next horizontal st] 13 times; slide all sts to opposite end of hook, turn. (29 lps)

Row 6: With variegated, rep Row 4.

Row 7: With variegated, working right to left, ch 1, sk first vertical bar, [draw up a lp in next horizontal st] 13 times, draw up a lp under next vertical bar, draw up a lp in next horizontal st, draw up a lp under next vertical bar, [draw up a lp in next horizontal st] 14 times; slide all sts to opposite end of hook, turn. (31 lps)

Row 8: Rep Row 4.

Row 9: With peacock, working right to left, ch 1, sk first vertical bar, [draw up a lp in next horizontal st] 14 times, draw up a lp under next vertical bar, draw up a lp in next horizontal st, draw up a lp under next vertical bar, [draw up a lp in next horizontal st] 15 times; slide all sts to opposite end of hook, turn. (33 lps)

Row 10: Rep Row 6.

Row 11: With variegated, working right to left, ch 1, sk first vertical bar, [draw up a lp in next horizontal st] 15 times, draw up a lp under next vertical bar, draw up a lp in next horizontal st, draw up a lp under next vertical bar, [draw up a lp in next horizontal st] 16 times; slide all sts to opposite end of hook, turn. (35 lps)

Row 12: Rep Row 4.

Row 13: With peacock, working right to left, ch 1, sk first vertical bar, [draw up a lp in next horizontal st] 16 times, draw up a lp under next vertical bar, draw up a lp in next horizontal st, draw up a lp under next vertical bar, [draw up a lp in next horizontal st] 17 times; slide all sts to opposite end of hook, turn. (37 lps)

Row 14: Rep Row 6.

Row 15: With variegated, working right to left, ch 1, sk first vertical bar, [draw up a lp in next horizontal st] 17 times, draw up a lp under next vertical bar, draw up a lp in next horizontal st, draw up a lp under next vertical bar, [draw up a lp in next horizontal st] 18 times; slide all sts to opposite end of hook, turn. (39 lps)

Row 16: Rep Row 4.

Row 17: With peacock, working right to left, ch 1, sk first vertical bar, [draw up a lp in next horizontal st] 18 times, draw up a lp under next vertical bar, draw up a lp in next horizontal st, draw up a lp under next vertical bar, [draw up a lp in next horizontal st] 19 times; slide all sts to opposite end of hook, turn. (41 lps)

Row 18: Rep Row 6.

Row 19: With variegated, working right to left, ch 1, sk first vertical bar, [draw up a lp in next horizontal st] 19 times, draw up a lp under next vertical bar, draw up a lp in next horizontal st, draw up a lp under next vertical bar, [draw up a lp in next horizontal st] 20 times; slide all sts to opposite end of hook, turn. (43 lps)

Row 20: Rep Row 4.

Row 21: With peacock, working right to left, ch 1, sk first vertical bar, [draw up a lp in next horizontal st] 20 times, draw up a lp under next vertical bar, draw up a lp in next horizontal st, draw up a lp under next vertical bar, [draw up a lp in next horizontal st] 21 times; slide all sts to opposite end of hook, turn. (45 lps)

Row 22: Rep Row 6.

Row 23: With variegated, working right to left, ch 1, sk first vertical bar, [draw up a lp in next horizontal st] 21 times, draw up a lp under next vertical bar, draw up a lp in next horizontal st, draw up a lp under next vertical bar, [draw up a lp in next horizontal st] 22 times; slide all sts to opposite end of hook, turn. (47 lps)

Row 24: Rep Row 4.

Row 25: With peacock, working right to left, ch 1, sk first vertical bar, [draw up a lp in next horizontal st] 22 times, draw up a lp

under next vertical bar, draw up a lp in next horizontal st, draw up a lp under next vertical bar, [draw up a lp in next horizontal st] 23 times; slide all sts to opposite end of hook, turn. (49 lps)

Row 26: Rep Row 6.

Row 27: With variegated, working right to left, ch 1, sk first vertical bar, [draw up a lp in next horizontal st] 23 times, draw up a lp under next vertical bar, draw up a lp in next horizontal st, draw up a lp under next vertical bar, [draw up a lp in next horizontal st] 24 times; slide all sts to opposite end of hook, turn. (51 lps)

Row 28: Rep Row 4.

Row 29: With peacock, ch 1, sk first vertical bar, [insert hook in next horizontal st, yo and draw through st and lp on hook] rep across to bind off, fasten off.

Continued on page 102

Baby Layette

Designs by Nazanin Fard

Skill Level: Intermediate

Size:

Jacket: newborn–3 months
Chest: 19 inches
Length to underarm: 7 inches
Sleeve length: 6 inches

Bonnet: 8 inches

Booties: newborn–3 months

Materials

- ▶ Lion Brand Baby soft yarn (5 oz per skein): 2 skeins white #100
- ▶ Size G/6 crochet hook or size needed to obtain gauge
- ▶ Tapestry needle
- ▶ Pencil

Gauge

5 dc = 1 inch
Check gauge to save time.

Pattern Notes

Weave in loose ends as work progresses.

Join rnds with a sl st unless otherwise stated.

Ch 3 counts as first dc throughout.

Pattern Stitches

Jacket pattern

Row 1: Ch 3, 2 dc in first st, *sk next 2 sts, 1 dc in next st, sk next 2 sts, 5 dc in next st (shell), rep from * across, ending with 3 dc in last st, turn.

Row 2: Ch 3, *5 dc in next single dc, 1 dc in 3rd dc of shell, rep from * across, ending with dc in 3rd ch, turn.

Rep Rows 1 and 2 for pattern.

Sleeve pattern

Rnd 1: Ch 3, 2 dc in first st, *sk next 2 sts, 1 dc in next st, sk next 2 sts, 5 dc in next st (shell), rep from * across, ending with 2 dc in same st as beg ch-3, sl st top of beg ch-3.

Rnd 2: Ch 3, 5 dc in next single dc, *dc in 3rd dc of next shell, 5 dc in next single dc, rep from * around, join in top of beg ch-3.

Rep Rnds 1 and 2 for pattern.

Jacket

Note: Jacket is crocheted from neckline down.

Row 1: Ch 61, sc in 2nd ch from hook, sc in each rem ch across, turn. (60 sc)

Row 2: Ch 1, sc in first sc, [ch 1, sk next sc, sc in each of next 3 sc] rep across, ending with ch 1, sc in last sc, turn. (15 ch-1 sps; 44 sc)

Row 3: Ch 1, sc in each sc and each ch-1 sp across, turn.

Row 4: Ch 1, sc in each st across, turn.

Row 5: Rep Row 4.

Row 6: Working in front lps for this row only, ch 1, reverse sc in each st across.

Row 7: Working in rem back lps only, ch 3, [dc in each of next 4 sts, 2 dc in next st] 11 times, dc in each of next 3 sts, turn. (70 sts)

Row 8: Ch 3, dc in each st across, turn.

Row 9: Ch 3, dc in each of next 3 sts, [2 dc in next st, dc in each of next 5 sts] rep across, turn. (81 sts)

Rows 10 & 11: Rep Rows 6 and 7.

Row 12: Ch 3, dc across, inc 11 dc evenly sp across, turn. (92 sts)

Row 13: Rep Row 12. (103 sts)

Row 14: Rep Row 6.

Row 15: Working in rem back lps only, ch 3, dc across, inc 11 dc evenly sp across, turn. (114 sts)

Row 16: Rep Row 12. (125 sts)

Row 17: Ch 3, dc across, inc 26 dc evenly sp across, turn. (151 sts)

Row 18: Ch 3, dc in each of next 23 dc (front), sk next 24 dc (sleeve), dc in each of next 55 dc (back), sk next 24 dc (sleeve), dc in each of next 24 dc (front), turn. (103 sts)

Rep Rows 1 and 2 of jacket pattern until section measures 7 inches. At the end of last rep, fasten off.

Sleeve

Make 2

Rep Rows 1 and 2 of sleeve pattern until from underarm sleeve measures 6 inches. At the end of last rep, fasten off.

Bonnet

Row 1: Ch 79, sc in 2nd ch from hook, sc in each rem ch across, turn.

Row 2: Ch 1, sc in each sc across, turn.

Rep Rows 1 and 2 of jacket pattern until piece measures 8 inches. At the end of last rep, fasten off.

Fold foundation ch in half, sew across edge of foundation ch.

Fold the side edge under about ½ inch and st across to make pocket for drawstring.

Bootie

Make 2

Rnd 1: Ch 15, 2 hdc in 3rd ch from hook, hdc in each of next 11 chs, 5 hdc in next ch, working on opposite side of foundation ch, hdc in next 11 chs, w hdc in last ch, join in top of beg ch. (32 sts)

Rnd 2: Ch 2, 2 hdc in next st, hdc in each of next 13 sts, 2 hdc in next st, hdc in next st, 2 hdc in next st, hdc in each of next 13 sts, 2 hdc in next st, join in top of beg ch-2. (36 sts)

This jacket, bonnet and booties set makes a pretty and practical gift for babies!

Rnd 3: Ch 2, 2 hdc in each of next 2 sts, hdc in each of next 12 sts, 2 hdc in each of next 2 sts, hdc in each of next 2 sts, 2 hdc in each of next 2 sts, hdc in each of next 12 sts, 2 hdc in each of next 2 sts, hdc in last st, join in top of beg ch-2. (44 sts)

Rnd 4: Ch 2, hdc in each st around, join in top of beg ch-2.

Rnds 5 & 6: Rep Rnd 4.

Rnd 7: Ch 2, hdc in each of next 15 sts, [dec 1 hdc over next 2 sts] 6 times, hdc in next 16 sts, join in top of beg ch-2. (38 sts)

Rnd 8: Ch 2, hdc in each of next 13 sts, [dec 1 hdc over next 2 sts] 5 times, hdc in each of next 14 sts, join in top of beg ch-2. (33 sts)

Rnd 9: Ch 2, hdc in each of next 12 sts, [dec 1 hdc over next 2 sts] 4 times, hdc in each of next 12 sts, join

in top of beg ch-2. (29 sts)

Rnd 10: Rep Rnd 4.

Rnd 11: Ch 2, hdc in each of next 2 sts, ch 1, sk 1 st, [hdc in each of next 4 sts, ch 1, sk 1 st] 5 times, join in top of beg ch-2.

Rnd 12: Ch 2, hdc in each hdc and each ch-1 sp around, join in top of beg ch-2.

Rnd 13: Ch 3, dc in same st, [2 dc in each of next 4

sts, dc in next st] 4 times, 2 dc in each of next 8 sts, join in top of beg ch-3. (54 dc)

Rnd 14: Rep Rnd 1 of sleeve pattern, fasten off.

Drawstring

For bonnet and jacket cut 2 lengths of yarn each 3 yds; tie ends in a knot. Secure knot on nail or doorknob. Place a pencil in opposite end and turn, twisting up

Continued on page 103

Raspberry Sherbet Afghan

Design by Darla Fanton

Skill Level: Intermediate

Size: 38 x 43½ inches

Materials

▶ Coats & Clark Red Heart Super Saver worsted weight yarn: 4 oz raspberry #375 (A), 3 oz each light raspberry #774 (B) and petal pink #373 (C), 9 oz white #311 (D)

▶ Size K/10½ flexible double-ended crochet hook or size needed to obtain gauge

▶ Size K/10½ crochet hook

▶ Tapestry needle

Create this warm and cozy afghan in your choice of colors. You'll love the reversibility of the Crochet on the Double™ style!

Gauge

7 sts = 2 inches; 7 rows = 2 inches

Check gauge to save time.

Pattern Notes

Weave in loose ends as work progresses.

When picking up lp in horizontal st, insert hook under top lp only.

Carry unused yarn along side edge, working over it before beg ch 1 of each odd numbered row.

Pattern Stitch

Long sc: Insert hook in indicated st, yo, draw up a lp level with working rnd, yo, draw through 2 lps on hook.

Afghan

Row 1: With flexible double-ended crochet hook and A, ch 108 loosely, working through back lps only, draw up lp in 2nd ch from hook, yo, draw up lp in same ch, *yo, sk next ch, draw up lp in next ch, yo, draw up a lp in same ch, rep from * across foundation ch, slide all sts to opposite end of hook, turn. (216 lps on hook)

Row 2: To work lps off hook, place D on hook with sl knot, working from left to right draw through first lp, [yo, draw through 4 lps on hook, yo, draw through 2 lps on hook] rep across until 1 lp rem on hook, do not turn.

Row 3: With D and working right to left, ch 1, sk first puff, [draw up a lp in next horizontal st, yo, draw up a lp in same st, yo, sk next horizontal st, sk next puff st] rep across, slide all sts to opposite end of hook, turn. (216 lps on hook)

Rows 4 & 5: With B, rep Rows 2 and 3.

Row 6: Pick up D, working from left to right, yo, draw through first lp, [yo, draw through 4 lps on hook, yo, draw through 2 lps on hook] rep across until 1 lp rem on hook, do not turn.

Row 7: Rep Row 3.

Rows 8 & 9: With C, rep Rows 2 and 3.

Rows 10 & 11: Rep Rows 6 and 7.

Row 12: With A, rep Row 6.

Row 13: With A, rep Row 3.

Rows 14 & 15: Rep Rows 6 and 7.

Row 16: With B, rep Row 6.

Row 17: Rep Row 5.

Rows 18 & 19: Rep Rows 6 and 7.

Row 20: With C, rep Row 6.

Row 21: Rep Row 9.

Rows 22–168: Rep Rows 10–21, ending last rep with a Row 12.

Row 169: To bind off, with A, working right to left, ch 1, sk first puff st, [draw up a lp in next horizontal st, yo, draw up a lp in same horizontal st, yo and draw through all 4 lps on hook, ch 1, sk next horizontal st, sk next puff st] rep across, transfer rem lp to standard hook to work edging, fasten off B, C and D.

First Side Edging

Row 1: Ch 3, turn work so you are working in ends of rows, dc evenly sp along side edge, ending with ch 3, sl st in foundation ch, fasten off.

Second Side Edging

Row 1: Attach A in opposite end of foundation ch with sl st, ch 3, dc evenly sp along edge, ending with a dc in base of Row 167, ch 3, sl st in top of Row 169, fasten off.

Border

Rnd 1: Attach B with sl st in any corner sp, ch 2 (counts as first hdc throughout), [hdc, ch 2, 2 hdc] in same corner sp, hdc evenly sp around entire outer edge, working [2 hdc, ch 2, 2 hdc] in each corner, sl st to join in top of beg ch-2, fasten off.

Rnd 2: Attach C in any corner ch-2 sp, ch 1, *[sc, ch 2, sc] in corner ch-2 sp, ch 2, sk next st, [sc in next st, sk next st, ch 2] rep across edge, rep from * around, sl st to join in beg sc, fasten off.

Rnd 3: Attach D in any corner ch-2 sp, ch 1, sc in

Continued on page 103

Ombre Blocks Cardigan

Design by Ann E. Smith

Skill Level: Intermediate

Size: 4, (6, 8)

Chest: 29 (30, 33) inches

Length: 16½ (18, 19½) inches

Materials

▶ Coats & Clark Red Heart Soft Baby worsted weight yarn (7 oz per solid skein and 6 oz per multicolor skein): 1 (2, 2) skeins white #7001 (MC), 1 (1, 2) skeins key west #7939 (CC)

▶ Size G/6 crochet hook or size needed to obtain gauge

▶ Size F/5 crochet hook

▶ 5 (¾-inch) buttons

▶ Tapestry needle

Crochet this delightful sweater in lovely pastels for the birthday girl or select autumn colors for back-to-school fun!

Gauge

In body pattern, 30 sts = 7 inches; 22 rows = 4 inches

Check gauge to save time.

Pattern Notes

Weave in loose ends as work progresses.

Use crochet hook size G unless otherwise indicated.

Instructions are given for smallest size with larger sizes in parentheses. When only 1 number is given, it applies to all sizes.

To change color at end of a row, with present color draw up a lp in last st, then with new color, yo and draw through both lps on hook. Carry color not in use loosely along edge.

Pattern Stitch

Fptr: Yo hook twice, insert hook front to back to front again around vertical post of indicated st 3 rows below, yo, draw up a lp, [yo, draw through 2 lps on hook] 3 times.

Body Pattern

Note: Body pattern is a multiple of 4 sts plus 3 sts; a rep of 4 rows.

Row 1 (RS): With CC, ch 1, sc in each sc across, turn.

Row 2: Rep Row 1, changing to MC in last st, turn.

Row 3: With MC, ch 1, sc in first sc, *fptr over skipped sc 3 rows below, sk sc behind fptr, sc in next sc, ch 1, sk 1 sc, sc in next sc, rep from * across, turn.

Row 4: With MC, ch 1, sc in each sc, sc in each tr, sc in each ch-1 sp across, changing to CC in last st, turn.

Rows 5 & 6: Rep Rows 1 and 2, changing to MC in last st on Row 2.

Row 7: With MC, ch 1, sc in first sc, ch 1, sk 1 sc, *fptr over skipped sc 3 rows below, sk sc behind fpdc, sc in next sc, ch 1, sk 1 sc, rep from * across, turn.

Row 8: Rep Row 4.

Rep Rows 1–8 for body pattern.

Back

Row 1 (RS): Beg at lower edge, with MC, ch 60 (64, 68), sc in 2nd ch from hook, sc in next 2 chs, *dc in next ch, sc in each of next 3 chs, rep from * across, turn. (59, 63, 67 sts)

Row 2: With MC, ch 1, sc in each sc and each dc across, changing to CC in last st, turn.

Row 3: With CC, ch 1, sc in each sc across, turn.

Row 4: Rep Row 3, changing to MC in last st, turn.

Row 5: With MC, ch 1, sc in first sc, ch 1, sk 1 sc, sc in next sc, *fptr over dc from Row 1, sk sc behind the fptr, sc in next sc, ch 1, sk 1 sc, sc in next sc, rep from * across, turn.

Row 6: With MC, ch 1, sc in each sc, ch 1-sp and tr across changing to CC in last st, turn.

Beg body pattern, working Rows 1–6 until piece measures approximately 15½ (17, 18½) inches from beg, ending with Row 4, fasten off.

Right Front

Row 1 (RS): Beg at lower edge with MC, ch 32 (32, 36), sc in 2nd ch from hook, [dc in next ch, sc in each of next 3 chs] rep across, ending with dc in next ch, sc in last ch, turn. (31, 31, 35 sts)

Rows 2–4: Rep Rows 2–4 of back.

Row 5: With MC, ch 1, sc in first sc, *fptr over dc from Row 1, sk sc behind the fptr, sc in next sc, ch 1, sk 1 sc, sc in next sc, rep from * across, ending fptr over dc from Row 1, sk sc behind the fptr, sc in last sc, turn.

Row 6: Rep Row 6 the same as for back.

Work in body pattern until piece measures approximately 9½ (11, 12½) inches from beg.

V-Neck shaping

Keeping to established pattern, dec st at neck edge every row 7 (3, 9) times, then every other row 5 (7, 4) times. Continue in pattern on rem 19 (21, 22) sts to same length as back ending with Row 4, fasten off.

Left Front

Work the same as for right front reversing neck shaping.

Sleeve

Make 2

Beg at the lower edge and above cuff, with MC, ch 32 (36, 40), rep foundation rows 1–6 as for back on the 31 (35, 39) sts. Including new sts into body pattern as they accumulate, inc 1 st each edge every other row 7 (5, 3) times, then every 4th row 3 (5, 7) times. Continue in pattern on 51 (55, 59) sts to approximately 9 (10, 11) inches from beg, ending with Row 4, fasten off.

Joining

Join shoulder seams. Place markers 6½ (7, 7½) inches each side of shoulder seam. Set in sleeve between markers. Join underarm and side seams.

Sleeve Edging

Rnd 1: With RS facing and crochet hook size F, attach MC in opposite side of foundation ch, ch 1, sc in each ch around, join in beg sc.

Rnd 2: Working in front lps only, sl st in each st around.

Rnd 3: Sl st into rem back lp, sl st in each st around, fasten off.

Lower Body Band

Row 1: With RS facing and with crochet hook size

Continued on page 103

Flowered Squares Baby Afghan

Design by Michele Wilcox

Skill Level: Beginner

Size: 28 inches square

Materials

▶ Worsted weight yarn: 8 oz each off-white and yellow

▶ Size G/6 crochet hook or size needed to obtain gauge

▶ Tapestry needle

Gauge

5 dc = 1½ inches; 2 dc rnds = 1 inch

Check gauge to save time.

Pattern Notes

Weave in loose ends as work progresses.

Join rnds with a sl st unless otherwise stated.

Squares

Note: Make 4 yellow squares with off-white flowers and 5 off-white squares with yellow flowers.

Rnd 1 (RS): With off-white (yellow), ch 6, sl st to join to form a ring, ch 1, 12 sc in ring, do not join. (12 sc)

Rnd 2: Working in front lps for this rnd only, [{sc, hdc} in next st, 2 dc in next st, {hdc, sc} in next st] 4 times, join in beg sc. (4 petals)

Rnd 3: Sl st into rem back lp of Rnd 1, working in back lps only, ch 4 (counts as first tr throughout), tr in same st as beg ch-4, *[dc, hdc, ch 1] in next st, [sl st, ch 1, hdc, dc] in next st **, 3 tr in next st, rep from * around, ending last rep at **, tr in same st as beg ch-4, join in top of beg ch-4, fasten off.

Rnd 4: Attach yellow (off-white) to any sl st between petals of Rnd 3, [ch 5, sl st between next 2 petals] rep around. (4 ch-5 sps)

Rnd 5: Sl st into ch-5 sp, ch 3 (counts as first dc throughout), [2 dc, ch 2, 3 dc] in same ch-5 sp, ch 1, [{3 dc, ch 2, 3 dc} in next ch-5 sp, ch 1] rep around, join in top of beg ch-3.

Rnd 6: Sl st into ch-2 sp, [ch 3, 2 dc, ch 2, 3 dc] in ch-2 sp, ch 1, 3 dc in next ch-1 sp, ch 1, [{3 dc, ch 2, 3 dc} in next ch-2 corner sp, ch 1, 3 dc in next ch-1 sp, ch 1] rep around, join in top of beg ch-3.

Rnd 7: Sl st into corner ch-2 sp, [ch 3, 2 dc, ch 2, 3 dc] in same corner ch-2 sp, *[ch 1, 3 dc in next ch-1 sp] twice, ch 1 **, [3 dc, ch 2, 3 dc] in next corner ch-2 sp, rep from * around, ending last rep at **, join in top of beg ch-3.

Rnd 8: Ch 3, [dc in each dc and each ch-1 sp to corner ch-2 sp, {dc, ch 3, dc} in corner ch-2 sp] rep around, join in top of beg ch-3. (68 dc; 4 ch-3 sps)

Rnds 9 & 10: Ch 3, dc in each dc around, working [dc, ch 3, dc] in each corner ch-3 sp, join in top of beg ch-3. (84 dc; 4 ch-3 sps) At the end of Rnd 10, fasten off.

Sew squares tog 3 x 3 alternating colors.

Border

Rnd 1 (RS): Attach yellow in any corner ch-3 sp, ch 6 (counts as first dc, ch 3 throughout) dc in same corner sp, *[dc in each of next 21 dc, dc in sp, dc in joining of 2 squares, dc in next sp] twice, dc in each of next 21 dc **, [dc, ch 3, dc] in next corner ch-3 sp, rep from * around, ending last rep at **, join in 3rd ch of beg ch-6.

Rnd 2: Sl st into corner ch-3 sp, ch 6, dc in same ch-3 sp, *dc in each dc across edge **, [dc, ch 3, dc] in corner ch-3 sp, rep from * around, ending last rep at **, join in 3rd ch of beg ch-6.

Rnd 3: Rep Rnd 2, fasten off.

Rnd 4: Attach off-white in any corner ch-3 sp, rep Rnd 2.

Rnd 5: Sl st into corner ch-3 sp, *ch 1, [hdc, dc, 6 tr, dc, hdc] in corner ch-3 sp, ch 1, sc in next dc, ch 3, sl st in first ch of ch-3, sc in next 2 dc, sk 1 dc, 5 dc in next dc, [sk 1 dc, sc in next 2 dc, ch 3, sl st in first ch of ch-3, sc in next 2 dc, sk 1 dc, 5 dc in next dc], rep across until 11 groups of 5 dc with 2 dc rem before corner, sk 1 dc, sc in next dc, ch 3, sl st in first ch of ch-3, sl st in corner, rep from * around, join, fasten off. ✄

Reversible Baby Bib

Continued from page 91

Edging

With hook size I and with predominantly variegated side facing, attach white with a sl st in the end of the foundation row, 2 dc in end of next row, [sl st in end of next row, 2 dc in end of next row] 6 times, 3 sc in end of next

row (for corner), [2 dc in next st, sk next st, sl st in next st, sk next st] 5 times, 2 dc in next st, sk next st, sl st in next st, [dc in next st] 2 times, sl st in next st, [sk next st, 2 dc in next st, sk next st, sl st in next st] 5 times, sk next st, 2 dc in next st, 3 sc in next st (for corner), [2 dc in end of next row, sl st in end of next row] 7 times, fasten off.

Ties

Row 1: With hook size I and peacock, ch 25, sl st in last sl st of edging, sl st in opposite side of each foundation ch, sl st in first sl st of edging, ch 26, turn.

Row 2: Sl st in 2nd ch from hook, sl st in each st across Row 1, fasten off. ✂

Chevron Ripple Baby Afghan

Continued from page 92

around entire outer edge working 2 sc over each end dc of a row and 3 sc in each corner st, join in beg sc, fasten off.

Afghan Back

Row 1 (RS): With pink, ch 157, sc in 2nd ch from hook, sc in each rem ch across, turn. (156 sc)

Note: Mark Row 1 as RS with safety pin.

Rows 2–6: Ch 1, sc in each sc across, turn.

Row 7 (RS): Ch 1, sc in each of next 34 sc, [ch 10, sc in next 5 sc] twice, ch 10, [sc in each of next 29 sc, {ch 10, sc in next 5 sc} twice, ch 10] twice, sc in each of next 34 sc, turn. (156 sc; 9 ch-10 sps)

Row 8: Holding ch-10 lps on RS as row progresses, ch 1, sc in each sc across, turn. (156 sc)

Rows 9–138: Rep Rows 7 and 8.

Row 139: Ch 1, sc in each sc across, turn.

Row 140: Ch 1, sc in each sc across, draw up a lp remove hook, do not fasten off.

Note: Afghan back and mesh overlay must be placed tog and the ch-10 lps braided before working next row.

Braiding

For best results, work on a flat surface, place WS of overlay over RS of afghan back, draw 1 ch-10 lp of back through each matching ch-2 sp of overlay, leaving last ch-2 sp free. [Take first lp, pass 2nd lp through first lp, pass 3rd lp through previous lp, {pass next lp through previous lp} rep across section of chs leaving last lp free to be worked into next row of back] rep with each row of chs until all sets are braided.

Row 141: Keeping overlay free, pick up dropped lp from Row 140, ch 1, sc in each of next 33 sc, *[draw next free lp through matching ch-2 sp to back, insert hook through lp and sc in 2 sc, sc in 3 sc] twice, draw next free lp through matching ch-2 sp, insert hook through lp and sc in 2 sc *, [sc in next 27 sc, rep from * to *] twice, sc in next 33 sc, turn.

Rows 142–146: Keeping overlay free, ch 1, sc in each sc across, turn.

Rnd 147: Keeping overlay free, ch 1, sc evenly sp around entire outer edge, working 3 sc in each corner st, join in beg sc, do not turn, draw up a lp and remove hook.

Edging

Rnd 148: Draw dropped lp through to front overlay of afghan and working through both thicknesses, ch 1, sc in each st around working 3 sc in each corner st, do not join, do not turn.

Rnd 149: [Sl st in 1 sc, sl st in sc in rnd below] rep around, working 3 sl sts in same sc rnd below for the 3 sc corner to maintain fullness, join, fasten off. ✂

Baby Layette

Continued from page 95

the yarn until it twists back on itself when relaxed. Holding ends tog fold twisted yarn in half. Release folded end and let yarn twist back on itself. Tie another knot at both ends of drawstring about ½ inch from end; trim ends. Thread drawstring through bottom edge of bonnet. Weave another drawstring through the sps around neckline of jacket. With 2 strands of yarn each 1½ yds long, make a drawstring for each bootie. Beg at center front, weave drawstring through ch-1 sps. ✂

Raspberry Sherbet Afghan

Continued from page 96

same ch-2 sp, long sc in the B corner sp below, sc in same ch-2 sp of Rnd 2, *ch 2, sk next st, long sc in skipped st of Rnd 1, rep from * around, for each corner work sc in ch-2 corner sp of Rnd 2, long sc in Rnd below, sc in same ch-2 sp of Rnd 2, sl st to join in beg sc, fasten off. ✂

Ombre Blocks Cardigan

Continued from page 99

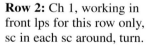

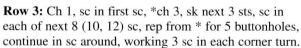

F, attach MC with sl st in first V-neck dec row on left front, ch 1, work 52 (60, 68) sc evenly sp to lower edge, 3 sc in corner, sc in each rem ch across foundation ch, 3 sc in corner, 52 (60, 68) sc evenly sp to first V-neck dec, turn.

Row 2: Ch 1, working in front lps for this row only, sc in each sc around, turn.

Row 3: Ch 1, sc in first sc, *ch 3, sk next 3 sts, sc in each of next 8 (10, 12) sc, rep from * for 5 buttonholes, continue in sc around, working 3 sc in each corner turn.

Row 4: Ch 1, sc in each st, working 3 sc in each ch-3 sp, turn.

Row 5: Ch 1, sc in each sc around, working 3 sc in each corner, fasten off.

Neck Band

Row 1: With RS facing, with crochet hook size F, attach MC with sl st just above band on right front, ch 1, work 38 sc evenly sp to shoulder, dec 1 sc over next 2 sts, work 22 (22, 24) sc evenly sp along back neck, dec 1 sc over next 2 sts, work 38 sc evenly sp to band, sl st in first sc row on band, turn.

Row 2: Ch 1, sk sl st, working in front lps for this row only, sc in next 37 sc, dec 1 sc over next 2 sts, sc in next 22 (22, 24) sc, dec 1 sc over next 2 sc, sc in each of next 37 sc, sl st in first row on band, turn.

Row 3: Ch 1, sk sl st, sc in next 36 sc, dec 1 sc over next 2 sc, sc in next 22 (22, 24) sc, dec 1 sc over next 2 sc, sc in next 36 sc, sl st in 2nd row on band, turn.

Row 4: Ch 1, sk sl st, sc in next 35 sc, dec 1 sc over next 2 sc, sc in next 22 (22, 24) sc, dec 1 sc over next 2 sc, sc in next 35 sc, sl st in next 2nd row on band, turn.

Rows 5–10: Ch 1, sk sl st, sc in each sc around, sl st in next band row, turn. At the end of Row 10, fasten off.

With RS facing and crochet hook size F, attach MC with sl st in any rem lp from band Row 2 along lower edge, Sl st in each rem lp around, fasten off.

With RS facing and crochet hook size F, attach MC with sl st in any sc on last band row of lower edge, sl st in each sc around entire body, fasten off.

Sew buttons opposite buttonholes. ✂

Gifts & Goodies

Giving a crocheted gift is the perfect way to show your affection for a family member or special friend! Crocheted gifts are as unique and endearing as the person who gives them—you!

Pansy Teacup Pincushion Set

Designs by Sue Childress

Skill Level: Beginner

Size:
Pincushion: 4 inches in diameter
Tape measure pocket: 2½ x 4 inches
Scissors case: 2 x 3 inches

Materials

- ▶ Madil Cotton Cable sport weight cotton yarn (50 grams/1.75 oz/123 yds per ball): 1 ball purple
- ▶ Size E/4 crochet hook or size needed to obtain gauge
- ▶ Teacup and saucer
- ▶ Polyester fiberfill
- ▶ 3½-inch embroidery scissors
- ▶ Retractable round tape measure approximately 2 inches in diameter
- ▶ 4 brass charms
- ▶ Hot-glue gun

Gauge

Rnds 1–3 of pincushion = 1⅜ inches

Check gauge to save time.

Pattern Notes

Weave in loose ends as work progresses.

Join each rnd with a sl st unless otherwise stated.

Pattern Stitches

Popcorn (pc): 5 dc in indicated st, draw up a lp, remove hook, insert hook in top of first dc of 5-dc group, pick up dropped lp, draw through st on hook, ch 1 to lock.

Pincushion

Rnd 1(RS): Ch 4, join to form a ring, ch 2 (counts as first hdc throughout), 11 hdc in ring, join in 2nd ch of beg ch-2. (12 hdc)

Rnd 2: Sl st into next hdc, ch 3 (counts as first dc throughout), [pc in next hdc, 2 dc in next hdc] 5 times, pc in next hdc, dc in same st as beg ch-3, join in 3rd ch of beg ch-3. (6 pc; 12 dc)

Rnd 3: Sl st into ch-1 sp of pc, ch 3, dc in same sp, [pc in each of next 2 dc, 2 dc in next ch-1 sp of pc] 5 times, pc in each of next 2 dc, join in 3rd ch of beg ch-3. (12 pc; 12 dc)

Rnd 4: Ch 3, dc in next dc, 3 dc in ch-1 sp of each of next 2 pc sts, [dc in each of next 2 dc, 3 dc in ch-1 sp of each of next 2 pc] rep around, join in 3rd ch of beg ch-3. (48 dc)

Rnd 5: Ch 1, sc in same dc as beg ch, sc in next dc, *sk next dc, 5 dc in next dc, sk next dc **, sc in each of next 3 dc, rep from * around, ending last rep at **, sc in next dc, join in beg sc, fasten off.

Fill cup firmly with fiberfill using glue to anchor layers. Referring to photo for placement, glue 2 charms to pincushion. Glue cover onto rim of cup. Glue cup to saucer.

Scissors Case

Rnd 1 (RS): Ch 4, join to form a ring, ch 3, 7 dc in ring, join in 3rd ch of beg ch-3. (8 dc)

Rnd 2: Ch 3, dc in each of next 2 dc, pc in next dc, dc in each of next 3 dc, pc in next dc, join in 3rd ch of beg ch-3. (6 dc; 2 pc)

Rnd 3: Ch 3, dc in next dc, pc in next dc, pc in ch-1 sp of next pc, dc in each of next 2 dc, pc in next dc, pc in ch-1 sp of next pc, join in 3rd ch of beg ch-3. (4 pc; 4 dc)

Rnd 4: Ch 3, 2 dc in next dc, 2 pc in ch-1 sp of next pc, dc in next dc, 2 dc in next dc, 2 pc in ch-1 sp of next pc, join in 3rd ch of beg ch-3. (6 dc; 4 pc)

Rnd 5: Ch 3, 2 dc in next dc, pc in next dc, pc in ch-1 sp of each of next 2 pc sts, dc in next dc, 2 dc in next dc, pc in next dc, pc in ch-1 sp of each of next 2 pc sts, join in 3rd ch of beg ch-3. (6 dc, 6 pc)

Rnd 6: Sl st in next dc, ch 3, 4 dc in same st as beg ch, sc in ch-1 sp of next pc, 5 dc in ch-1 sp of next pc, sc in ch-1 sp of next pc, sk next dc, 5 dc in next dc, sc in ch-1 sp of next pc, 5 dc in ch-1 sp of next pc, sc in ch-1 sp of next pc, join in 3rd ch of beg ch-3.

Rnd 7: Sl st in next 2 dc, ch 3, 4 dc in same dc, 2 sc in next sc, [5 dc in 3rd dc of next 5-dc group, 2 sc in next sc] rep around, join in 3rd ch of beg ch-3, turn.

Hanging loop

Sl st in next sc, ch 10, sl st

in same sc, sc in each ch of ch-10, sl st in next sc, fasten off.

Glue a charm to front of case; insert scissors.

Tape Measure Pocket

Make 2

Row 1: Ch 5, 2 dc in 3rd ch from hook, pc in next ch, 3 dc in last ch, turn. (1 pc; 6 dc)

Row 2: Ch 3, dc in same dc, [dc in next st, 2 dc in next st] twice, 2 dc in last dc, turn. (10 dc)

Row 3: Ch 3, dc in next dc, [pc in next dc, dc in each of next 2 dc] twice, pc in next dc, 2 dc in last dc, turn. (3 pc; 8 dc)

Row 4: Ch 3, dc in same st as beg ch, dc in next st, [2 dc in next st, dc in next st] rep across, turn. (17 dc)

Row 5: Ch 3, dc in next dc, [pc in next dc, dc in each of next 2 dc] rep across, turn. (5 pc; 12 dc)

Row 6: Ch 1, sc in each st across, turn. (17 sc)

Row 7: Ch 1, sc in next sc, [sk next sc, 5 dc in next sc, sk next sc, sc in next sc] rep across, fasten off.

At the end of 2nd piece, do not fasten off.

Joining

Holding WS tog, matching rows and working through both thicknesses, ch 1, 2 sc in end of each row to Row 1, 3 sc in opposite side of foundation ch at base of pc, 2 sc in end of each row across opposite side.

Handle

Ch 35, using care not to twist handle, sl st in top edge of opposite side, turn, ch 2, [sk 1 ch, sc in next ch, ch 2] rep across, join in base of ch, fasten off.

Glue a charm on front of pocket; insert tape measure. ✄

Victorian Picture Frames

Designs by Norma Gale

Creamy Yellow Frame

Skill Level: Intermediate

Size: 8 inches in diameter

Materials

- ▶ DMC Cebelia crochet cotton size 30: 75 yds creamy yellow #745
- ▶ Size 11 steel crochet hook or size needed to obtain gauge
- ▶ 8-inch-diameter clear plate
- ▶ 9-inch-diameter piece of plastic foam
- ▶ Waxed paper
- ▶ Straight pins
- ▶ Pewter Plasti-Kote Odds n' Ends fast-dry spray enamel
- ▶ Lightweight cardboard
- ▶ Masking tape
- ▶ ZIG Memory System #MSB15 2 Way Glue chisel-tip permanent/temporary glue pen
- ▶ Clear acrylic spray
- ▶ Aleene's Laminate IT laminating liquid
- ▶ Paintbrush
- ▶ 4 x 6-inch photo
- ▶ Easel or plate holder

These wonderful frames are a great way to show off your crochet skills and display cherished family photos!

Gauge

14 sc = 1 inch; 5 dc rnds = 1 inch

Check gauge to save time.

Pattern Notes

Weave in loose ends as work progresses.

Join each rnd with a sl st unless otherwise stated.

Pattern Stitch

P: Ch 3, sl st in top and side bar of previous sc.

Frame

Rnd 1: With creamy yellow, ch 144, being careful not to twist ch, join to form a ring, ch 1, sc in same ch, 2 sc in next ch, [sc in next ch, 2 sc in next ch] rep around, join in beg sc. (216 sc)

Rnd 2: Ch 3 (counts as first dc throughout), dc in next st, ch 2, sk next 2 sts, [dc in each of next 2 sts, ch 2, sk next 2 sts] rep around, join in 3rd ch of beg ch-3. (54 2-dc groups)

Rnd 3: Ch 3, dc in next dc, ch 2, sk next ch sp, [dc in each of next 2 dc, ch 2, sk next ch sp] rep around, join in 3rd ch of beg ch-3.

Rnds 4–6: Ch 3, dc in next st, ch 3, sk next ch sp, [dc in each of next 2 dc, ch 3, sk next ch sp] rep around, join in 3rd ch of beg ch-3.

Rnds 7–10: Ch 3, dc in next st, ch 4, sk next ch sp, [dc in each of next 2 dc, ch 4, sk next ch sp] rep around, join in 3rd ch of beg ch-3.

Rnd 11: Ch 1, sc in same st, sc in next st, 5 sc in next ch sp, [sc in each of next 2 sts, 5 sc in next ch sp] rep around, join in beg sc.

Rnd 12: Ch 1, [sc in each of next 2 sc, p, sk next st] rep around, join in beg sc, fasten off.

Finishing

Place waxed paper over plastic foam. Dampen crochet piece and pin onto waxed paper; let dry.

Place masking tape around outside edge of plate, approximately half way between front and back of plate; fold excess tape to inside front of plate.

From cardboard, cut a circle approximately 3 3/4 inches in diameter; apply 2 Way Glue around outer edge on one side, approximately 1/4 inch wide. Let dry to temporary bond. Place sticky side down on center back side of plate. Press edges down firmly. Place plate upside-down on newspaper and spray with pewter enamel. Let dry, then apply a 2nd coat. Let dry completely.

Apply 1 or 2 coats of clear acrylic spray, let dry.

Remove masking tape and cardboard circle. With RS of plate up, use a paint-brush to apply a coat of Aleene's Laminate IT over painted area only. Working quickly, place crocheted piece on top of laminate and press into place.

Carefully and slowly, paint a coat of laminate over crocheted piece. Be sure piece is saturated and watch for air bubbles; let dry.

Cut photo to size of opening. Apply 2 Way glue to outside edge of photo front; let dry to temporary bond. Place photo in frame from backside of plate. If you wish to mount the picture permanently, place in frame immediately. Press edges firmly.

Peach Frame

Skill Level: Intermediate

Size: 8 inches in diameter

Materials

► DMC Cebelia crochet cotton size 30: 75 yds peach #754

► Size 11 steel crochet hook or size needed to obtain gauge

► 8-inch-diameter clear plate

► 9-inch-diameter piece plastic foam

► Waxed paper

► Straight pins

► Antique gold Plasti-Kote Odds n' Ends fast-dry spray enamel

► Lightweight cardboard

► Masking tape

► ZIG Memory System #MSB15 2 Way Glue chisel-tip permanent/temporary glue pen

► Clear acrylic spray

► Aleene's Laminate IT laminating liquid

► Paintbrush

► 4 x 6-inch photo

► Easel or plate hanger

Gauge

14 sc = 1 inch; 5 dc rnds = 1 inch

Check gauge to save time.

Pattern Notes

Weave in loose ends as work progresses.

Join each rnd with a sl st unless otherwise stated.

Frame

Rnd 1: Ch 144, being careful not to twist ch, join to form a ring, ch 1, sc in same ch, 2 sc in next ch, [sc in next ch, 2 sc in next ch] rep around, join in beg sc. (216 sc)

Rnd 2: Ch 3 (counts as first dc throughout), dc in each of next 2 sts, ch 5, sk next 5 sts, [dc in each of next 3 sts, ch 5, sk next 5 sts] rep around, join in 3rd ch of beg ch-3. (27 3-dc groups)

Rnds 3 & 4: Sl st in next dc, ch 3, dc in next st, dc in next ch sp, ch 5, [sk next dc, dc in each of next 2 sts, dc in next ch sp, ch 5] rep around, join in 3rd ch of beg ch-3.

Rnd 5: Sl st in next dc, ch 3, dc in next st, 2 dc in next ch sp, ch 5, [sk next dc, dc in each of next 2 sts, 2 dc in next ch sp, ch 5] rep around, join in 3rd ch of beg ch-3.

Rnd 6: Sl st in next dc, ch 3, dc in each of next 2 sts, 2 dc in next ch sp, ch 5, [sk next dc, dc in each of next 3 sts, 2 dc in next ch sp, ch 5] rep around, join in 3rd ch of beg ch-3.

Rnd 7: Sl st in next dc, ch 3, dc in each of next 3 sts, dc in next ch sp, ch 5, [sk next dc, dc in each of next 4 sts, dc in next ch sp, ch 5] rep around, join in 3rd ch of beg ch-3.

Rnd 8: Sl st in next dc, ch 3, dc in each of next 3 sts, 2 dc in next ch sp, ch 5, [sk next dc, dc in each of next 4 sts, 2 dc in next ch sp, ch 4] rep around, join in 3rd ch of beg ch-3.

Rnd 9: Sl st in next dc, ch 3, dc in each of next 4 dc, dc in next ch sp, ch 5, [sk next dc, dc in each of next 5 sts, dc in next ch sp, ch 5] rep around, join in 3rd ch of beg ch-3.

Rnd 10: Sl st in next dc, ch 3, dc in each of next 4 sts, 2 dc in next ch sp, ch 5, [sk next dc, dc in each of next 5 sts, 2 dc in next ch sp, ch 5] rep around, join in 3rd ch of beg ch-3.

Rnd 11: Sl st in next dc, ch 3, dc in each of next 5 sts, 2 dc in next ch sp, ch 5, [sk next dc, dc in each of next 6 sts, 2 dc in next ch sp, ch 5] rep around, join in 3rd ch of beg ch-3.

Rnd 12: Ch 1, sc in each dc and each ch around, join in beg sc, fasten off.

Finishing

Follow finishing instructions for creamy yellow frame using antique gold spray enamel instead of pewter.

Black Frame

Skill Level: Intermediate

Size: 8 inches in diameter

Materials

► DMC Cebelia crochet cotton size 30: 85 yds black #310

► Size 11 steel crochet hook or size needed to obtain gauge

► 8-inch-diameter clear plate

► 9-inch-diameter piece plastic foam

► Waxed paper

► Straight pins

► Gold leaf Plasti-Kote Odds n' Ends fast dry spray enamel

► Lightweight cardboard

Continued on page 128

Sachet

Design by Gloria Graham

Skill Level: Beginner

Size: 6 inches in diameter

Materials

- ▶ Crochet cotton size 10: 65 yds white, 25 yds blue, 10 yds green
- ▶ Size 7 steel crochet hook or size needed to obtain gauge
- ▶ 2 (4¼-inch-diameter) fabric circles
- ▶ 5mm white pearl
- ▶ 18 inches ⅜-inch-wide white ribbon
- ▶ 24 inches ⅛-inch-wide white ribbon
- ▶ Sewing needle and thread
- ▶ Polyester fiberfill
- ▶ Tapestry needle

Fill this elegant sachet with your favorite scent and place it in your closet or dresser!

Gauge

Rnds 1–9 of front = 2¼ inches in diameter

Check gauge to save time.

Pattern Notes

Weave in loose ends as work progresses.

Join each rnd with a sl st unless otherwise stated.

Pattern Stitches

V-st: [Dc, ch 2, dc] in indicated st.

Beg V-st: [Ch 5 (for first dc, ch-2), dc] in indicated st.

Shell: [2 dc, ch 2, 2 dc] in indicated st.

Beg shell: [Ch 3 (for first dc), dc, ch 2, 2 dc] in indicated st.

P: Ch 3, sl st in top of last st.

Front

Rnd 1 (RS): With blue, ch 6, join to form a ring, ch 1, 12 sc in ring, join in beg sc. (12 sc)

Rnd 2: Ch 1, *sc in next st, [hdc, dc, 3 tr, dc, hdc] in next st, rep from * around, join in beg sc. (6 petals)

Rnd 3: Ch 1, sc in same st as beg ch, ch 4, [sc in next sc, ch 4] rep around, join in beg sc. (6 ch sps)

Rnd 4: Sl st into ch sp, ch 1, sc in same sp, ch 4, [sc in next ch sp, ch 4] rep around, join in beg sc.

Rnd 5: Ch 1, [sc, hdc, dc, 3 tr, dc, hdc] in each ch-4 sp around, join in beg sc.

Rnd 6: Ch 1, sc in same st as beg ch, ch 5, [sc in next sc, ch 5] rep around, join in beg sc.

Rnd 7: Sl st into ch-5 sp, ch 1, sc in same sp, ch 5, [sc in next ch sp, ch 5] rep around, join in beg sc.

Rnd 8: Ch 1, [sc, hdc, dc, 5 tr, dc, hdc] in each ch-5 sp around, join in beg sc, fasten off.

Rnd 9: Attach green at base of any center tr of 5-tr group of Rnd 8, ch 1, sc in same st, ch 5, [sc in base of next center tr of 5-tr group, ch 5] rep around, join in beg sc.

Rnd 10: Ch 1, [sc, hdc, dc, 2 tr, ch 1, 2 tr, dc, hdc, sc] in each ch-5 sp around, join in beg sc, fasten off.

Rnd 11: Attach white in any ch-1 sp of previous rnd, ch 1, sc in same sp, ch 6, sc in each of next 2 sc, ch 6, [sc in next ch-1 sp, ch 6, sc in each of next 2 sc, ch 6] rep around, join in beg sc.

Rnd 12: Ch 1, sc in next ch sp, ch 5, sl st in 3rd ch from hook, ch 3, [sc in next ch sp, ch 5, sl st in 3rd ch from hook, ch 3] rep around, join in beg sc.

Rnd 13: Ch 10 (counts as first dc, ch-7), [dc in next sc, ch 7] rep around, join in 3rd ch of beg ch-10.

Rnd 14: Ch 3, 9 dc in next ch-7 sp, [dc in next dc, 9 dc in next ch-7 sp] rep around, join in 3rd ch of beg ch-3. (120 dc)

Rnd 15: Ch 1, sc in each st around, join in beg sc.

Rnd 16: Ch 4, tr in each of next 2 sts, ch 4, sk next 3 sts, [tr in each of next 3 sts, ch 4, sk next 3 sts] rep around, join in 4th ch of beg ch-4.

Rnd 17: Ch 1, [sc in each of next 3 tr, 4 sc in next ch-4 sp] rep around, join in beg sc.

Continued on page 128

Votive Cup Holders

Designs by Paula Clark

Skill Level: Beginner

Size: Fits a tapered votive cup 2 inches in diameter at base

Materials

► South Maid crochet cotton size 10: 15 yds white #1, 30 yds victory red #494 and myrtle green #484

► Size 2 steel crochet hook or size needed to obtain gauge

► Tapered votive cups 2 inches in diameter at base

► Fabric stiffener

► Plastic wrap

With three different votive cup holders to choose from, you're sure to find a pattern and color to match any decor!

Gauge

7 dc = 1 inch; 2 dc rnds = ½ inch

Check gauge to save time.

Pattern Notes

Weave in loose ends as work progresses.

Join each rnd with a sl st unless otherwise stated.

Pattern Stitches

Shell: [2 dc, ch 2, 2 dc] in indicated st.

Beg shell: [Ch 3 (for first dc), dc, ch 2, 2 dc] in indicated st.

V-st: [Dc, ch 2, dc] in indicated st.

P: Ch 2, sl st in last sc.

Holder No. 1

Rnd 1 (RS): With victory red, ch 5, join to form a ring, ch 3 (counts as first dc throughout), 17 dc in ring, join in 3rd ch of beg ch-3. (18 dc)

Rnd 2: Ch 3, 4 dc in same st as beg ch, *sk next dc, 2 sc between next 2 dc, sk next dc **, 5 dc in next dc, rep from * around, ending last rep at **, join in 3rd ch of beg ch-3 (12 sc; 30 dc)

Rnd 3: Sl st in next 2 dc, ch 1, *[sc, ch 3, sc] in center dc of next 5-dc group, ch 5, rep from * around, join in beg sc.

Rnd 4: Sl st into ch-2 sp, beg shell in same sp, *dc in each of next 5 chs **, shell in next ch-2 sp, rep from * around, ending last rep at **, join in 3rd ch of beg ch-3.

Rnd 5: Sl st into ch-2 sp of shell, beg shell in shell, *ch 1, sk next 2 dc, sc in next dc, ch 2, sk next dc, V-st in next dc, ch 2, sk next dc, sc in next dc, ch 1, sk next 2 dc **, shell in next shell, rep from * around, ending last rep at **, join in 3rd ch of beg ch-3.

Rnd 6: Sl st into ch-2 sp of shell, beg shell in shell, *ch 1, shell in next V-st, ch 1 **, shell in next shell, rep from * around, ending last rep at **, join in 3rd ch of beg ch-3.

Rnd 7: Sl st into ch-2 sp of shell, beg shell in shell, sc in next ch-1 sp, [shell in next shell, sc in next ch-1 sp] rep around, join in 3rd ch of beg ch-3.

Rnd 8: Sl st into ch-2 sp of shell, beg shell in shell, ch 1, [shell in next shell, ch 1] rep around, join in 3rd ch of beg ch-3.

Rnd 9: Sl st into ch-2 sp of shell, beg shell in shell, sc in next ch-1 sp, [shell in next shell, sc in next ch-1 sp] rep around, join in 3rd ch of beg ch-3.

Rnd 10: Sl st into ch-2 sp of shell, ch 1, *[3 sc, p, 2 sc] in ch-2 sp of shell, sc in each of next 5 sts, rep from * around, join in beg sc, fasten off.

Holder No. 2

Rnd 1 (RS): With myrtle green, ch 5, join to form a ring, ch 1, 12 sc in ring, join in beg sc. (12 sc)

Rnd 2: Ch 4 (counts as first dc, ch-1 throughout), dc in same sc, sk next sc, *[dc, ch 1, dc] in next sc, sk next sc, rep from * around, join in 3rd ch of beg ch-4. (12 dc; 6 ch-1 sps)

Rnd 3: Sl st into ch-1 sp, ch 4, [dc, ch 1, dc] in same sp as beg ch, [{dc, ch 1} twice, dc] in each ch-1 sp around, join in 3rd ch of beg ch-4. (18 dc; 12 ch-1 sps)

Rnd 4: Sl st into ch-1 sp, ch 4, dc in same ch sp, [dc, ch 1, dc] in each rem ch-1 sp around, join in 3rd ch of beg ch-4. (24 dc; 12 ch-1 sps)

Rnd 5: Sl st into ch-1 sp, ch 3, 4 dc in same sp, sc between next 2 dc, [5 dc in next ch-1 sp, sc between next 2 dc] rep around, join in 3rd ch of beg ch-3.

Rnd 6: Working in back lps this rnd only, sl st in next 2 dc, ch 1, [sc in 3rd dc of next 5-dc group, ch 5] rep around, join in beg sc.

Rnd 7: Sl st into next ch-5 sp, ch 1, [sc, 5 dc, sc] in each ch-5 sp around, join in beg sc.

Rnd 8: Holding petals of Rnd 7 forward and working in sc sts of Rnd 6, ch 1, [sc in next sc of Rnd 6, ch 5] rep around, join in beg sc. (12 ch-5 sps)

Rnd 9: Sl st into ch-5 sp,

ch 3, 4 dc in same sp, 5 dc in each rem ch-5 sp around, join in 3rd ch of beg ch-3. (60 dc)

Rnd 10: Ch 3, dc in each dc around, join in 3rd ch of beg ch-3.

Rnd 11: Ch 1, sc in same dc as beg ch, ch 5, sk next 4 dc, [sc in next dc, ch 5, sk next 4 dc] rep around, join in beg sc. (12 ch-5 sps)

Rnd 12: Sl st into ch-5 sp, ch 1, [sc, 5 dc, sc] in each ch-5 sp around, join in beg

sc, fasten off.

Holder No. 3

Rnd 1 (RS): With white, ch 5, join to form a ring, ch 4 (counts as first dc, ch-1 throughout), [dc in ring, ch 1] 11 times, join in 3rd ch of beg ch-4. (12 dc; 12 ch-1 sps)

Rnd 2: Sl st into ch-1 sp, ch 1, sc in same sp, [ch 3, sc in next ch-1 sp] rep around, ending with ch 1, hdc in beg sc to position hook in center of last ch

sp. (12 ch-3 sps)

Rnds 3–6: Ch 1, sc in same sp as beg ch, [ch 3, sc in next ch-3 sp] rep around, ending with ch 1, hdc in beg sc.

Rnd 7: Ch 1, sc in same ch sp as beg ch, ch 3, [sc in next ch-3 sp, ch 3] rep around, join in beg sc.

Rnd 8: Sl st into ch-3 sp, ch 4, [dc, ch 1, dc] in same ch-3 sp, [{dc, ch 1} twice, dc] in each ch-3 sp

around, join in 3rd ch of beg ch-4.

Rnd 9: Sl st into ch-1 sp, ch 1, [sc, ch 3, sc] in each ch-1 sp around, join in beg sc, fasten off.

Shaping

Cover votive cup with plastic wrap. Saturate crocheted piece with fabric stiffener and stretch over bottom of votive cup.

Dry completely and remove plastic wrap. ✂

Mini Victorian Dresser Box

Design by Carol Alexander
for Crochet Trends & Traditions

Skill Level: Beginner

Size: 1¾ inches high x 3 inches in diameter

Materials

▶ J. & P. Coats Knit-Cro-Sheen crochet cotton size 10: 100 yds cream #42, small amount each medium celery #27 and almond pink #35

▶ J. & P. Coats Pearl Knit-Cro-Sheen crochet cotton size 10: 100 yds ecru/pearl #61P

▶ Size 4 steel crochet hook or size needed to obtain gauge

▶ 6mm pearl bead

▶ Fabric stiffener

▶ Plastic wrap

▶ 6-oz plastic yogurt cup measuring 2⅛ inches across bottom

▶ Small round container measuring approximately 2⅝ inches across top

▶ Hot-glue gun

▶ Tapestry needle

This decorative little box is perfect for keeping small dresser items such as jewelry or coins close at hand. It can even be a mini mending kit, holding small spools of thread and sewing needles for emergency repairs!

Gauge

With 2 strands crochet cotton held tog, Rnds 1–4 of bottom = 1⅛ inches

Rose motif = 1¾ inches

Check gauge to save time.

Pattern Notes

Weave in loose ends as work progresses.

Join each rnd with a sl st unless otherwise stated.

Box is worked with 2 strands held tog throughout.

Box Bottom

Rnd 1: Beg at bottom center, with 1 strand each cream and ecru/pearl held tog, ch 3, 11 hdc in first ch of ch-3, join in 3rd ch of beg ch-3. (12 hdc)

Rnd 2: Ch 2 (counts as first hdc throughout), hdc in same st as beg ch, 2 hdc in each hdc around, join in 2nd ch of beg ch-2. (24 hdc)

Rnd 3: Ch 2, hdc in same st as beg ch, hdc in next st, [2 hdc in next st, hdc in next st] rep around, join in 2nd ch of beg ch-2. (36 hdc)

Rnd 4: Ch 2, hdc in same st as beg ch, hdc in each of next 2 sts, [2 hdc in next st, hdc in each of next 2 sts] rep around, join in 2nd ch of beg ch-2. (48 hdc)

Rnd 5: Working in back lps this rnd only, ch 2, hdc in each st around, join in 2nd ch of beg ch-2.

Rnds 6–9: Ch 2, hdc in each st around, join in 2nd ch of beg ch-2.

Rnd 10: Ch 1, sc in each st around, join in beg sc, fasten off.

Bottom trim

Rnd 1: With Rnd 10 of box facing, attach 1 strand each cream and ecru/pearl in rem free lp of Rnd 4 at joining, ch 1, sc in same st as joining, *ch 2, [yo, insert hook in same st as ch-2, yo, draw up a lp] 4 times, yo, draw through 8 lps on hook, yo, draw through rem 2 lps on hook (cl made), sk next 2 sts **, sc in next st, rep from * around, ending last rep at **, join in beg sc. (16 cls)

Rnd 2: Ch 1, sc in same sc as joining, *ch 2, sc in next ch-2 sp, ch 2 **, sc in next sc, rep from * around, ending last rep at **, join in beg sc, fasten off. (32 ch-2 sps)

Lid

Rnds 1–4: Rep Rnds 1–4 of box bottom. (48 hdc)

Rnds 5 & 6: Ch 2, hdc in each st around, join in 2nd ch of beg ch-2.

Rnd 7: Ch 1, sc in same st as joining, *ch 2, [yo, insert hook in same st as ch-2, yo, draw up a lp] 4 times, yo, draw through 8 lps on hook, yo, draw through rem 2 lps on hook (cl made), sk next 2 sts **, sc in next st, rep from * around, ending last rep at **, join in beg sc. (16 cls)

Rnd 8: Rep Rnd 2 of bottom trim.

Shaping

Following fabric stiffener instructions, stiffen box bottom and lid to shape.

To shape box, turn a 6-oz plastic yogurt cup (measuring approximately 2⅛ inches across bottom) upside down, cover with plastic wrap and place box bottom over it. To shape lid, cover any small round container

measuring approximately 2⅝ inches across top and cover with plastic wrap, place lid over it.

Rose Motif

Rnd 1: With almond pink, ch 5, join to form a ring, ch 1, 16 sc in ring, join in beg sc. (16 sc)

Rnd 2: Ch 1, sc in same st as beg ch, ch 2, sk next sc, [sc in next sc, ch 2, sk next sc] 7 times, join in beg sc. (8 ch-2 sps)

Rnd 3: [Sl st, ch 2, 3 dc, ch 2, sl st] in each ch-2 sp around, fasten off. (8 petals)

Rnd 4: Working in front of Rnd 3 in skipped sts of Rnd 1, attach almond pink in any sc, ch 1, [sc, ch 1, 2 dc, ch 1, sc] in each sc around, join in beg sc, fasten off. (8 petals)

Leaves
First leaf

Attach medium celery to center back of any outside petal of Rnd 3 of rose motif, ch 3, in same place work [2 tr, ch 2, sc around top of post of last tr made, tr, ch 3, sl st], fasten off.

Second leaf

Attach medium celery to center back of next outside petal, rep first leaf.

Glue rose motif to top center of lid. Glue pearl bead to center of rose. ✂

Li'l Bear's Outfit

Design by Tammy Hildebrand

Skill Level: Beginner

Size: Fits 12-inch bear

Materials

▶ Lion Brand Chenille Sensations chenille yarn: 2 oz purple #147 (MC), ½ oz Milan #402 (CC)

▶ Size G/6 crochet hook or size needed to obtain gauge

▶ 10mm shank button

▶ 3 purple ribbon rosettes

▶ 1½ yds ³⁄₁₆-inch-wide lavender picot-edge ribbon

▶ 1½ yds ⅛-inch-wide pink ribbon

▶ Tapestry needle

In chenille hat and dress, this charming bear is all dressed up and would make a treasured gift!

Gauge

8 dc = 2 inches

Check gauge to save time.

Pattern Notes

Weave in loose ends as work progresses.

Join each rnd with a sl st unless otherwise stated.

Pattern Stitches

Shell: [2 dc, ch 1, 2 dc] in indicated st.

Beg shell: [Ch 3 (for first dc), dc, ch 1, 2 dc] in indicated st.

V-st: [Dc, ch 1, dc] in indicated st.

Beg V-st: [Ch 4 (for first dc, ch-1), dc] in same st.

P: Ch 2, sl st in first ch of ch-2.

Dress

Row 1 (RS): Beg at neckline with MC, ch 34, sc in 2nd ch from hook, sc in each rem ch across, turn. (33 sc)

Row 2: Ch 3 (counts as first dc throughout), [2 dc in next st, dc in next st] 16 times, turn. (49 dc)

Row 3: Ch 3, dc in next dc, [2 dc in next dc, dc in each of next 2 dc] 15 times, dc in last dc, turn. (65 dc)

Row 4: Ch 3, dc in same st as beg ch, dc in each rem dc across, turn. (66 dc)

Rnd 5 (RS): Ch 3, dc in each of next 6 dc, ch 1, sk next 20 dc (armhole opening), dc in each of next 13 dc, ch 1, sk next 20 dc (armhole opening), dc in each of next 6 dc, join in 3rd ch of beg ch-3. (26 dc)

Rnd 6: Ch 3, dc in same st as beg ch, [ch 1, sk next dc, 2 dc in next dc] 3 times, 2 dc in next ch-1 sp, [2 dc in next dc, ch 1, sk next dc] 6 times, 2 dc in next dc, 2 dc in next ch-1 sp, [2 dc in next dc, ch 1, sk next dc] 3 times, join in 3rd ch of beg ch-3. (32 dc)

Rnd 7: Ch 3, dc in next dc, [2 dc in next ch-1 sp, dc in each of next 2 dc] 3 times, dc in each of next 4 dc, [2 dc in next ch-1 sp, dc in each of next 2 dc] 6 times, dc in each of next 4 dc, [2 dc in next ch-1 sp, dc in each of next 2 dc] twice, 2 dc in next ch-1 sp, join in 3rd ch of beg ch-3. (56 dc)

Rnd 8: Ch 1, sc in same st as beg ch, sk next dc, shell in next dc, [sk next dc, sc in next dc, sk next dc, shell in next dc] 13 times, join in beg sc. (14 sc; 14 shells)

Rnd 9: Ch 3, shell in ch-1 sp of next shell, [dc in next sc, shell in next ch-1 sp] rep around, join in 3rd ch of beg ch-3. (14 dc; 14 shells)

Rnd 10: Beg V-st in same st as joining, shell in ch-1 sp of next shell, [V-st in next single dc between shells, shell in ch-1 sp of next shell] rep across, join in 3rd ch of beg ch-4. (14 V-sts; 14 shells)

Rnds 11 & 12: Beg V-st in ch-1 sp, shell in ch-1 sp of next shell, [V-st in ch-1 sp of next V-st, shell in ch-1 sp of next shell] rep around, join in 3rd ch of beg ch-4, at the end of Rnd 12, fasten off.

Rnd 13: Attach CC in any st of Rnd 12, ch 1, sc in same st, p, [sc in next st, p] rep in each st around, join in beg sc, fasten off.

Neckline Trim

Rnd 1 (RS): Attach CC with a sl st in rem lp on opposite side of foundation ch, p, [sl st in next ch, p] rep around neckline, sc evenly sp down back opening, sc evenly sp up opposite side of back opening, ch 1 (for buttonhole), join in beg sc, fasten off.

Sew button opposite buttonhole.

Sleeve Trim

Make 2

Rnd 1: Attach CC with a sl st in first skipped st of Rnd 5, p, [sl st in next st, p] 19 times, fasten off.

Cut a 20-inch length each of lavender and pink ribbon. Holding both strands tog, starting at center front, weave through ch-1 sps of Rnd 6. Making sure dress is removable from bear, knot at center front. Sew a rosette centered over knot.

Sew a rosette at center front neckline.

Hat

Rnd 1: With MC, ch 3, join to form a ring, ch 3, 11 dc in ring, join in top of beg ch-3. (12 dc)

Rnd 2: Ch 3 (counts as first dc throughout), 2 dc in next dc, [dc in next dc, 2 dc

in next dc] 5 times, join in 3rd ch of beg ch-3. (18 dc)

Rnd 3: Ch 3 (counts as first hdc, ch-1), sk next dc, [hdc in next dc, ch 1, sk next dc] rep around, join in 2nd ch of beg ch-3. (9 hdc; 9 ch-1 sps)

Rnd 4: Sl st into ch-1 sp, beg shell in same sp, sl st in next hdc, [shell in next ch-1 sp, sl st in next hdc] rep around, join in 3rd ch of beg ch-3, fasten off.

Holding rem lengths of ribbon tog, weave through ch-1 sps of Rnd 3; knot ends tog. Sew a rosette over knot. ✂

Stitch these lovely frames in spring pastels to give as gifts or to display your favorite photos—a perfect extra to add to your Easter baskets!

Easter Egg Frames

Designs by Kathryn Clark

Skill Level: Beginner

Size: 3 x 4 inches

Materials

► Crochet cotton size 10: 50 yds each lavender, pink and peach, 35 yds pale yellow, small amount each light green, light blue and lavender

► Size 7 steel crochet hook or size needed to obtain gauge

► Fabric stiffener

► Self-adhesive vinyl paper

► 4-inch square of lightweight cardboard

► Paper towel

► Plastic wrap

► Heavy cardboard

► Rustproof straight pins

► Hot-glue gun

► Small peach silk flower with leaves

► ⅛-inch-wide satin ribbon: 18 inches white; 10 inches each white, pink and yellow

► ¼-inch-wide picot-edge ribbon: 18 inches off-white; 8 inches white

► 3 (¼-inch) jump rings

► 2 x 3-inch oval mirror

Gauge

8 dc = 1 inch; 4 rows = 1 inch

Check gauge to save time.

Pattern Notes

Weave in loose ends as work progresses.

Join each rnd with a sl st unless otherwise stated.

Lavender Photo Frame

Back

Rnd 1: With lavender, ch 11, 2 dc in 4th ch from hook, 2 dc in next ch, dc in each of next 4 chs, 2 dc in next ch, 3 dc in last ch, working on opposite side of foundation ch, 2 dc in next ch, dc in each of next 4 chs, 2 dc in last ch, join in 4th ch of beg ch-4. (22 sts)

Rnd 2: Ch 3 (counts as first dc throughout), [dc, tr] in same st as beg ch, 2 tr in next st, [tr, 2 dc] in next st, 2 dc in each of next 2 sts, dc in each of next 4 sts, 2 dc in each of next 2 sts, [2 dc, tr] in next st, 2 tr in next st, [tr, 2 dc] in next st, 2 dc in each of next 2 sts, dc in each of next 4 sts, 2 dc in each of next 2 sts, join in 3rd ch of beg ch-3. (40 sts)

Rnd 3: Ch 3, dc in same st as beg ch, dc in next st, [2 dc in next st, dc in next st] 6 times, dc in each of next 4 sts, [2 dc in next st, dc in next st] 8 times, dc in each of next 4 sts, 2 dc in next st, dc in next st, join in 3rd ch of beg ch-3. (56 sts)

Rnd 4: Ch 3, dc in same st as beg ch, dc in each of next 2 sts, [2 dc in next st, dc in each of next 2 sts] 6 times, dc in each of next 4 sts, [2 dc in next st, dc in each of next 2 sts] 8 times, dc in each of next 4 sts, 2 dc in next st, dc in each of next 2 sts, join in 3rd ch of beg ch-3, fasten off. (72 sts)

With RS facing, count 5 sts to the right of beg ch-3; mark with scrap of CC cotton.

Cover front and back of 4-inch square of lightweight cardboard with self-adhesive vinyl paper. Trace frame back onto covered cardboard and cut out just inside the line about ¹⁄₁₆-inch. This will be used as a shaping form and as pattern for cutting photo to fit frame.

Front

Rnd 1: With lavender, ch 56, join to form a ring, taking care not to twist ch, ch 3 (counts as first dc throughout), [2 dc in next st, dc in each of next 2 sts] 4 times, dc in each of next 4 sts, [2 dc in next st, dc in each of next 2 sts] 8 times, dc in each of next 4 sts, [2 dc in next st, dc in each of next 2 sts] 3 times, 2 dc in next st, dc in next st, join in 3rd ch of beg ch-3. (72 sts)

Rnd 2: Ch 1, sc in same st, ch 4, sk next 2 sts, [sc in next st, ch 4, sk next 2 sts] 4 times, holding front and back with WS tog, matching next st with marked st on back and working through both thicknesses, [sc in next st, ch 4, sk next 2 sts] 15 times, working sts in front only, [sc in next st, ch 4, sk next 2 sts] 4 times, join in beg sc.

Rnd 3: Sl st into ch-4 sp, ch 1, [sc, hdc, 2 dc] in same sp, ch 2, *[sc, hdc, 2

dc] in next ch-4 sp, ch 2, rep from * around, join in beg sc, fasten off.

Stiffening

Cover heavy cardboard with plastic wrap for pinning board. Soak frame in fabric stiffener. Blot excess stiffener with paper towel. Place shaping form inside frame; pin frame to shape on pinning board. Allow to dry completely.

Finishing

Beg and ending at center top, weave a ½-yard length of ⅛-inch-wide white satin ribbon through Rnd 2 of frame front; tie ends in a bow at top of frame. Attach jump ring to top of frame and tie 10-inch length of ⅛-inch-wide white satin ribbon through ring for hanging lp. Using the shaping form, cut

picture and insert between front and back.

Pink Photo Frame

Back

With pink, follow instructions for lavender photo frame back.

Front

Rnd 1: With pink, ch 56, join to form a ring, taking care not to twist ch, ch 3, [2 dc in next st, dc in each of next 2 sts] 4 times, dc in each of next 4 sts, [2 dc in next st, dc in each of next 2 sts] 8 times, dc in each of next 4 sts, [2 dc in next st, dc in each of next 2 sts] 3 times, 2 dc in next st, dc in next st, join in 3rd ch of beg ch-3. (72 sts)

Rnd 2: Ch 1, [sc, ch 3, sc] in same st as beg ch, ch 3, sk next 2 sts, [{sc, ch 3, sc}

in next st, ch 3, sk next 2 sts] 4 times, holding front and back with WS tog, matching next st with marked st on egg back and working through both thicknesses, [{sc, ch 3, sc} in next st, ch 3, sk next 2 sts] 15 times, working in sts of front only, [{sc, ch 3, sc} in next st, ch 3, sk next 2 sts] 3 times, [sc, ch 3, sc] in next st, join with dc in beg sc.

Rnd 3: Ch 1, [sc, ch 3, sc] over post of joining dc, ch 4, sk next ch-3, *[sc, ch 3, sc] in next ch-3 sp, ch 4, sk next ch-3 sp, rep from * around, join in beg sc, fasten off.

Stiffening

Follow stiffening instructions for lavender photo frame.

Finishing

Tie 8-inch length of ¼-inch-wide white picot-edge

satin ribbon in a bow; glue to top of frame. Attach jump ring to top of frame and tie 10-inch length of ⅛-inch-wide pink satin ribbon through ring for hanging lp. Using the shaping form, cut picture and insert between front and back.

Multicolored Photo Frame

Back

With pale yellow, follow instructions for lavender photo frame back.

Front

Rnd 1: With pale yellow, follow instructions for Rnd 1 of pink photo frame front, fasten off. (72 sts)

Rnd 2: Attach light green in first st of previous rnd, ch 6, dc in same st as beg ch, sk next 2 sts, [{dc, ch 3, *Continued on page 129*

Continued on page 129

Blooming Hearts Gift Set

Designs by Lauri Grammer

Skill Level: Beginner

Size:

Key Chain: 2¼ x 2¾ inches, excluding chain

Pin: 1½ x 1¾ inches

Coin Purse: 4¼ x 2⅜ inches

Materials

▶ J. & P. Coats Knit-Cro-Sheen crochet cotton size 10: 75 yds cream #42, 50 yds almond pink #35

▶ Size 7 steel crochet hook or size needed to obtain gauge

▶ Snake link key chain

▶ 1-inch pin back

▶ 4-inch off-white zipper

▶ Sewing needle and cream thread

▶ Tacky glue

▶ Polyester fiberfill

▶ Tapestry needle

Gauge

5 sc rows and 4 sc stitches = ½ inch
Check gauge to save time.

Pattern Notes

Weave in loose ends as work progresses.

Join each rnd with a sl st unless otherwise stated.

Key Chain

Heart

Make 2

Row 1 (RS): Beg at bottom with almond pink, ch 2, sc in 2nd ch from hook, turn. (1 sc)

Row 2: Ch 1, 3 sc in sc, turn. (3 sc)

Row 3: Ch 1, sc in each sc across, turn.

Row 4: Ch 1, 2 sc in first sc, sc in next sc, 2 sc in last sc, turn. (5 sc)

Row 5: Rep Row 3.

Row 6: Ch 1, 2 sc in first sc, sc in each sc across to last sc, 2 sc in last sc, turn. (7 sc)

Rows 7–20: Rep Rows 5 and 6. (21 sc at end of Row 20)

Row 21: Rep Row 3.

Left lobe

Row 22 (WS): Ch 1, sc in each of next 10 sc, leaving rem sts unworked, turn. (10 sc)

Row 23: Ch 1, sc dec over next 2 sc, sc in each of next 8 sc, turn. (9 sc)

Row 24: Ch 1, sc in each of next 7 sc, sc dec over next 2 sc, turn. (8 sc)

Row 25: Ch 1, sc dec over next 2 sc, sc in each rem sc across, turn. (7 sc)

Row 26: Rep Row 25. (6 sc)

Row 27: Ch 1, sc dec over next 2 sc, sc in each of next 2 sc, sc dec over next 2 sc, fasten off. (4 sc)

Right lobe

Row 22 (WS): Sk next sc of Row 21, attach almond pink with a sl st in next sc, ch 1, sc in same st as beg ch, sc in each of next 9 sc, turn. (10 sc)

Row 23: Ch 1, sc in each of next 8 sc, sc dec over next 2 sc, turn. (9 sc)

Row 24: Ch 1, sc dec over next 2 sc, sc in each of next 7 sc, turn. (8 sc)

Row 25: Ch 1, sc in next 6 sc, sc dec over next 2 sc, turn. (7 sc)

Row 26: Ch 1, sc in each of next 5 sc, sc dec over next 2 sc, turn. (6 sc)

Row 27: Ch 1, sc dec over next 2 sc, sc in each of next 2 sc, sc dec over next 2 sc, fasten off. (4 sc)

Edging

Rnd 1 (RS): Attach almond pink in skipped sc at center of Row 21, ch 1, sc in same sc as beg ch-1, sc evenly sp around outer edge of heart, working 3 sc in center bottom point of heart, join in beg sc, fasten off.

Finishing

With cream, embroider 3 lazy-daisy st, 6-petal flowers on RS of 1 heart.

With WS facing and working through both thicknesses, sew hearts tog with length of almond pink, stuffing with fiberfill before closing. Attach key chain to center top of heart between lobes.

Pin

Heart

Make 2

Rows 1–13: Rep Rows 1–13 of key chain heart. (13 sc)

Left lobe

Row 14 (WS): Ch 1, sc in each of next 6 sc, leaving rem sc unworked, turn. (6 sc)

Row 15: Ch 1, sc dec over next 2 sc, sc in each of next 4 sc, turn. (5 sc)

Row 16: Ch 1, sc in each sc across, turn.

Row 17: Ch 1, sc dec over next 2 sc, sc in next sc, sc dec over next 2 sc, fasten off. (3 sc)

Right lobe

Row 14 (WS): Working in rem sts of Row 13, sk next sc, attach almond pink with a sl st in next sc, ch 1, sc in same sc as beg ch-1, sc in each of next 5 sc, turn. (6 sc)

Hearts and flowers—two of the most treasured symbols of love—come to radiant life in this dainty trio. This is one gift set that you may choose to make for yourself!

Row 15: Ch 1, sc in each of next 4 sc, sc dec over next 2 sc, turn. (5 sc)

Row 16: Ch 1, sc in each sc across, turn.

Row 17: Ch 1, sc dec over next 2 sc, sc in next sc, sc dec over next 2 sc, fasten off. (3 sc)

Edging

Rnd 1: Attach almond pink with a sl st in skipped sc of Row 13, ch 1, sc in same st as beg ch-1, sc evenly sp around outer edge, working 3 sc in center bottom point of heart, join in beg sc, fasten off.

Finishing

With tapestry needle and cream, embroider 2 lazy-daisy st, 6-petal flowers on RS of 1 heart.

With tapestry needle and almond pink, holding hearts with WS tog and working through both thicknesses, sew around outer edge, stuffing with fiberfill before closing. Glue pin back to back of heart.

Coin Purse

First Side

Row 1 (RS): With cream, ch 40, sc in 2nd ch from hook, sc in each rem ch across, turn. (39 sc)

Rows 2–25: Ch 1, sc in each sc across, turn, at the end of Row 25, fasten off.

Second Side

Row 1 (RS): Working in rem lps across opposite side of foundation ch on first side, attach cream in first ch, ch 1, sc in each ch across, turn. (39 sc)

Rows 2–25: Rep Rows 2–25 of first side.

Heart

Rows 1–17: Rep Rows 1–17 of heart for pin.

Edging

Rnd 1: Rep Rnd 1 of edging for heart pin.

Finishing

With tapestry needle and cream, embroider 2 lazy-daisy st, 6-petal flowers on RS of heart.

Fold coin purse with foundation ch at the fold. Using tapestry needle and cream, sew short sides tog. With almond pink, sew heart to RS of coin purse. With sewing needle and thread, sew zipper into opening, following manufacturer's instructions. ✂

Swan Bonbon Dish

Design by Maggie Petsch

Skill Level: Intermediate

Size: 6 inches long x 3¾ inches tall

Materials

- ► Crochet cotton size 10 (225 yds per ball): 1 ball white, small amount black
- ► Size 7 steel crochet hook or size needed to obtain gauge
- ► Small amount polyester fiberfill
- ► Fabric stiffener
- ► Tapestry needle

Gauge

12 sc = 1 inch
Check gauge to save time.

Pattern Notes

Weave in loose ends as work progresses.

Join each rnd with a sl st unless otherwise stated.

Pattern Stitches

Sc5tog: Draw up a lp in each of next 5 sts, yo, draw through all 6 lps on hook.

Sc3tog: Draw up a lp in each of next 3 sts, yo, draw through all 4 lps on hook.

Sc2tog: Draw up a lp in each of next 2 sts, yo, draw through all 3 lps on hook.

Split sc2tog: Draw up a lp in next st, sk next st, draw up a lp in next st, yo, draw through all 3 lps on hook.

P: Ch 3, sl st in top of last st made.

Body

Rnd 1 (RS): With white, ch 21, sc in 2nd ch from hook, sc in each of next 18 chs, [sc, ch 1, sc] in last ch, working on opposite side of foundation ch, sc in each of next 18 chs, [sc, ch 1] in same st as beg sc, join in beg sc. (40 sc)

Rnd 2: Ch 1, sc in same st as joining, sc in each of next 19 sc, 3 sc in next ch-1 sp, sc in each of next 20 sc, 3 sc in next ch-1 sp, join in beg sc. (46 sc)

Rnd 3: Ch 1, sc in same st as joining, sc in each of next 19 sc, 2 sc in each of next 3 sc, sc in each of next 20 sc, 2 sc in each of next 3 sc, join in beg sc. (52 sc)

Rnd 4: Ch 1, sc in same sc as joining, sc in each of next 20 sc, *[2 sc in next sc, sc in next sc] twice, 2 sc in next sc *, sc in each of next 21 sc, rep from * to *, join in beg sc. (58 sc)

Rnd 5: Ch 1, sc in same st as joining, sc in each of next 21 sc, *[2 sc in next sc, sc in each of next 2 sc] twice, 2 sc in next sc *, sc in each of next 22 sc, rep from * to *, join in beg sc. (64 sc)

Rnd 6: Ch 1, sc in same st as joining, sc in each of next 22 sc, *[2 sc in next sc, sc in each of next 3 sc] twice, 2 sc in next sc *, sc in each of next 23 sc, rep from * to *, join in beg sc. (70 sc)

Rnd 7: Ch 1, sc in same st as joining, sc in each of next 23 sc, *[2 sc in next sc, sc in each of next 4 sc] twice, 2 sc in next sc *, sc in each of next 24 sc, rep from * to *, join in beg sc. (76 sc)

Rnd 8: Ch 1, sc in same st as joining, sc in each of next 30 sc, 3 sc in next sc, sc in each of next 31 sc, [2 sc in next sc, sc in each of next 5 sc] twice, 2 sc in next sc, join in beg sc. (81 sc)

Rnd 9: Ch 1, sc in same st as joining, sc in each of next 31 sc, 3 sc in next sc, sc in each of next 32 sc, [2 sc in next sc, sc in each of next 6 sc] twice, 2 sc in next sc, sc in next sc, join in beg sc. (86 sc)

Rnd 10: Ch 1, sc in same st as joining, sc in each of next 32 sc, 3 sc in next sc, sc in each of next 34 sc, [2 sc in next sc, sc in each of next 7 sc] twice, 2 sc in next sc, sc in next sc, join in beg sc. (91 sc)

Rnd 11: Ch 1, sc in same st as joining, sc in each of next 34 sc, 3 sc in next sc, sc in each of next 35 sc, [2 sc in next sc, sc in each of next 8 sc] twice, 2 sc in next sc, sc in next sc, join in beg sc. (96 sc)

Rnd 12: Ch 1, sc in same st as joining, sc in each of next 25 sc, 3 sc in next sc, sc in each of next 36 sc, [2 sc in next sc, sc in each of next 9 sc] twice, 2 sc in next sc, sc in each of next 2 sc, join in beg sc. (101 sc)

Rnd 13: Ch 1, sc in same st as joining, sc in each of next 36 sc, 3 sc in next sc, sc in each of next 38 sc, [2 sc in next sc, sc in each of next 10 sc] twice, 2 sc in next sc, sc in each of next 2 sc, join in beg sc. (106 sc)

Rnd 14: Ch 1, sc in same st as joining, sc in each of next 37 sc, 3 sc in next sc, sc in each of next 40 sc, [2 sc in next sc, sc in each of next 11 sc] twice, 2 sc in next sc, sc in each of next 2 sc, join in beg sc. (111 sc)

Rnd 15: Ch 1, sc in same st as joining, sc in each of next 38 sc, 5 sc in next sc, sc in each of next 17 sc, turn, sk last sc made, sc in

each of next 18 sc, 5 sc in next sc, sc in each of next 17 sc, turn, sk last sc made, sc in each of next 17 sc, 3 sc in next sc, sc in each rem sc around, join in beg sc. (119 sc)

Rnd 16: Ch 1, sc in same st as joining, sc in each of next 40 sc, sc5tog, sc in each rem sc around, join in beg sc. (115 sts)

Rnd 17: Ch 1, sc in same st as joining, sc in each of

next 38 sc, sc5tog, sc in each rem st around, join in beg sc. (111 sts)

Rnd 18: Ch 1, sc in same st as joining, sc in each of next 13 sc, sc2tog, sc in each of next 6 sts, sc3tog, sc in each of next 6 sts, sc2tog, sc in each rem sc around, join in beg sc. (107 sts)

Rnd 19: Ch 1, sc in same st as joining, sc in each of next 37 sc, split sc2tog, sc

in each rem st around, join in beg sc. (105 sts)

Rnd 20: Ch 1, sc in same st as joining, sc in each of next 36 sts, split sc2tog, sc in each rem st around, join in beg sc. (103 sts)

Rnd 21: Ch 1, sc in same st as joining, sc in each of next 35 sts, split sc2tog, sc in each rem st around, join in beg sc. (101 sts)

Rnd 22: Ch 1, sc in same st as joining, sc in each of

next 34 sts, split sc2tog, sc in each rem st around, join in beg sc, turn. (99 sts)

Rnd 23: Sl st in each of last 6 sts made, turn, sc over each of next 6 sl sts and in next sc, turn, *sc in each of next 7 sc, turn, sk first sc, sc in each of next 6 sc, turn, sc in each of next 4 sc, sk next sc, sc in next sc, turn, sk first sc, sc in each of next 4 sc, sl st over end st of each of last 4 rows * (first scallop made), sc in each of next 7 unworked sts on last rnd, turn, rep from * to *, sc in each of next 7 unworked sc on last rnd, turn, sc in each of next 6 sc, turn, sk first sc, sc in each of next 5 sc, turn, sc in each of next 3 sc, sk next sc, sc in next sc, turn, sk first sc, sc in each of next 3 sc, sl st over end sts of each of last 4 rows, sc in each of next 7 unworked sc on last rnd, turn, sc in each of next 6 sc, turn, sk first sc, sc in each of next 3 sc, sk next sc, sc in next sc, sl st over end sts of each of last 2 rows, sc in each of next 7 unworked sts on last rnd, turn, sc in each of next 6 sts, turn, sk next 2 sts, sc in each of next 4 sts, sl st over end sts of each of last 2 rows, sc in each of next 6 unworked sts on last rnd, turn, sc in each of next 5 sts, turn, sk 2 sts, sc in each of next 3 sts, sl st over end sts of each of last 2 rows, sc in each of next 8 unworked sts on last rnd, turn, sk first st, sc in each of next 5 sc, turn, sc in each of next 3 sc, sl st in each of next 2 sc, sl st over end sts of each of last 2 rows, sc in each of next 7 unworked sc sts on last rnd, turn, sk first sc, sc in each of next 6 sc, turn; sc in each of next 4 sc, sl st in each of next 2 sc, sl st over end sts of each of next 2 rows, sc in each of next 7 unworked sts on last rnd, turn, sk first sc, sc in each of next 6 sc, turn, sc in next st, sk next st, sc in each of next 3 sts, sl st in next st, sl st over end sts of each of last 2 rows, sc in each of next 7 unworked sts on last rnd, turn, sk first sc, sc in each of next 6 sc, turn, sc in each of next 5 sc, turn, sc in next sc, sk next sc, sc in each of next 3 sc, turn, sc in each of next 3 sc, sl st in next sc, sl st over end sts of each of last 4 rows, **sc in each of next 7 unworked sts on last rnd, turn, sc in each of next 7 sc, turn, sc in each of next 6 sc, turn, sc in next sc, sk next sc, sc in each of next 4 sc, turn, sc in each of next 4 sc, sl st in next sc, sl st over end sts of each of last 4 rows, rep from **, sc in each of next 4 unworked sts on last rnd, 2 sc in next st, sc in each of next 5 sts, 2 sc in next st, sc in each of next 4 sts, turn, sk next sc, sc in each of next 16 sc, turn, sk next sc, sc in each of next 15 sc, turn, sk next sc, sc in each of next 14 sc, turn, sk next sc, sc in each of next 13 sc, turn, sk next sc, sc in each of next 12 sc, turn, sk next sc, sc in each of next 11 sc, turn, sk next sc, sc in each of next 10 sc, turn, sk next sc, sc in each of next 9 sc, sl st over end sts of each of last 8 rows.

Rnd 24: [Work 5 sc evenly sp up side of scallop, sc in each of next 2 sc, {p, sc in next sc} twice, sc in each of next 4 sl sts] twice, 5 sc evenly sp up side of next scallop, sc in next sc, [p, sc in next sc] twice, sc in each of next 4 sl sts, 3 sc evenly sp up side of next scallop, sc in each of next 3 sc, p, sc in next sc, sc in each of next 2 sl sts, 3 sc evenly sp up side of next scallop, sc in each of next 4 sc, sc in each of next 2 sl sts, 3 sc evenly sp up side of next scallop, sc in each of next 3 sc, sc in each of next 2 sl sts, sc in each of next 2 sc, 3 sc evenly sp up side of next scallop, sc in each of next 3 sc, 4 sc evenly sp down side of same scallop, 3 sc evenly sp up side of next scallop, sc in each of next 4 sc, 4 sc evenly sp down side of same scallop, 3 sc evenly sp up side of next scallop, p, sc in each of next 4 sc, 3 sc evenly sp down side of same scallop, 5 sc evenly sp up side of next scallop, [p, sc in next sc] twice, sc in next sc, 4 sc evenly sp down side of same scallop, [5 sc evenly sp up side of next scallop, {p, sc in next sc} twice, sc in each of next 2 sc, 4 sc evenly sp down side of same scallop] twice, sc over end st of each of next 8 rows, sc in each of next 9 sc, sc in each of next 8 sl sts, join in beg sc, fasten off.

Beak, Head & Neck

Beg at tip of beak with white, ch 4, join to form a ring, ch 1, 6 sc in ring, [2 sc in next st, sc in each of next 2 sts] twice, sc in each of next 24 sts, [2 sc in next st, sc in each of next 2 sts] 7 times, 2 sc in next st (16 sts around at this point), sc in each of next 25 sts, [2 sc in next st, sc in each of next 4 sts] twice, 2 sc in next st, sc in each of next 7 sts, [2 sc in next st, sc in each of next 5 sts] twice, 2 sc in next st, sc in each of next 8 sts, 2 sc in next st, sc in each of next 3 sts, 2 sc in next st, sc in each of next 4 sts, 2 sc in next st, sc in each of next 3 sts, 2 sc in next st (26 sts around at this point), sc in each of next 62 sts, [sk next st, sc in each of next 8 sts] 3 times, [sk next st, sc in each of next 7 sts] 3 times, [sk next st, sc in each of next 6 sts] 3 times, [sk next st, sc in each of next 5 sts] twice, sk next st, sc in each of next 10 sts, stuff beak and head firmly with fiberfill, sk next st, sc in each of next 400 sts, stopping occasionally to stuff neck firmly with fiberfill, [sc in each of next 2 sts, 2 sc in next st] twice, sc in each of next 10 sts, 2 sc in next st, sc in each of next 3 sts, 2 sc in next st, sc in each of next 11 sts, 2 sc in next st, sc in each of next 4 sts, 2 sc in next st, sc in each of next 12 sts, 2 sc in next st, sc in each of next 5 sts, 2 sc in next st, sc in each of next 13 sts, 2 sc in next st, [sc in each of next 2 sts, 2 sc in next st] twice, sc in each of next 15 sts, 2 sc in next st, [sc in each of next 3 sts, 2 sc in next st] twice, sc in each of next 16 sts, 2 sc in next st, sc in each of next 4 sts, 2 sc in next st, sc in each of next 23 sts, 2 sc in next st, sc in each of next 30 sts, 2 sc in next st, sc in each of next 31 sts, 2 sc in next st, sc in each of next 32 sts, 2 sc in next st, sc in each of next 11 sts, turn, sc in each of next 11 sts, 2 sc in next st, sc in each of next 12 sts, turn, sc in each of next 26 sts, turn, sk next sc, sc in each of next 23 sc, sk next sc, sc in next sc, turn, sk first sc, sc in each of next 21 sc, sk next sc, sc in next sc, turn, sk first sc, sc in each of next 19 sc, sk next sc, sc in next sc, turn, sk first sc, sc in each of next 17 sc, sk next sc, sc in next sc, turn, sk first sc, sc in each of next 15 sc, sk next sc, sc in next sc, turn, sk first 2 sc, sc in each of next 11 sc, sk 2 sc, sc in next sc, turn, sk next 2 sc, sc in each of next 7 sc, sk next 2 sc, sc in next sc, turn, sk first sc, sc in each of next 5 sc, sk next sc, sc in next sc, mark last sc made, sc evenly sp around opening to marked st, remove marker, sc in marked st, join in next sc, leaving a length of thread, fasten off.

Finishing

With tapestry needle and black, work 1 French knot on each side of head for eyes. With tapestry needle and rem length, using photo as a guide, sew neck opening to neck flap on body, centering top back of neck opening over top of neck flap and completing stuffing with fiberfill as neck is joined to body.

Apply fabric stiffener. Shape neck to desired shape as piece dries. ✄

Bookmarks for Book Lovers

Designs by Sandy Scoville

Skill Level: Beginner

Size:

Jewels: 2 x 9 inches

Snowflake: 2½ inches in diameter, excluding tassel

Materials

► Crochet cotton size 10: 50 yds blue, 30 yds white

► Size 6 steel crochet hook or size needed to obtain gauge

► Tapestry needle

These quick and easy bookmarks make great gifts. Give one along with the latest best seller or include it in a greeting card on any occasion!

Gauge

9 dc = 1 inch

Check gauge to save time.

Pattern Notes

Weave in loose ends as work progresses.

Join each rnd with a sl st unless otherwise stated.

Jewels Bookmark

Row 1 (RS): With blue, ch 4, join to form a ring, ch 4 (counts as first tr throughout), 6 tr in ring, turn. (7 tr)

Row 2: Ch 4, 3 tr in same st as beg ch, sk next 2 tr, sc in back lp only of next tr, sk next 2 tr, 4 tr in next tr, turn.

Row 3: Ch 1, sc in first tr, sk next 3 tr, 7 tr in next sc, sk next 3 tr, sc in last tr, turn.

Row 4: Ch 4, 3 tr in same sc, sc in back lp only of center tr of 7-tr group, 4 tr in last sc, turn.

Rows 5–28: Rep Rows 3 and 4 alternately.

Row 29: Rep Row 3.

Rnd 30: Ch 1, sc in same sc, sk next 3 tr, 11 tr in back lp only of next tr, sk next 3 tr, sc in next sc, working around rem of bookmark, [9 tr in same sc as next 4-tr group, sc in same sc as next 4-tr group] 7 times, 9 tr in opposite side of foundation ch, sc in same tr as next 4-tr group, [9 tr in same sc as next 4-tr group, sc in same sc as next 4-tr group] 7 times, join in beg sc, fasten off.

Snowflake Bookmark

Rnd 1 (RS): With white, ch 6, join to form a ring, ch 1, 12 sc in ring, join in beg sc. (12 sc)

Rnd 2: Ch 1, working in back lps this rnd only, sc in same st as beg ch, ch 11, sk next sc, [sc in next st, ch 11, sk next sc] rep around, join in beg sc. (6 ch-11 sps)

Rnd 3: Ch 1, working in ch-11 sp, *sc in each of next 3 chs of ch-11 sp, ch 3, sc in next ch, ch 5, sc in next ch, [hdc, 5 dc, hdc] in next ch, sc in next ch, ch 5, sc in next ch, ch 3, sc in each of next 3 chs, rep from * around, join in beg sc, fasten off.

Tassel Loop

With WS facing, attach white in ch-5 sp to left of any 5-dc group, ch 1, sc in same sp, ch 5, sc in next ch-5 sp, turn, sl st in each of next 3 chs, ch 40, sl st in same ch as last sl st, sl st in next 2 chs, sl st in next sc, fasten off.

Tassel

Cut 21 strands of white cotton each 10 inches in length. Fold 20 strands in half at center over ch-40 sp; wrap rem 10 inch strands about ¼ inch below fold. Secure ends; weave into tassel. Trim ends evenly. ✂

Pretty 'n' Pink Floral Basket

Design by Sue Childress

Skill Level: Beginner

Size: Flowers range from 1½–3½ inches in diameter

Materials

- On Line Gipsy sport weight crochet yarn (50 grams per ball): 1 ball dark pink #08 (A)
- Grignasco Marina sport weight crochet yarn (50 grams per ball): 1 ball pale pink #596 (B)
- Trendsetter Sunshine size 10 rayon/nylon blend (50 grams per ball): 2 balls pale pink #20 (C)
- Grignasco crochet cotton size 5 (50 grams per ball): 1 ball light green #822
- Size D/3 crochet hook
- 8-inch-diameter x 2-inch-thick plastic foam circle
- Glue
- 3 bags white gypsophila
- 10 x 12-inch basket
- 3 yds 2½-inch-wide pink sheer wire-edged ribbon
- 36 (10–12-inch) pieces floral wire
- Floral tape
- Pearl stamens
- Tapestry needle

Gauge

Work evenly and consistently

Pattern Notes

Weave in loose ends as work progresses.

Join each rnd with a sl st unless otherwise stated. Leave a 2-inch length at beg and ending of each petal and leaf to help in assembly.

Rose

Make 12

Petal No. 1

Row 1: With A, ch 5, 10 tr in 4th ch from hook, turn.

Row 2: [Ch 2, sc in next tr] rep across, fasten off.

Petal No. 2

Make 2 for each rose

Row 1: With B, ch 8, 4 tr in 4th ch from hook, 5 dtr in next ch, 3 tr in each of next 3 chs, turn.

Row 2: [Ch 3, sc in next st] rep across, fasten off.

Petal No. 3

Make 2 for each rose

Row 1: With C, ch 10, 4 tr in 4th ch from hook, 4 tr in next ch, 3 tr in each of next 3 chs, tr in each of next 2 chs, turn.

Row 2: [Ch 3, sc in next st] rep across, fasten off.

Calyx

Make 24

Rnd 1: With light green, ch 6, join to form a ring, ch 3 (counts as first dc throughout), 10 dc in ring, join in 3rd ch of beg ch-3.

Rnd 2: Ch 3, [2 dc in next dc, dc in next dc] rep around, ending with 2 dc in last dc, join in 3rd ch of beg ch-3.

Rnd 3: [Ch 3, sc in same dc, sc in each of next 2 dc] rep around, join, fasten off.

Leaf

Make 2 for each rose and 1 for each rosebud

Rnd 1: With light green, ch 9, hdc in 4th ch from hook, dc in each of next 5 chs, 3 dc in next ch, working on opposite side of foundation ch, dc in each of next 4 chs, hdc in next ch, sc in same ch, fasten off.

Bud

Make 12

Row 1: With A, ch 5, 17 tr in 4th ch from hook, turn.

Row 2: [Ch 3, sc in next tr] rep across, fasten off.

Ribbon Accents

Make 12

Cut 12 (4-inch) pieces of ribbon. Fold piece of ribbon in half; gather cut ends and glue to a length of floral wire. Wrap with floral tape, inserting pearl stamens as you progress down entire length of wire.

Assembling Roses & Buds

Using glue, roll each petal around next, beg with petal No. 1, then 2 and finally 3. Draw ends of petals through center of calyx and attach wire, wrapping with floral tape and attaching leaves as you progress down length of wire.

Finishing

Glue plastic foam circle in bottom of basket. Arrange gypsophila in basket and push ends into plastic foam. Add roses, buds and ribbon accents as desired in basket. With rem ribbon, make a large bow and attach to front of basket. ✄

Create this beautiful floral basket to use as a centerpiece at a baby or bridal shower or to simply add cheer to your home! Choose your favorite color or shade to match your decor!

Victorian Picture Frames

Continued from page 110

- ► Masking tape
- ► ZIG Memory System #MSB15 2 Way Glue chisel-tip permanent/temporary glue pen
- ► Clear acrylic spray
- ► Aleene's Laminate IT Laminating Liquid
- ► Paintbrush
- ► 4 x 6-inch photo
- ► Easel or plate holder

Gauge

14 sc = 1 inch; 5 dc rnds = 1 inch

Check gauge to save time.

Pattern Notes

Weave in loose ends as work progresses.

Join each rnd with a sl st unless otherwise stated.

Pattern Stitches

4-dc cl: [Yo hook, insert hook in indicated st, yo, draw up a lp, yo, draw through 2 lps on hook] 4 times, yo, draw through all 5 lps on hook, ch 1 to lock.

Beg 4-dc cl: Ch 2 (counts as first dc), [yo hook, insert hook in indicated st, yo, draw up a lp, yo, draw through 2 lps on hook] 3 times, yo, draw through all 4 lps on hook.

P: Ch 3, sl st in top and side bar of previous sc.

Frame

Rnd 1: Ch 144, being careful not to twist ch, join to form a ring, ch 1, sc in same ch, 2 sc in next ch, [sc in next ch, 2 sc in next ch] rep around, join in beg sc. (216 sc)

Rnd 2: Ch 3 (counts as first dc throughout), 3 dc in

same st, ch 2, sk next 5 sts, [4 dc in next st, ch 2, sk next 5 sts] rep around, join in 3rd ch of beg ch-3. (36 4-dc groups)

Rnd 3: Ch 4 (counts as first tr throughout), tr in each of next 3 sts, ch 3, sk next ch sp, [tr in each of next 4 sts, ch 3, sk next ch sp] rep around, join in 4th ch of beg ch-4.

Rnd 4: Beg 4-dc cl over next 4 tr, ch 1, sk next ch, 4 dc in next ch, ch 1, sk next ch, [4-dc cl over next 4 tr, ch 1, sk next ch, 4 dc in next ch, ch 1, sk next ch] rep around, join in top of beg cl.

Rnd 5: Sl st in next ch and next st, ch 4, tr in each of next 3 sts, ch 3, [sk to next 4-dc group, tr in each of next 4 sts, ch 3] rep around, join in 4th ch of beg ch-4.

Rnd 6: Rep Rnd 4.

Rnd 7: Sl st in next ch and next st, ch 4, tr in each of next 3 sts, ch 5, [sk to next 4-dc group, tr in each of next 4 sts, ch 5] rep around, join in 4th ch of beg ch-4.

Rnd 8: Beg 4-dc cl over next 4 tr, ch 2, sk next 2 chs, 4 dc in next ch, ch 2, sk next 2 chs, [4-dc cl over next 4 tr, ch 2, sk next 2 chs, 4 dc in next ch, ch 2, sk next 2 chs] rep around, join in top of beg cl.

Rnd 9: Sl st in next 2 chs and next st, ch 4, tr in each of next 3 sts, ch 5, [sk to next 4-dc group, tr in each of next 4 sts, ch 5] rep around, join in 4th of beg ch-4.

Rnd 10: Ch 1, sc in same st as joining, sc in next st, p, sc in each of next 2 sts, sc in next 3 chs, p, [sc in next 2 chs, sc in next 2 sts, p, sc in next 2 sts, sc in next 3 chs, p] rep around, ending with sc in last 2 chs, join in beg sc, fasten off.

Finishing

Follow finishing instructions for creamy yellow frame, using gold leaf spray enamel instead of pewter. ✂

Sachet

Continued from page 111

Rnd 18: Ch 1, *sc in next sc, hdc in next st, dc in next st, [2 tr, p] in next st, 2 tr in next st, 2 tr in next st, dc in next st, hdc in next st, rep from * around, join in beg sc, fasten off.

Back

Rnd 1 (RS): With white, ch 6, join to form a ring, ch 5 (counts as first dc, ch-2), [dc, ch 2] 7 times in ring, join in 3rd ch of beg ch-5.

Rnd 2: Sl st into ch-2 sp, beg V-st in same sp, ch 1, [V-st in next ch-2 sp, ch 1] rep around, join in 3rd ch of beg ch-5.

Rnd 3: Sl st into ch-2 sp of V-st, beg shell in same sp, [shell in next V-st] rep around, join in 3rd ch of beg ch-3. (8 shells)

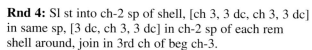

Rnd 4: Sl st into ch-2 sp of shell, [ch 3, 3 dc, ch 3, 3 dc] in same sp, [3 dc, ch 3, 3 dc] in ch-2 sp of each rem shell around, join in 3rd ch of beg ch-3.

Rnd 5: Sl st into ch-3 sp, [ch 3, dc, ch 2, {2 dc, ch 2} twice] in same sp, *[2 dc, ch 2] 3 times in next ch-3 sp, rep from * around, join in 3rd ch of beg ch-3.

Rnd 6: Sl st into ch-2 sp, beg shell in same sp, shell in next ch-2 sp, ch 1, sk next ch-2 sp, *[shell in next ch-2 sp] twice, ch 1, sk next ch-2 sp, rep from * around, join in 3rd ch of beg ch-3. (16 shells)

Rnd 7: Ch 3, dc in next dc, *2 dc in next ch sp, dc in each of next 4 dc, 2 dc in next ch sp, dc in each of next 2 dc, 3 dc in next ch-1 sp **, dc in each of next 2 dc, rep from * around, ending last rep at **, join in 3rd ch of

beg ch-3. (120 dc)

Rnds 8 & 9: Rep Rnds 15 and 16 of front.

Finishing

Sew fabric circles with RS tog, leaving an opening for turning. Turn RS out; stuff lightly with fiberfill. Add scent; stitch opening closed.

Sew white pearl to center of flower with sewing needle and white thread.

Holding front and back tog with fabric disc between layers, weave 3/8-inch-wide ribbon through ch sps of both thicknesses over and under tr groups; secure ends. Secure 1/8-inch-wide ribbon above joining of woven ribbon and tie ends into a double bow. ✄

Easter Egg Frames

Continued from page 119

dc} in next st, sk next 2 sts] 4 times, holding front and back with WS tog, matching next st with marked st on back and working through both thicknesses, [{dc, ch 3, dc} in next st, sk next 2 sts] 15 times, working sts in front only, [{dc, ch 3, dc} in next st, sk next 2 sts] 4 times, join in 3rd ch of beg ch-6, fasten off.

Rnd 3: Attach light blue in any ch sp, ch 1, 3 sc in same sp, ch 1, [3 sc in next ch sp, ch 1] rep around, join in beg sc, fasten off.

Rnd 4: Attach lavender in ch-1 sp, ch 1, sc in same sp, ch 4, [sc in next ch-1 sp, ch 4] rep around, join in beg sc, fasten off.

Stiffening

Follow stiffening instructions for lavender photo frame.

Finishing

Attach jump ring to center top of frame. Tie a 10-inch length of ⅛-inch-wide yellow satin ribbon through ring for hanging lp. Using shaping form, cut picture and insert between front and back.

Peach Mirror Frame

Back

With peach, follow instructions for lavender photo frame back.

Front

Rnd 1: With peach, follow instructions for Rnd 1 of pink photo frame. (72 sts)

Rnd 2: Ch 4 (counts as first dc, ch-1 throughout), [dc, ch 1, dc] in same st as beg ch, ch 2, sk next 2 sts, sc in next st, *ch 2, sk next 2 sts, [dc, ch 1, dc] in next st, ch 2, sk next 2 sts, sc in next st *, ch 2, sk next 2 sts, [dc, ch 1, dc] in next st, ch 2, sk next 2 sts, holding front and back with WS tog, matching next st with marked st on back and working through both thicknesses, sc in next st, rep from * to * 3 times, ch 2, sk next 2 sts, [[dc, ch 1} twice, dc] in next st, ch 2, sk next 2 sts, sc in next st, rep from * to * 3 times, working in sts of front only, rep from * to * twice, ch 2, join in 3rd ch of beg ch-4.

Rnd 3: Sl st into ch-1 sp, ch 4, [dc, ch 1] twice in next dc, dc in next ch-1 sp, ch 3, [sc, ch 3, sc] in next sc, ch 3 *, [dc, ch 1, dc] in ch-1 sp between next 2 dc, ch 3, [sc, ch 3, sc] in next sc, ch 3 *, rep from * to * 4 times, dc in ch-1 sp between next 2 dc, ch 1, [dc, ch 4, sl st in 4th ch from hook, dc] in next dc, ch 1, dc in next ch-1 sp, ch 3, [sc, ch 3, sc] in next sc, ch 3, rep from * to * 5 times, join in 3rd ch of beg ch-4, fasten off.

Stiffening

Follow stiffening instructions for lavender photo frame.

Finishing

Referring to photo for placement, tie 18-inch length of ¼-inch-wide off-white picot-edge ribbon in a double-lp bow with 4-inch-long tails. Glue bow to center top of frame; tack ribbon tails to sides of frame. Glue small silk flower over center of bow. Insert mirror between front and back. ✄

The Toy Shoppe

Let their imagination run wild as puppets come to life and teddy bears enjoy tea parties with nursery rhyme characters. Kids of all ages will delight in this collection of toys that will bring hours of fun!

Mr. Brown the Bear

Design by Michele Wilcox

Skill Level: Beginner

Size: 14 inches tall

Materials

► Worsted weight yarn: 3 oz brown, 2 oz each yellow and light blue

► Size G/6 crochet hook or size needed to obtain gauge

► Small amount black #3 pearl cotton

► 2 (6mm) animal eyes

► Polyester fiberfill

► Tapestry needle

Ever the gentleman, Mr. Brown the Bear looks quite debonair in his stylish turtleneck and pants—ready to brave the cold of winter!

Gauge

4 sc = 1 inch; 4 sc rnds = 1 inch

Check gauge to save time.

Pattern Notes

Weave in loose ends as work progresses.

Do not join rnds unless otherwise indicated. Use a scrap of CC yarn as a marker.

Head & Body

Rnd 1 (RS): With brown, ch 2, 6 sc in 2nd ch from hook. (6 sc)

Rnd 2: Work 2 sc in each sc around. (12 sc)

Rnd 3: [Sc in next sc, 2 sc in next sc] rep around. (18 sc)

Rnd 4: [Sc in each of next 2 sc, 2 sc in next sc] rep around. (24 sc)

Rnd 5: Sc in each sc around.

Rnd 6: [Sc in each of next 3 sc, 2 sc in next sc] rep around. (30 sc)

Rnd 7: [Sc in each of next 4 sc, 2 sc in next sc] rep around. (36 sc)

Rnd 8: Rep Rnd 5.

Rnd 9: [Sc in each of next 5 sc, 2 sc in next sc] rep around. (42 sc)

Rnds 10–17: Rep Rnd 5.

Rnd 18: [Sc in each of next 5 sc, dec 1 sc over next 2 sc] rep around. (36 sc)

Rnd 19: [Sc in each of next 4 sc, dec 1 sc over next 2 sc] rep around. (30 sc)

Insert eyes between Rnds 10 and 11, spacing 8 sc sts apart.

Rnd 20: [Sc in each of next 3 sc, sc dec over next 2 sc] rep around. (24 sc)

Rnd 21: [Sc in each of next 2 sc, sc dec over next 2 sc] rep around. (18 sc)

Stuff head with fiberfill.

Rnd 22: Rep Rnd 5, sl st in next st, fasten off.

Rnd 23: Attach yellow, rep Rnd 3. (36 sc)

Rnds 24 & 25: Rep Rnd 5.

Rnd 26: [Sc in each of next 5 sc, 2 sc in next sc] rep around. (42 sc)

Rnds 27–29: Rep Rnd 5.

Rnd 30: [Sc in each of next 6 sc, 2 sc in next sc] rep around. (48 sc)

Rnds 31–36: Rep Rnd 5, at the end of Rnd 36, fasten off.

Rnd 37: Attach light blue, rep Rnd 5.

Rnds 38–43: Rep Rnd 5.

Rnd 44: [Sc in each of next 6 sc, sc dec over next 2 sc] rep around. (42 sc)

Rnds 45–48: Rep Rnds 18–21. (18 sc)

Stuff body with fiberfill.

Rnd 49: [Sc dec over next 2 sc] rep around, sl st in next st, leaving a length of yarn, fasten off. (9 sc)

Weave rem length through sts; pull to close opening and secure.

Turtleneck

Row 1: With yellow, ch 8, sc in 2nd ch from hook, sc in each rem ch across, turn. (7 sc)

Rows 2–36: Ch 1, working in back lps only, sc in each st across, turn, at the end of Row 36, leaving a length of yarn, fasten off.

Sew edge to neckline, sew center back seam and fold downward to form turtleneck.

Waistband

Row 1: With yellow, ch 6, sc in 2nd ch from hook, sc in each rem ch across, turn. (5 sc)

Rows 2–48: Ch 1, working in back lps this row only, sc in each st across, turn, at the end of Row 48, leaving a length of yarn, fasten off.

Sew around waistline and sew ends tog.

Snout

Rnds 1 & 2: Rep Rnds 1 and 2 of head and body. (12 sc)

Rnd 3: Sc in each sc around.

Rnd 4: Rep Rnd 3 of head and body. (18 sc)

Rnds 5 & 6: Sc in each sc around, at the end of Rnd 6, leaving a length of yarn, fasten off.

Sew snout to head, centered slightly below eyes and stuffing with fiberfill before closing. With black cotton, embroider satin-st nose and straight sts centered below nose in an upside-down Y for mouth.

To slightly indent eyes, thread needle with a length

of brown yarn. Insert needle into back of head straight through and out at first eye, over 1 st and back through head through same st as entry. Pull gently to indent slightly, knot to secure and weave ends into head. Rep with the 2nd eye.

Ear
Make 2

Rnd 1: With brown, ch 2, 6 sc in 2nd ch from hook. (6 sc)

Rnd 2: 2 sc in each sc around. (12 sc)

Rnds 3–5: Sc in each sc around, at the end of Rnd 5, sl st in next st, leaving a length of yarn, fasten off. Fold Rnd 5 flat; working through both thicknesses, sew closed. Sew ear to head.

Leg
Make 2

Rnd 1: With brown, ch 12, sc in 2nd ch from hook, sc in each of next 9 chs, 3 sc in last ch, working in rem lps on opposite side of foundation ch, sc in each of next 9 chs, 2 sc in last ch. (24 sc)

Rnd 2: 2 sc in next sc, sc in each of next 9 sc, 2 sc in each of next 3 sc, sc in each of next 9 sc, 2 sc in each of next 2 sc. (30 sc)

Rnd 3: [Sc in each of next 4 sc, 2 sc in next sc] rep around. (36 sc)

Rnd 4: Sc in each sc around.

Rnds 5–7: Rep Rnd 4.

Rnd 8: Sc in each of next 12 sc, [sc dec over next 2 sc] 6 times, sc in each of next 12 sc. (30 sc)

Rnd 9: Sc in each of next 9 sc, [sc dec over next 2 sc] 6 times, sc in next 9 sc. (24 sc)

Rnd 10: [Sc in each of next 6 sc, sc dec over next 2 sc] rep around. (21 sc)

Rnds 11–21: Rep Rnd 4, at the end of Rnd 21, leaving a length of yarn, fasten off. Stuff leg with fiberfill. Keeping toe end of foot centered in front, fold Rnd 21 flat and sew closed. Sew leg to bottom of bear.

Pants Leg
Make 2

Rnd 1: With light blue, ch 30, sl st to join to form a ring, ch 1, sc in each ch around. (30 sc)

Rnds 2–8: Sc in each sc around, at the end of Rnd 8, fasten off.

Rnd 9: Attach light blue in rem lp on opposite side of foundation ch, ch 1, sc in each of next 30 chs, sl st to join in beg sc, leaving a length of yarn, fasten off.

With Rnd 9 at top and Rnd 8 at the bottom, place pants leg over foot and up to top of leg; sew Rnd 9 to body.

Arm
Make 2

Rnd 1: With brown, ch 2, 6 sc in 2nd ch from hook. (6 sc)

Rnd 2: 2 sc in each sc around. (12 sc)

Rnd 3: [Sc in each of next 3 sc, 2 sc in next sc] rep around. (15 sc)

Rnd 4: Sc in each sc around.
Continued on page 156

Bitty Mouse & Pansy Pig Puppets

Designs by Dot Drake

Skill Level: Beginner

Size:

Mouse: 9 x 9½ inches, excluding ears

Pig: 10½ x 11½ inches, excluding ears

Materials

► Brushed worsted weight yarn (3 oz per skein): 2 skeins each light green and light peach, 1 skein each dark peach and variegated yellow/pale green/white

► Size H/8 crochet hook or size needed to obtain gauge

► Size G/6 crochet hook

► Small safety pin

► 2 (⅝-inch) black shank buttons

► 2 (⅜-inch) brown shank buttons

► Sewing needle and brown and black thread

► 6-strand pink embroidery floss

► Small spray flowers

► 1 yd 1-inch-wide pink sheer wire-edged ribbon

► ¾ yd ⅜-inch-wide yellow satin ribbon

► 3-inch triangle of yellow craft foam

► Scrap of polyester fiberfill

► Craft glue

► Tapestry needle

E*ncourage your child's imagination with these two adorable puppets!*

Gauge

With smaller hook and 2 strands of yarn held tog, 7 sts = 2 inches; 7 rnds = 2½ inches

With larger hook and 2 strands of yarn held tog, 10 sts = 3 inches; 5 rows = 2 inches

Check gauge to save time.

Pattern Notes

Weave in loose ends as work progresses.

Join each rnd with a sl st unless otherwise stated.

Inside will be RS when completed.

Puppet is not recommended for children under 3 years of age.

Bitty Mouse

Body

Rnd 1: Beg at bottom with smaller hook and 2 strands of light green, ch 32, join to form a ring, ch 1, sc in each ch around, join in beg sc. (32)

Rnd 2: Working in back lps only throughout, ch 1, sc in each sc around, join in beg sc.

Rnds 3–11: Rep Rnd 2.

Note: Do not join rnds 12–16; mark rnds with small safety pin.

Rnd 12: Ch 1, [sc in each of next 15 sc, ch 10, sc in 3rd ch from hook, sc in each of next 7 chs (arm), sk next sc on body] twice. (46 sc)

Rnd 13: Sc in each sc around, working 8 sc in rem lps on opposite side of foundation ch of each arm, and 3 sc in ch-2 sp at end of each arm. (68 sc)

Rnd 14: Sc in each sc around, working 2 sc in each sc of 3-sc group at end of each arm. (74 sc)

Rnds 15–17: Sc in each sc around. At the end of Rnd 17, join in next st, fasten off.

Fold piece flat with RS tog; mark center front and center back 11 sc sts. Matching rem 24 sts and working through both thicknesses, sew 12 sts across each arm.

Head Front

Rnd 1: With 2 strands of light green and smaller hook, ch 2, 5 sc in 2nd ch from hook, join in beg sc. (5 sc)

Rnd 2: Working in back lps only throughout, ch 1, 2 sc in each sc around, join in beg sc. (10 sc)

Rnd 3: Ch 1, [2 sc in next sc, sc in each of next 4 sc] twice, join in beg sc. (12 sc)

Rnd 4: Ch 1, 2 sc in first sc, [sc in each of next 4 sc, 2 sc in next sc] twice, sc in last sc, join in beg sc. (15 sc)

Rnd 5: Ch 1, [2 sc in next sc, sc in each of next 4 sc] 3

times, join in beg sc. (18 sc)

Rnd 6: Ch 1, 2 sc in first sc, [sc in each of next 4 sc, 2 sc in next sc] 3 times, sc in each of next 2 sc, join in beg sc. (22 sc)

Rnd 7: Ch 1, 2 sc in first sc, [sc in each of next 4 sc, 2 sc in next sc] 4 times, sc in next sc, join in beg sc. (27 sc)

Rnd 8: Ch 1, 2 sc in first sc, [sc in each of next 5 sc, 2 sc in next sc] 4 times, sc in each of next 2 sc, join in beg sc. (32 sc)

Rnds 9–11: Ch 1, sc in each sc around, join in beg sc, at the end of Rnd 11, fasten off.

Facial Features

With WS facing, sew brown buttons between Rnds 6 and 7 spacing 1½ inches apart.

With pink embroidery floss, embroider satin st nose over Rnd 1; embroider mouth below nose, using straight sts and outline st.

For whiskers, cut several strands of brown sewing thread and knot through sts on each side of nose.

Head Back

Rnd 1: With smaller hook and 2 strands of light green, ch 2, 5 sc in 2nd ch from hook, join in beg sc. (5 sc)

Rnd 2: Working in back lps only throughout, ch 1, 2 sc in each sc around, join in beg sc. (10 sc)

Rnd 3: Ch 1, [sc in next sc, 2 sc in next sc] rep around, join in beg sc. (15 sc)

Rnd 4: Ch 1, [2 sc in next sc, sc in each of next 2 sc] rep around, join in beg sc. (20 sc)

Rnd 5: Ch 1, [2 sc in next sc, sc in each of next 3 sc] 5 times, join in beg sc. (25 sc)

Rnd 6: Ch 1, 2 sc in first sc, [sc in each of next 3 sc, 2 sc in next sc] 6 times, join in beg sc, fasten off. (32 sc)

With RS tog, working through both thicknesses and matching sts, sew head back to 21 sts across top of head front, leaving 11 sts free across bottom of each head front and head back.

Sew free sts to corresponding sts on body front and back.

Bottom Trim

Rnd 1: With smaller hook, working in rem lps on opposite side of foundation ch, attach 2 strands of variegated in any ch, working on the inside edge so that WS of work faces out, ch 1, sc in each ch around, join in beg sc, fasten off.

Ear

Make 2 each light green and variegated

Rnd 1: With smaller hook and 2 strands of yarn, ch 2, 7 sc in 2nd ch from hook, do not join, use safety pin for marker. (7 sc)

Rnd 2: Working in back lps only throughout, 2 sc in each sc around. (14 sc)

Rnd 3: [2 sc in next sc, sc in next sc] rep around. (21 sc)

Rnd 4: [2 sc in next sc, sc in each of next 2 sc] rep around, sl st in next sc, fasten off. (28 sc)

Rnd 5: Holding 1 each ear color with WS facing out and variegated section facing, attach 2 strands light green, working through both thicknesses, sl st in each st around, fasten off.

Sew ears to top of head. Tie yellow ribbon around

neckline in a bow.

Tail

With smaller hook and 1 strand of light green, ch 30, sc in 2nd ch from hook, sc in each rem ch across, fasten off.

Make a fringe of variegated about 2½ inches long and knot into end of tail. Sew tail to back body.

Finishing

Cut little "nibble" holes in craft foam triangle for cheese; glue to front of hand.

Place yellow ribbon around neck and tie in a bow at center front.

Pansy Pig

Body

Rnd 1: Beg at bottom with larger hook and 2 strands of light peach, ch 32, join to form a ring, ch 1, sc in each ch around, join in beg sc. (32 sc)

Rnds 2–12: Working in back lps only throughout, ch 1, sc in each sc around, join in beg sc.

Rnds 13–18: Rep Rnds 12–17 of mouse body.

Head Front

Rnd 1: With larger hook and 2 strands light peach, ch 2, 7 sc in 2nd ch from hook, join in beg sc. (7 sc)

Rnd 2: Working in back lps only throughout, ch 1, 2 sc in each sc around, join in beg sc. (14 sc)

Rnd 3: Ch 1, [2 sc in next sc, sc in next sc] rep around, join in beg sc. (21 sc)

Rnd 4: Ch 1, [2 sc in next sc, sc in each of next 2 sc] rep around, join in beg sc. (28 sc)

Rnd 5: Ch 1, [2 sc in next sc, sc in each of next 3 sc] rep around, join in beg sc. (35 sc)

Rnds 6–8: Ch 1, sc in each sc around, join in beg sc, at the end of Rnd 8, fasten off.

Snout

Rnds 1 & 2: With larger hook and 2 strands dark peach, rep Rnds 1 and 2 of head front for Pansy pig. (14 sc)

Rnds 3 & 4: Ch 1, sc in each sc around, join in beg sc, at the end of Rnd 4, fasten off.

Stuff snout with fiberfill and sew to center front of head.

With pink embroidery floss, embroider nostrils with straight sts.

Sew black buttons above snout.

Head Back

Rnd 1: With larger hook and 2 strands of light peach, ch 2, 6 sc in 2nd ch from hook, join in beg sc. (6 sc)

Rnd 2: Working in back lps only throughout, ch 1, 2 sc in each sc around, join in beg sc. (12 sc)

Rnd 3: Ch 1, [2 sc in next sc, sc in next sc] rep around, join in beg sc. (18 sc)

Rnd 4: Ch 1, [2 sc in next sc, sc in each of next 2 sc] rep around, join in beg sc. (24 sc)

Rnd 5: Ch 1, [2 sc in next sc, sc in each of next 3 sc] rep around, join in beg sc. (30 sc)

Rnd 6: Ch 1, [2 sc in next sc, sc in each of next 5 sc] rep around, join in beg sc, fasten off. (35 sc)

With RS tog, working through both thicknesses and matching sts, sew head back to 24 sts across top of head front, leaving 11 sts free across bottom of each head front and head back.

Sew free sts to corresponding sts on body front and back.

Bottom Trim

With larger hook and 2 strands dark peach, rep bottom trim instructions for mouse.

Ear

Make 2

Row 1: With smaller hook and 1 strand dark peach, ch 9, sc in 2nd ch from hook, sc in each rem ch across, turn. (8 sc)

Row 2: Ch 1, sk first sc, sc in each rem sc across, turn. (7 sc)

Rows 3–8: Rep Row 2. (1 sc)

Rnd 9: Working around outer edge of ear, ch 1, sc evenly sp around, working 2 sc in each of 3 corner points, join in beg sc, fasten off.

Sew ears to top of head.

Tail

With larger hook and 2 strands dark peach, ch 12, 2 sc in 2nd ch from hook, 2 sc in each rem ch across, fasten off.

Sew tail to center back of body approximately 1½ inches from bottom edge.

Finishing

Sew flowers to hand. Place pink ribbon around neckline and tie in a bow at center front. ✄

Baby's First Football

Design by Diane Poellot

Skill Level: Beginner

Size: 6½ inches long

Materials

▶ Worsted weight yarn: 2 oz brown, small amount white

▶ Size G/6 crochet hook or size needed to obtain gauge

▶ Polyester fiberfill

▶ Tapestry needle

Dad will love to throw a few passes to his budding sports fan with this football. Soft and cushy, this quick-and-easy pattern could easily make a great last-minute gift!

Gauge

4 sc = 1 inch; 4 sc rows = 1 inch

Check gauge to save time.

Pattern Note

Weave in loose ends as work progresses.

Panel

Make 3

Row 1: With brown, leaving a length at beg, ch 2, 2 sc in 2nd ch from hook, turn. (2 sc)

Row 2: Ch 1, sc in each sc across, turn.

Row 3: Ch 1, 2 sc in each sc across, turn. (4 sc)

Row 4: Rep Row 2.

Row 5: Ch 1, 2 sc in first sc, sc in each rem sc across to last sc, 2 sc in last sc, turn. (6 sc)

Row 6: Rep Row 2, fasten off.

Row 7: With white, rep Row 5. (8 sc)

Row 8: Rep Row 2, leaving a length of yarn, fasten off.

Row 9: With brown, rep Row 5. (10 sc)

Rows 10–12: Rep Row 2.

Row 13: Rep Row 5. (12 sc)

Row 14: Rep Row 2.

Row 15: Rep Row 5. (14 sc)

Rows 16 & 17: Rep Row 2.

Row 18: Ch 1, sc dec over next 2 sts, sc in each rem sc across to last 2 sc, sc dec over next 2 sc, turn. (12 sc)

Row 19: Rep Row 2.

Row 20: Rep Row 18. (10 sc)

Rows 21–23: Rep Row 2, at the end of Row 23, fasten off.

Row 24: With white, rep Row 18. (8 sc)

Row 25: Rep Row 2, leaving a length of yarn, fasten off.

Row 26: With brown, rep Row 18. (6 sc)

Row 27: Rep Row 2.

Row 28: Rep Row 18. (4 sc)

Row 29: Rep Row 2.

Row 30: Ch 1, [sc dec over next 2 sc] twice, turn. (2 sc)

Row 31: Ch 1, sc dec over next 2 sc, leaving a length of yarn, fasten off. (1 sc)

Sew panels tog with tapestry needle and matching yarn colors.

Finishing

With white, beg between 5th and 6th sc sts on Row 9 of 1 panel, work 13 surface chs up center of panel; leaving a long length of yarn, fasten off.

Thread tapestry needle with rem length; work 2 straight sts under every other surface ch across for laces. ✂

Curlicue Dress

Designs by Jo Ann Maxwell

Skill Level: Intermediate

Size: Fits 11½-inch fashion doll

Materials

▶ #5 pearl cotton: 900 yds yellow, 350 yds pale pink

▶ Size 5 steel crochet hook or size needed to obtain gauge

▶ 18 inches 1-inch-wide sheer pink ribbon

▶ 3 clear snap fasteners

▶ 10 yellow ribbon roses with leaves

▶ 2–3 small white feathers

▶ Glue

▶ Spray starch

▶ Sewing needle and thread

▶ Tapestry needle

Your doll will deserve a place of honor dressed in this beautiful gown. Reminiscent of a true Southern belle, the costume is complete with matching bonnet and fan!

Gauge

7 dc = 1 inch; 3 dc rnds = 1 inch

Check gauge to save time.

Pattern Notes

Weave in loose ends as work progresses.

Join each rnd with a sl st unless otherwise stated.

Dress

Bodice

Row 1 (RS): Beg at waistline with yellow, ch 26, sc in 2nd ch from hook, sc in each rem ch across, turn. (25 sc)

Rows 2 & 3: Ch 1, sc in each sc across to last sc, 2 sc in last sc, turn. (27 sc)

Row 4: Ch 1, sc in each of next 8 sc, 3 sc in next sc, sc in each of next 9 sc, 3 sc in next sc, sc in each of next 8 sc, turn. (31 sc)

Row 5: Ch 1, sc in each of next 9 sc, 3 sc in next sc, sc in each of next 11 sc, 3 sc in next sc, sc in each of next 9 sc, turn. (35 sc)

Row 6: Ch 1, sc in each sc across, turn.

Rows 7–9: Rep Row 6.

Row 10: Ch 1, sc in each of next 13 sc, 3 sc in next sc, sc in each of next 7 sc, 3 sc in next sc, sc in each of next 13 sc, turn. (39 sc)

Row 11: Ch 1, sc in each of next 14 sc, 3 sc in next sc, sc in each of next 9 sc, 3 sc in next sc, sc in each of next 14 sc, turn. (43 sc)

Row 12: Rep Row 6.

Row 13: Ch 1, sc in each of next 8 sc, ch 10, sk next 4 sts (armhole), sc in each of next 19 sc, ch 10, sk next 4 sts (armhole), sc in each of next 8 sc, turn. (35 sc)

Row 14: Ch 1, sc in each of next 6 sc, sc dec over next 2 sc, sc in each of next 10 chs, sc dec over next 2 sc, sc in each of next 7 sc, sl st in next sc, sc in each of next 7 sc, sc dec over next 2 sc, sc in each of next 10 chs, sc dec over next 2 sc, sc in each of next 6 sc, turn. (51 sts)

Row 15 (RS): Ch 1, sc in each of next 6 sc, sl st in next st, sc in each of next 10 sc, sl st in next st, sc in each of next 6 sts, sk next 3 sts, sc in each of next 6 sts, sl st in next st, sc in each of next 10 sc, sl st in next st, sc in each of next 6 sc, fasten off.

Skirt

Row 1 (RS): Working in rem lps on opposite side of foundation ch, attach yellow with a sl st in first ch, ch 1, sc in each ch across, turn. (25 sc)

Row 2: Working in front lps this row only, ch 3 (counts as first dc throughout), 2 dc in same st as beg ch-3, [2 dc in next st, 3 dc in next st] rep across, turn. (63 dc)

Row 3: Ch 3, dc in each st across, turn.

Row 4: Ch 3, 2 dc in next dc, [dc in each of next 3 dc, 2 dc in next dc] rep across, dc in last st, turn. (79 dc)

Rnd 5 (RS): Ch 3, dc in each dc around, join in 3rd ch of beg ch-3, do not turn.

Rnd 6: Ch 3, dc in same st as beg ch-3, [dc in each of next 4 sts, 2 dc in next st] rep around, ending with dc in each of last 3 dc, join in 3rd ch of beg ch-3. (95 dc)

Rnd 7: Rep Rnd 5.

Rnd 8: Working in back lps this rnd only, ch 3, dc in same st as beg ch-3, [dc in each of next 4 sts, 2 dc in next st] rep around, join in 3rd ch of beg ch-3. (114 dc)

Rnd 9: Rep Rnd 5.

Rnd 10: Ch 3, dc in same st as beg ch-3, [dc in each of next 6 sts, 2 dc in next st] rep around, ending with dc in last st, join in 3rd ch of beg ch-3. (131 dc)

Rnd 11: Rep Rnd 5.

Rnd 12: Ch 3, dc in same st as beg ch-3, [dc in each of next 6 dc, 2 dc in next dc] rep around, ending with dc in each of next 4 dc, join in 3rd ch of beg ch-3. (150 dc)

Rnd 13: Rep Rnd 5.

Rnd 14: Working in back lps this rnd only, ch 3, dc in same st as beg ch-3, [dc in each of next 6 sts, 2 dc in next st] rep around, ending with dc in each of last 2 sts, join in 3rd ch of beg ch-3. (172 dc)

Rnd 15: Rep Rnd 5.

Rnd 16: Ch 3, dc in same st as beg ch-3, [dc in each of next 6 dc, 2 dc in next dc] rep around, ending with dc in each of last 3 dc, join in 3rd ch of beg ch-3. (197 dc)

Rnds 17 & 18: Rep Rnd 5.

Rnd 19: Ch 3, dc in same st as beg ch-3, [dc in each of next 6 dc, 2 dc in next dc] rep around, ending with dc in each of last 7 dc, join in 3rd ch of beg ch-3. (225 dc)

Rnd 20: Working in back lps this rnd only, ch 3, dc in each st around, join in 3rd ch of beg ch-3.

Rnd 21: Rep Rnd 5.

Rnd 22: Rep Rnd 19. (257 dc)

Rnds 23–25: Rep Rnd 5.

Bottom ruffle

Rnd 26: Ch 1, sc in same st as beg ch-1, ch 4, [sc in next st, ch 4] rep around, join in beg sc.

Rnds 27 & 28: Sl st into ch sp, ch 1, sc in same sp, ch 4, [sc in next ch sp, ch 4] rep around, join in beg sc.

Rnds 29–32: Sl st into ch sp, ch 1, sc in same sp, ch 5, [sc in next ch sp, ch 5] rep around, join in beg sc, fasten off.

Rnd 33: Attach pale pink in 3rd ch of ch-5 sp, [ch 3, dc, ch 2, 2 dc] in same ch, ch 2, [sc, ch 3, sc] in next

ch-5 sp, ch 2, *[2 dc, ch 2, 2 dc] in 3rd ch of next ch-5 sp, ch 2, [sc, ch 3, sc] in next ch-5 sp, rep from * around, join in 3rd ch of

beg ch-3, fasten off.

Top ruffle

Attach yellow with a sl st in any rem front lp of Rnd

7 of skirt, ch 1, rep Rnds 26–33 of bottom ruffle.

Rem ruffles

Rep instructions for top

ruffle in Rnd 13 and Rnd 19 of skirt.

Waistline Curls

Row 1: Working in rem free lps of Row 1 of skirt, attach pale pink at back waistline, ch 1, sc in same st as beg ch-1, *ch 14, 3 hdc in 3rd ch from hook, 3 hdc in each rem ch across, sl st in same sc as ch-14 **, sc in next st on Row 1, rep from * around, ending last rep at **, fasten off.

Rnd 2: Twist first curl around 5 times, attach pale pink in ch-2 sp at end of curl, ch 1, sc in same ch-2 sp, ch 5, [twist next curl around 5 times, sc in ch-2 sp at end of curl, ch 5] rep around, join in beg sc.

Rnd 3: Ch 1, *sc in sc, ch 3, sl st in top of sc, ch 2, [2 dc, ch 2, 2 dc] in 3rd ch of next ch-5 sp, ch 2, rep from * around, join in beg sc, fasten off.

Sleeve

Make 2

Rnd 1: Attach yellow with a sl st in first skipped st of armhole on Row 13 of bodice, ch 1, sc in each of next 4 skipped sc, ch 3, [sc in next ch, ch 3] 3 times, [sc, ch 3] twice in each of next 4 chs, [sc, ch 3] in each of next 3 chs, join in beg sc. (15 ch sps)

Rnd 2: Ch 1, sc in each of next 4 sc, sc in next ch sp, ch 4, [sc in next ch sp, ch 4] 13 times, sc in last ch sp, join in beg sc. (14 ch sps)

Rnd 3: Ch 1, sc in each of next 4 sc, ch 4, [sc in next ch sp, ch 4] rep around, join in beg sc. (15 ch sps)

Rnds 4–7: Rep Rnds 2 and 3.

Rnd 8: Ch 1, sc in each of next 4 sc, sc in each ch sp around, join in beg sc. (19 sc)

Rnd 9: Ch 1, sc in same sc as beg ch-1, [sk next sc, sc in next sc] rep around, join in beg sc. (10 sc)

Rnds 10 & 11: Ch 1, sc in each sc around, join in beg sc, at the end of Rnd 11, fasten off.

Rnd 12: Attach pale pink, ch 5 (counts as first dc, ch-2), dc in same st, ch 2, [dc, ch 2] twice in each rem st around, join in 3rd ch of beg ch-5.

Rnd 13: Sl st into ch-2 sp, ch 1, sc in same sp, ch 3, [sc in next ch-2 sp, ch 3] rep around, join in beg sc, fasten off.

Hat

Rnd 1: With yellow, ch 4, 19 dc in 4th ch from hook, join in 4th of beg ch-4. (20 dc)

Rnd 2: Ch 3 (counts as first dc throughout), dc in same st as beg ch-3, dc in next st, [2 dc in next st, dc in next st] rep around, join in 3rd ch of beg ch-3. (30 dc)

Rnd 3: Ch 2 (counts as first hdc), hdc in each st around, join in 2nd of beg ch-2.

Rnd 4: Ch 1, sc in each st around, join in beg sc.

Rnd 5: Working in back lps this rnd only, ch 3, dc in same st as beg ch-3, 2 dc in each st around, join in 3rd ch of beg ch-3. (60 dc)

Rnd 6: Ch 3, dc in each dc around, join in 3rd ch of beg ch-3, fasten off.

Rnd 7: Attach pale pink in any dc, ch 3, [dc, ch 2, 2 dc] in same st as beg ch-3, *ch 1, sk 1 dc, sc in next dc, ch 3, sl st in top of last sc, ch 1 **, [2 dc, ch 2, 2 dc] in next dc, rep from * around, ending last rep at **, join in 3rd ch of beg ch-3, fasten off.

Fan

Row 1: With yellow, ch 12, join to form a ring, ch 8, 8 dc in same st as beg ch-3, turn. (9 dc)

Row 2: Ch 4 (counts as first dc, ch-1), dc in next dc, [ch 1, dc in next dc, fasten off, attach pale pink, turn.

Row 3: Ch 1, sc in same dc as beg ch-1, [ch 3, sc in next dc] rep across, fasten off.

Finishing

With sewing needle and thread, sew 3 snap fasteners down back opening of dress. Wet dress and squeeze out excess water, using care not to squeeze curls at waistline. Place dress on doll; shape ruffles as desired and spray with starch. Shape ruffles as needed during drying; spray again with starch and allow to dry completely.

Cut 4½-inch piece of ribbon for sleeve; fold ends to center and st at center to secure, gather ribbon at center and wrap thread several times around center to secure, fasten off. Glue bow to center top of shoulder above sleeve. Glue a ribbon rose to center of bow. Rep for 2nd sleeve.

Spray hat with starch; shape and allow to dry completely. Fold rem 9 inches of ribbon into a bow; glue to brim. Glue feathers as desired over bow; glue 7 ribbon roses in a cluster over bow.

Spray fan with starch and dry completely. Glue a rose above handle. ✂

Ladybug Ball

Design by Michele Wilcox

Skill Level: Beginner

Size: 5 inches in diameter

Materials

▶ Bernat Berella 4 worsted weight yarn: 2 oz China rose #8923, 1 oz black #8994

▶ Size G/6 crochet hook or size needed to obtain gauge

▶ Polyester fiberfill

▶ 12mm blue animal eyes

▶ Tapestry needle

This is one bug kids will love to play with—and her big eyes and ever-present spots make this one bug Mom won't mind having in the house!

Gauge

4 sc = 1 inch; 4 rnds = 1 inch

Check gauge to save time.

Pattern Notes

Weave in loose ends as work progresses.

Join each rnd with a sl st unless otherwise stated.

Lady Bug

Rnd 1 (RS): With black, ch 2, 6 sc in 2nd ch from hook, join in beg sc. (6 sc)

Rnd 2: Ch 1, 2 sc in each sc around, join in beg sc. (12 sc)

Rnd 3: Ch 1, [sc in next sc, 2 sc in next sc] rep around, join in beg sc. (18 sc)

Rnd 4: Ch 1, [sc in each of next 2 sc, 2 sc in next sc] rep around, join in beg sc. (24 sc)

Rnd 5: Ch 1, sc in next sc, 2 sc in next sc, [sc in each of next 3 sc, 2 sc in next sc] 5 times, sc in each of next 2 sc, join in beg sc. (30 sc)

Rnd 6: Ch 1, [sc in each of next 4 sc, 2 sc in next sc] rep around, join in beg sc. (36 sc)

Rnd 7: Ch 1, sc in each of next 2 sc, 2 sc in next sc, [sc in each of next 5 sc, 2 sc in next sc] 5 times, sc in each of next 3 sc, join in beg sc. (42 sc)

Rnd 8: Ch 1, sc in each sc around, join in beg sc.

Rnd 9: Rep Rnd 8, fasten off black.

Attach eyes through Rnd 5 spacing 1¼ inches apart.

Thread tapestry needle with a length of China rose; embroider V-shaped mouth centered below eyes.

Rnd 10: Attach China rose, rep Rnd 8.

Rnd 11: Ch 1, [sc in each of next 6 sc, 2 sc in next sc] rep around, join in beg sc. (48 sc)

Rnds 12–20: Rep Rnd 8.

Rnd 21: Ch 1, [sc in each of next 6 sc, sc dec over next 2 sc] rep around, join in beg sc. (42 sc)

Rnds 22–24: Rep Rnd 8.

Rnd 25: Ch 1, [sc in each of next 5 sc, sc dec over next 2 sc] rep around, join in beg sc. (36 sc)

Rnd 26: Ch 1, [sc in each of next 4 sc, sc dec over next 2 sc] rep around, join in beg sc. (30 sc)

Rnd 27: Ch 1, [sc in each of next 3 sc, sc dec over next 2 sc] rep around, join in beg sc. (24 sc)

Rnd 28: Ch 1, [sc in each of next 2 sc, sc dec over next 2 sc] rep around, join in beg sc. (18 sc)

Stuff ball with fiberfill.

Rnd 29: Ch 1, [sc in next sc, sc dec over next 2 sc] rep around, join in beg sc. (12 sc)

Rnd 30: Ch 1, [sc dec over next 2 sc] 6 times, join, leaving a length of yarn, fasten off.

Sew opening closed.

Continued on page 156

Nursery Rhyme Dolls

Designs by Vicky Tignanelli

Little Boy Blue

Little Boy Blue, come blow your horn,

The sheep's in the meadow,
the cow's in the corn.

Where is the boy who looks after the sheep?

He's under a haystack, fast asleep.

Will you wake him? No, not I,

For if I do, he's sure to cry.

Skill Level: Intermediate

Size: Fits 9½-inch Expressions cloth-bodied doll

Materials

► Sport weight yarn: 1 oz medium blue, ½ oz light blue, small amount each black and medium brown

► Size G/6 crochet hook or size needed to obtain gauge

► 3 black E beads

► 4 (⅜-inch) black buttons

► Size 4/0 snap fastener

► Small safety pin

► Sewing needle and thread

► Tapestry needle

Gauge

5 sc = 1 inch; 5 sc rows = 1 inch

Check gauge to save time.

Pattern Notes

Weave in loose ends as work progresses.

Join each rnd with a sl st unless otherwise stated.

Little Boy Blue and Mary with her Little Lamb—two favorite nursery rhyme characters are created in these delightful patterns. Crochet just one or both sets to give with copies of the rhymes to your favorite little person!

Shirt & Pants

Row 1: Beg at neck with light blue, ch 19, sc in 2nd ch from hook, sc in each rem ch across, turn. (18 sc)

Row 2: Ch 1, 2 sc in each sc across, turn. (36 sc)

Rows 3 & 4: Ch 1, sc in each st across, turn.

Row 5: Ch 3 (counts as first dc throughout), dc in each of next 6 dc, ch 4, sk next 4 sts (armhole), dc in each of next 14 sts, ch 4, sk next 4 sts (armhole), dc in each of next 7 sts, turn. (28 dc; 2 ch-4 sps)

Row 6: Ch 3, dc in each dc and each ch across, turn. (36 dc)

Rnd 7: Ch 3, dc in each dc around, join in 3rd ch of beg ch-3, do not turn, fasten off, attach medium blue.

Rnds 8–11: Ch 3, dc in each dc around, join in 3rd ch of beg ch-3.

Rnd 12: Ch 3, dc in each dc around, join in 3rd ch of beg ch-3, then join in 18th dc to form crotch.

Right leg

Note: Do not join Rnds 1–7; mark each rnd with small safety pin.

Rnd 1: Ch 1, hdc in each of next 18 sts. (18 hdc)

Rnds 2–7: Hdc in each hdc around.

Rnd 8: Sc in each hdc around, sl st in next st, fasten off.

Left leg

Rnds 1–8: Attach medium blue at crotch, rep Rnds 1–8 of right leg.

Sleeve

Make 2

Rnd 1 (RS): Attach light blue at underarm, ch 3 (counts as first dc throughout), work 14 dc evenly sp around armhole opening, join in 3rd ch of beg ch-3. (15 dc)

Rnd 2: Ch 3, dc in each of next 2 dc, dc dec over next 2 sts, [dc in each of next 3 sts, dc dec over next 2 sts] twice, join in 3rd ch of beg ch-3. (12 dc)

Rnd 3: Ch 3, dc in each dc around, join in 3rd ch of beg ch-3, fasten off.

Rnd 4: Attach medium blue, ch 2 (counts as first hdc throughout), hdc in each st around, join in 2nd ch of beg ch-2.

Rnd 5: Ch 2, hdc in each st around, join in top of beg ch-2, fasten off.

Neckline Edging

With RS facing, attach medium blue in rem lp on opposite side of foundation ch at left back, ch 1, sc in each ch across, turn. (18 sc)

Left Collar

Row 1: Ch 1, [sc in next sc, 2 sc in next sc] 4 times, sc in next sc, turn. (13 sc)

Rows 2–6: Ch 1, sc in each sc across, turn, at the end of Row 7, fasten off.

in beg sc. (30 sc)

Row 6: Ch 1, sc in each of next 14 sts, turn. (14 sc)

Row 7: Ch 1, sc in each of next 14 sc, turn.

Row 8: Ch 1, sc in next sc, hdc in next sc, 2 dc in each of next 10 sc, hdc in next sc, sc in next sc, fasten off. (24 sts)

Shoe

Make 2

Note: *Do not join Rnds 1–4; mark rnds with small safety pin.*

Rnd 1: With black, ch 7, sc in 2nd ch from hook, hdc in each of next 3 chs, dc in next ch, 6 dc in last ch, working on opposite side of foundation ch, dc in next ch, hdc in each of next 3 chs, sc in next ch. (16 sts)

Rnds 2 & 3: Hdc in each st around.

Rnd 4: Sc in each of next 4 sts, sc dec over next 2 sts] 4 times, sc in each of next 4 sts. (12 sc)

Rnd 5: Sc in each sc around, join in next sc, fasten off.

Horn

Rnd 1: With medium brown, ch 4, 3 dc in 4th ch from hook, join in 4th ch of beg ch-4. (4 dc)

Rnd 2: Ch 3 (counts as first dc throughout), 2 dc in next dc, dc in next dc, 2 dc in next dc, join in 3rd ch of beg ch-3. (6 dc)

Rnd 3: Ch 1, sc in first st, hdc in next st, 2 dc in each of next 2 sts, hdc in next st, sc in next st, join in beg sc. (8 sts)

Rnd 4: Ch 1, sc in first st, hdc in next st, 2 dc in each

Right Collar

Rows 1–6: With RS facing, attach medium blue in first sc at left back, rep Rows 1–6 of left collar.

Finishing Shirt & Pants

Using photo as a guide, with sewing needle and thread, sew snap fastener to back opening; sew 3 E beads down center front of shirt; sew black buttons to front of shirt at waist of pants.

Cap

Rnd 1: Beg at crown with medium blue, ch 4, 14 dc in 4th ch from hook, join in 4th ch of beg ch-4. (15 dc)

Rnd 2: Ch 3 (counts as first dc), dc in same st as beg ch-3, 2 dc in each rem dc around, join in 3rd ch of beg ch-3. (30 dc)

Rnd 3: Ch 2 (counts as first hdc throughout), hdc in same st, 2 hdc in each of next 13 sts, hdc in each rem st around, join in 2nd ch of beg ch-2. (44 hdc)

Rnd 4: Ch 2, hdc in each hdc around, join in 2nd ch of beg ch-2.

Rnd 5: Ch 1, [sc dec over next 2 sts] 14 times, sc in each rem hdc around, join

of next 4 sts, hdc in next st, sc in next st, join in beg sc. (12 sts)

Rnd 5: Ch 3, dc in each st around, join in 3rd ch of beg ch-3, ch 16 for handle, sl st in opposite side of foundation ch, fasten off.

Mary Had a Little Lamb

Mary had a little lamb,
Its fleece was white as snow.
Everywhere that Mary went,
The lamb was sure to go.
It followed her to school one day,
Which was against the rule.
It made the children laugh and play,
To see a lamb at school.

Skill Level: Intermediate

Size: Fits 9½-inch Expressions cloth-bodied doll

Materials

► Sport weight yarn: ½ oz each red and off-white, ¼ oz white, small amounts medium brown, dark green, black and light blue

► Size G/6 crochet hook or size needle to obtain gauge

► 30 inches ¼-inch-wide red picot-edge ribbon

► ¼-inch silver bell

► 12-inch white chenille stem

► 1½ x 1⅝-inch piece lightweight cardboard

► Polyester fiberfill

► Size 4/0 snap fastener

► Pencil

► Hot-glue gun

► Small safety pin

► Sewing needle and thread

► Tapestry needle

Gauge
5 sc = 1 inch; 5 sc rows = 1 inch
Check gauge to save time.

Pattern Notes
Weave in loose ends as work progresses.
Join each rnd with a sl st unless otherwise stated.

Dress
Pinafore

Row 1 (RS): Beg at neckline with red, ch 19, sc in 2nd ch from hook, sc in each rem ch across, turn. (18 sc)

Row 2: Ch 1, 2 sc in each sc across, fasten off. (36 sc)

Row 3: Working in back lps this row only, attach off-white, ch 1, sc in each st across, turn.

Row 4: Ch 1, sc in each st across, turn.

Row 5: Ch 3 (counts as first dc throughout), dc in each of next 6 sts, ch 4, sk next 4 sts (armhole), dc in each of next 14 sts, ch 4, sk next 4 sts (armhole), dc in each of next 7 sts, turn. (28 dc; 2 ch-4 sps)

Row 6: Rep Row 4.

Rnd 7: Working in back lps this row only, ch 3, 2 dc in next st, [dc in next st, 2 dc in next st] rep around, join in 3rd ch of beg ch-3. (54 dc)

Rnds 8–12: Ch 3, dc in each st around, join in 3rd ch of beg ch-3.

Rnd 13: Working in front lps this rnd only, ch 3, dc in each st around, join in 3rd ch of beg ch-3, fasten off.

Skirt

Rnd 1 (WS): Working in rem free lps of Rnd 12, attach red, ch 3, [2 dc in next st, dc in next st] rep around, join in 3rd ch of beg ch-3. (81 dc)

Rnd 2: Ch 3, dc in each dc around, join in top of beg ch-3, fasten off.

Sleeve
Make 2

Note: Do not join rnds, use safety pin to mark rnds.

Rnd 1 (RS): Attach red at center underarm, ch 1, work 20 sc evenly sp around armhole opening. (20 sc)

Rnd 2: Sc in each sc around.

Rnds 3–5: Rep Rnd 2.

Rnd 6: [Sc dec over next 2 sts] 10 times. (10 sc)

Rnds 7–10: Rep Rnd 2, at the end of Rnd 10, fasten off.

Neckline Edging

With RS facing, attach red at left back in opposite side of foundation ch, ch 2, 2 hdc in next ch, [hdc in next ch, 2 hdc in next ch] rep across, fasten off. (27 hdc)

Finishing Dress

Using photo as a guide, embroider lazy daisy sts with tapestry needle and dark green over Rnd 12 of pinafore to form V shapes evenly sp around; embroider a French knot with red in center of each dark green V.

With sewing needle and thread, sew snap fastener to back opening.

Bonnet

Rnd 1: Beg at crown with red, ch 4, 14 dc in 4th ch from hook, join in 3rd ch of beg ch-3. (15 dc)

Rnd 2: Ch 3 (counts as first dc throughout), dc in same st as beg ch, 2 dc in each st around, join in 3rd ch of beg ch-3. (30 dc)

Rnd 3: Ch 3, 2 dc in next st, [dc in next st, 2 dc in

next st] rep around, join in 3rd ch of beg ch-3. (45 dc)

Row 4: Ch 1, [sc in each of next 2 sts, sc dec over next 2 sts] 9 times, leaving rem 9 sts unworked, turn. (27 sc)

Brim

Row 5: Ch 3, dc in each of next 26 sc, turn. (27 dc)

Row 6: Ch 1, sc in first st, [ch 1, sk next st, sc in next st, rep across, turn. (14 sc; 13 ch-1 sps)

Row 7: Ch 1, sc in next sc, [sc in ch-1 sp, sc in next sc] rep across, turn. (27 sc)

Row 8: Ch 1, sc in next sc, [2 sc in next sc, sc in next sc] rep across, turn. (40 sc)

Row 9: Ch 1, sc in each sc across, do not turn.

Row 10: Ch 1, working along bottom of hat, work 12 sc dec evenly sp to opposite side of brim.

Row 11: Working around brim, [sc in next st, 2 sc in next st] rep across, turn. (60 sc)

Row 12: Ch 1, sc in each sc across, do not turn.

Row 13: Ch 1, reverse sc in each sc of brim, fasten off. Using tapestry needle, weave 18 inches of red ribbon through ch-1 sps of Row 6.

Shoe

Make 2

Note: Do not join Rnds 1–10; mark rnds with small safety pin.

Rnd 1: With medium brown, ch 7, sc in 2nd ch from hook, hdc in each of next 3 chs, dc in next ch, 6 dc in last ch, working on

opposite side of foundation ch, dc in next ch, hdc in each of next 3 chs, sc in last ch. (16 sts)

Rnds 2 & 3: Hdc in each st around.

Rnd 4: Sc in each of next 4 sts, [sc dec over next 2 sts] 4 times, sc in each of next 4 sts. (12 sts)

Rnds 5–11: Sc in each st around, at the end of Rnd 11, sl st in next st, fasten off.

Buttons

Using photo as a guide, with black, embroider 3 French knots down right side of right shoe and 3 French knots down left side of left shoe.

Lunch Basket

Note: Do not join rnds, use safety pin to mark rnds.

Rnd 1: With medium brown, ch 2, 6 sc in 2nd

ch from hook. (6 sc)

Rnd 2: 2 sc in each sc around. (12 sc)

Rnd 3: Rep Rnd 2. (24 sc)

Rnd 4: Sc in each sc around.

Rnd 5: Rep Rnd 4.

Basket will turn inward; turn RS out to continue.

Rnd 6: [Sc in next sc, sc dec over next 2 sc] rep around. (16 sc)

Rnd 7: Rep Rnd 4.

Rnd 8: Rep Rnd 2. (32 sc)

Rnd 9: Rep Rnd 2, ch 15 (for handle) join with a sc in st on opposite side of Rnd 9, fasten off.

Cover

Row 1: With white, ch 9, sc in 2nd ch from hook, sc in each rem ch across, turn. (8 sc)

Rows 2–7: Ch 1, sc in each sc across, turn, at the end of Row 7, do not turn.

Rnd 8: Working around outer edge, [ch 2, sk next st or row end, sc in next st or row end] rep around, join in base of beg ch-2, fasten off.

Using photo as a guide, with light blue, embroider straight sts horizontally between rows of cover; embroider straight sts vertically between rows to complete checkerboard design.

Shape basket with fingers, turning edge outward and down slightly and flattening bottom. Stuff basket lightly with fiberfill. Glue cover over top of basket.

Slate

Front

Row 1 (WS): With black, ch 9, sc in 2nd ch from hook, sc in each rem ch across, turn. (8 sc)

Rows 2–8: Ch 1, sc in each sc across, turn, at the end of Row 8, fasten off.

Rnd 9 (RS): Attach medium brown in any corner, sc evenly sp around outer edge, join in beg sc, fasten off.

Back

Row 1: With medium

brown, ch 10, sc in 2nd ch from hook, sc in each rem ch across, turn. (9 sc)

Rows 2–10: Ch 1, sc in each sc across, turn, at the end of Row 10, do not turn.

For handle, sl st in each of first 3 sts, ch 8, sl st in each of last 3 sts, fasten off.

Using photo as a guide, with white, embroider straight sts to make letters and numbers on slate front.

Holding front and back tog with cardboard sandwiched between, with medium brown yarn, whip-stitch around entire outer edge.

Lamb

Note: Do not join Rnds 1–15: mark rnds with small safety pin.

Body

Rnd 1: Beg at tail end with white, ch 2, 6 sc in 2nd ch from hook. (6 sc)

Rnd 2: 2 sc in each st around. (12 sc)

Rnd 3: [Sc in next st, 2 sc in next st] rep around. (18 sc)

Rnd 4: [Sc in each of next 2 sc, 2 sc in next sc] rep around. (24 sc)

Rnd 5: Sc in each st around.

Rnd 6: Rep Rnd 5.

Rnd 7: [Sc in each of next 2 sc, sc dec over next 2 sts] rep around. (18 sc)

Rnds 8 & 9: Rep Rnd 5. Piece will turn inward; turn RS out to continue.

Rnd 10: [Sc in next sc, sc dec over next 2 sc] rep around. (12 sc)

Rnd 11: Rep Rnd 5.

Rnd 12: Rep Rnd 2. (24 sc)

Rnd 13: Rep Rnd 5.

Rnd 14: Working in back lps this rnd only, sc in each st around.

Rnd 15: [Sc dec over next 2 sts] rep around. (12 sc)

Rnd 16: Rep Rnd 5, join in beg sc, fasten off.

Face

Rnd 1: With white, ch 2, 6 sc in 2nd ch from hook. (6 sc)

Rnd 2: Sc in each sc around.

Rnd 3: 2 sc in each sc around. (12 sc)

Turn RS out to continue, shaping end with blunt end of pencil.

Rnds 4–6: Rep Rnd 2. At the end of Rnd 6, sl st in next st, leaving a length of yarn, fasten off.

Ear

Make 2

Note: Do not ch 1 at beg of rows.

Row 1: With white, ch 5, sc in 2nd ch from hook, sc in each rem ch across, turn. (4 sc)

Row 2: Sk first sc, sc in each of next 2 sc, turn. (2 sc)

Row 3: Sk first sc, sc in next sc.

Rnd 4: Working around outer edge of ear, sc in each st and row end around, leaving a length of yarn, fasten off.

Leg

Make 4

Rnd 1: With white, ch 2,

3 sc in 2nd ch from hook. (3 sc)

Rnd 2: Work 2 sc in each sc around. (6 sc)

Rnd 3: Sc in each sc around.

Work will beg to turn inward; turn RS out to continue, shaping end with blunt end of pencil.

Rnd 4: Attach white in any sc, ch 1, sc in each sc around. (6 sc)

Rnds 5–7: Sc in each sc around.

Rnd 8: Sc in each of next 2 sc, sc dec over next 2 sc, sc in each of next 2 sc, join in beg sc, fasten off.

Tail

With white, ch 4, sc in 2nd ch from hook, sc in each rem ch across, leaving a length of yarn, fasten off. (3 sc)

Finishing Lamb

Using photo as a guide, with black, embroider straight sts for eyes and nose on face. Lightly stuff body and face with fiberfill.

Cut chenille stem into 4 (3-inch) lengths; fold each length in half and insert blunt end first into each leg. Trim ends even with top of each leg.

With tapestry needle and rem yarn ends, tack 2 corners on each ear tog.

Whipstitch face, legs, ears and tail to body.

Thread rem length of ribbon through lp of bell; tie ribbon in 1½-inch bow, trimming ends at a slight angle. Glue bow under face. ✁

Victorian Rose Teddy Bear

Designs by Beverly Mewhorter

Skill Level: Beginner

Size: Fits 10-inch bear

Materials

► Coats & Clark Super Saver worsted weight yarn: 2 oz rose pink #372

► Size H/8 crochet hook or size needed to obtain gauge

► 3 silk roses

► 42 inches ¼-inch-wide white ribbon

► 12 inches 4mm pre-strung pearl beads

► Hot-glue gun

► Tapestry needle

Gauge

4 dc sts = 1 inch

Check gauge to save time.

Pattern Notes

Weave in loose ends as work progresses.

Join each rnd with a sl st unless otherwise stated.

Dress

Bodice

Row 1: Beg at waistline, ch 37, sc in 2nd ch from hook, sc in each of next 5 chs, ch 16, sk next 7 chs of foundation ch, sc in each of next 10 chs, ch 16, sk next 7 chs of foundation ch, sc in each of next 6 chs, turn.

Row 2: Ch 1, sc in each of next 6 sc, sc in each of next 16 chs, sc in each of next 10 sc, sc in each of next 16 chs, sc in each of next 6 sc, turn. (54 sc)

Row 3: Ch 1, sc in each sc across, turn.

Row 4: Ch 1, [sc dec over next 2 sc] rep across, turn. (27 sc)

Row 5: Ch 1, [sc dec over next 2 sc] 13 times, sc in next sc, fasten off. (14 sc)

Skirt

Row 1: Attach rose pink in rem lp on opposite side of foundation ch of bodice, ch 1, sc in each ch across, turn. (36 sc)

Row 2: Ch 3 (counts as first dc throughout), dc in same st as beg ch-3, 2 dc in each rem st across, turn. (72 dc)

Rows 3–6: Ch 3, dc in each dc across, turn, at the end of Row 6, fasten off.

Matching ends of rows, sew back seam across Rows 1–6.

Place dress on bear. Insert a 14-inch length of ribbon through sts at neckline edge of back opening; tie ends in a bow to close.

Cut 2 lengths of ribbon each 14 inches long. Holding ribbons tog, tie in a bow and glue to center front neckline of dress. Glue 1 rose to center of bow.

Hat

Rnd 1: Ch 4, 11 dc in 4th ch from hook, join in 4th ch of beg ch-4. (12 dc)

Rnd 2: Ch 3, dc in same st as beg ch-3, 2 dc in each rem st around, join in 3rd ch of beg ch-3. (24 dc)

Rnd 3: Ch 3, dc in same st as beg ch-3, dc in next dc, [2 dc in next dc, dc in next dc] rep around, join in 3rd ch of beg ch-3. (36 dc)

Rnd 4: Ch 3, dc in each dc around, join in 3rd ch of beg ch-3.

Rnd 5: Sl st in each st around, fasten off.

Cut pre-strung pearl beads into 4-inch lengths. Make 3 lps and glue to Rnd 3 of hat. Glue 2 flowers over center of beads where ends meet. Place hat on bear. ✂

Cleopatra Fashion Doll Gown

Design by Beverly Mewhorter

Skill Level: Beginner

Size: Fits 11½-inch fashion doll

Materials

- ▶ J. & P. Coats Metallic Knit-Cro-Sheen crochet cotton size 10: 200 yds each gold/gold #90G and ecru/gold #61G
- ▶ J. & P. Knit-Cro-Sheen crochet cotton size 10: 100 yds black #12
- ▶ Size 7 steel crochet hook or size needed to obtain gauge
- ▶ 3 yds 5mm gold pre-strung half beads
- ▶ 18 inches pre-strung gold sequins
- ▶ 2 red oval rhinestones
- ▶ Hot-glue gun
- ▶ 6 snap fasteners
- ▶ Sewing needle and thread
- ▶ Tapestry needle

Gold Metallic Knit-Cro-Sheen and sequins give a truly rich look to this beautiful gown. The matching headpiece and wrist cuffs add authentic-looking accents!

Gauge

7 sc = 1 inch; 8 sc rows = 1 inch

Check gauge to save time.

Pattern Note

Weave in loose ends as work progresses.

Dress

Bodice

Row 1: Beg at waistline with gold/gold, ch 23, sc in 2nd ch from hook, sc in each rem ch across, turn. (22 sc)

Row 2: Ch 1, sc in each st across, turn.

Row 3: Rep Row 2.

Row 4: Ch 1, [sc in each of next 2 sts, 2 sc in next st] rep across, turn. (29 sc)

Rows 5–10: Rep Row 2.

Row 11: Ch 1, sc in each of next 4 sc, [2 sc in next sc, sc in each of next 4 sc] rep across, turn. (34 sc)

Rows 12 & 13: Rep Row 2.

Row 14: Ch 1, [sc in each of next 5 sc, 2 sc in next sc] rep across, ending with sc in each of last 4 sc, turn. (39 sc)

Row 15: Ch 1, sc in each of next 6 sc, ch 10, sk next 4 sc (armhole opening), sc in each of next 19 sc, ch 10, sk next 4 sc (armhole opening), sc in each of next 6 sc, turn. (31 sc; 2 ch-10 sps)

Row 16: Ch 1, sc in each of next 6 sc, sc in each of next 10 chs, [sc in next sc, sc dec over next 2 sc] 6 times, sc in next sc, sc in each of next 10 chs, sc in each of next 6 sc, fasten off. (45 sc)

Skirt

Row 1: Working in rem lps on opposite side of foundation ch of bodice, attach gold/gold, ch 1, sc in same ch as beg ch, sc in each of next 21 chs, turn. (22 sc)

Row 2: Ch 1, sc in first sc, 2 sc in next sc, [sc in next sc, 2 sc in next sc] rep across, turn. (33 sc)

Row 3: Ch 1, sc in each sc across, turn.

Rows 4 & 5: Rep Row 3.

Row 6: Ch 1, [sc in each of next 5 sc, 2 sc in next sc] rep across, ending with sc in each of last 3 sc, turn. (38 sc)

Rnd 7: Ch 1, sc in each sc around, join in beg sc, turn.

Rnds 8–28: Rep Rnd 7.

Row 29: Ch 1, 3 sc in each sc across, turn. (114 sc)

Rnds 30–50: Rep Rnd 7, at the end of Rnd 50, fasten off.

Rnds 51 & 52: With black, rep Rnd 7, at end of Rnd 52, fasten off.

Rnd 53: Attach gold/gold, rep Rnd 7.

Rnd 54: Ch 1, reverse sc in each st around, join in beg reverse sc, fasten off.

Sew 3 snap fasteners evenly sp down back opening.

Using photo as a guide, glue a 5-inch length of sequins down center front of dress to Rnd 28. Glue a 7-inch length of sequins around Rnd 28 of dress. Place dress on doll.

Collar

Row 1: With black, ch 31, sc in 2nd ch from hook, sc in each rem ch across, turn. (30 sc)

Row 2: Ch 1, [sc in each of next 2 sc, 2 sc in next sc] rep across, turn. (40 sc)

Row 3: Ch 1, sc in each sc across, turn.

Row 4: Ch 1, [sc in each of next 3 sc, 2 sc in next sc] rep across, turn. (50 sc)

Row 5: Rep Row 3.

Row 6: Ch 1, [sc in each of next 4 sc, 2 sc in next sc] rep across, turn. (60 sc)

Row 7: Rep Row 3, fasten off.

Row 8: Attach gold/gold in first sc, ch 1, reverse sc in each st across, fasten off.

Cut 8 groups of 3 gold beads and glue evenly sp around collar. Glue a red rhinestone at front center. Using care that collar fits around neckline, sew 2 snap fasteners evenly sp down back opening. With snaps at back, place collar on doll; tack each side of collar to shoulder straps of dress.

Wrist Cuff

Make 2

Row 1: With gold/gold, ch 5, sc in 2nd ch from hook, sc in each rem ch across, turn. (4 sc)

Rows 2–7: Ch 1, sc in each sc across, turn.

Row 8: Working through both thicknesses, holding Row 7 to opposite side of foundation ch, sl st in each st across, fasten off.

Glue 3 sets of 2 gold beads evenly sp around cuff. Slip cuff over hand onto wrist of doll.

Cape

Row 1: Beg at top of cape with ecru/gold, ch 13, sc in 2nd ch from hook, sc in each rem ch across, turn. (12 sc)

Row 2: Ch 3 (counts as first dc throughout), 2 dc in same st as beg ch-3, 3 dc in each rem sc across, turn. (36 dc)

Row 3: Ch 3, dc in each dc across, turn.

Row 4: Rep Row 3.

Row 5: Ch 3, 2 dc in next dc, [dc in next dc, 2 dc in next dc] rep across, turn. (54 dc)

Rows 6 & 7: Rep Row 3.

Josephine's Coronation Gown
Pattern begins on next page

Row 8: Rep Row 5. (81 dc)

Rows 9–28: Rep Row 3, at the end of Row 28, fasten off.

Edging

Rnd 1: Attach gold/gold in rem lp on opposite side of foundation ch, ch 1, 3 sc in same st, sc in each rem ch across top, 3 sc in corner, sc evenly sp around outer edge, working 3 sc in each bottom corner, join in beg sc, fasten off.

Rnd 2: Attach black in center sc of any corner, ch 1, [3 sc in center corner st, sc in each sc across to next corner] rep around, join in beg sc, fasten off.

Rnd 3: Rep Rnd 2, do not fasten off.

Rnd 4: Ch 1, reverse sc in each st around outer edge, join in beg sc, fasten off.

Cut 8 lengths of gold beads each 6½ inches long; glue to back of cape from top to bottom in a fanned-out design.

Cut a 30-inch-length of gold beads; glue from top inside edge Row 1 of cape, down side, across bottom edge and up opposite side back to Row 1.

Sew left back top edge of cape to left back of shoulder strap. Attach right edge of cape to right back shoulder strap with a snap fastener.

Headpiece

Rnd 1: With gold/gold, ch 4, 11 dc in 4th ch from hook, join in 4th of beg ch-4. (12 dc)

Rnd 2: Ch 3 (counts as first dc throughout), dc in same st as beg ch-3, 2 dc in each rem dc around, join in 3rd ch of beg ch-3. (24 dc)

Rnd 3: Ch 1, [sc in next dc, 2 sc in next dc] rep around, join in beg sc. (36 sc)

Rnd 4: Working in back lps this rnd only, ch 3, dc in each st around, join in 3rd ch of beg ch-3.

Rnd 5: Ch 3, dc in each dc around, join in 3rd ch of beg ch-3.

Row 6: Ch 3, dc in each of next 20 dc, leaving rem sts unworked, turn. (21 dc)

Rows 7–9: Ch 3, dc in each of next 20 dc, turn.

Rnd 10: Ch 1, 2 sc in same dc as beg ch-1, sc in each of next 19 dc, 2 sc in next dc, sc evenly sp in ends of rows, sc in each rem dc of Rnd 5, sc evenly sp in ends of rows, join in beg sc, fasten off.

Cobra

For first section, holding 2 strands of gold/gold tog, ch 8, fasten off.

For 2nd section, holding 2 strands of gold/gold tog, ch 4, 2 dc in 4th ch from hook, ch 3, sl st in dc, fasten off.

Glue first section in a circle with beg and ending of ch between Rnds 4 and 5. Glue 2nd section with ch-3 sp centered in ch-8 lp.

With 2 strands of gold/gold, ch 12, fasten off. Shape into a U and glue to back top of cobra. Glue red rhinestone to center of U-shape.

Cut 8 sections of 4 gold beads each. Glue evenly sp across backdrop of headpiece. Glue a 6-inch length of sequins over Rnd 5 of headpiece. Place headpiece on doll. ✄

Josephine's Coronation Gown

Design by Beverly Mewhorter
Photo on page 149

Skill Level: Beginner

Size: Fits 11½-inch fashion doll

Materials
▶ J. & P. Coats Metallic Knit-Cro-Sheen crochet cotton size 10: 150 yds each white/gold #1G and gold/gold #90G

▶ J. & P. Coats Knit-Cro-Sheen crochet cotton size 10: 125 yds Spanish red #126

▶ Size 7 steel crochet hook or size needed to obtain gauge

▶ 312 plus 2 (optional) 4mm gold beads

▶ 2 straight pins (optional)

▶ 12 inches 1-inch-wide white-and-gold lace

▶ 25 inches ¼-inch-wide gold ribbon

▶ 24 inches gold pre-strung sequins

▶ 3 snap fasteners

▶ Hot-glue gun

▶ Tapestry needle

In this beautiful white gown and Spanish red cape, the queen's regal beauty will stand out at the Coronation Ball!

Gauge
7 sc = 1 inch
Check gauge to save time.

Pattern Notes
Weave in loose ends as work progresses.

Join each rnd with a sl st unless otherwise stated.

Pattern Stitch
Sl st2tog: Insert hook front to back through next st and back to front through next st, yo, draw through all sts on hook.

Dress

Bodice
Row 1: Beg at bottom with white/gold, ch 37, sc in 2nd ch from hook, sc in each rem ch across, turn. (36 sc)

Row 2: Ch 1, sc in each of next 12 sc, 2 sc in each of next 12 sc, sc in each of next 12 sc, turn. (48 sc)

Row 3: Ch 1, sc in each st across, turn.

Row 4: Ch 1, sc in each of next 10 sc, ch 10, sk next 4 sc, sc in each of next 26 sc, ch 10, sk next 4 sc, sc in each of next 7 sc, turn. (40 sc; 2 ch-10 sps)

Row 5: Ch 1, sc in each of next 7 sc, sc in each of next 10 chs, sc in each of next 2 sc, [sc dec over next 2 sc] 11 times, sc in each of next 2 sc, sc in each of next 10 chs, sc in each of next 7 sc, turn. (49 sc)

Row 6: Ch 1, sl st in each of next 19 sc, [sl st2tog] 5 times, sl st in each of next 20 sc, fasten off.

Skirt
Row 1: Attach white/gold with a sl st in rem lp on opposite side of foundation ch of bodice, ch 1, sc in

each ch across, turn. (36 sc)

Row 2: Ch 1, [sc in next sc, 2 sc in next sc] rep across, turn. (54 sc)

Rows 3–8: Ch 1, sc in each sc across, turn.

Rnd 9: Ch 1, sc in each sc around, join in beg sc, turn.

Rnds 10–59: Rep Rnd 9. At the end of Rnd 59, fasten off.

Rnd 60: Attach gold/gold, rep Rnd 9.

Rnd 61: Ch 3 (counts as first dc throughout), 2 dc in same st, 3 dc in each rem st around, join in 3rd ch of beg ch-3, turn.

Rnd 62: Ch 3, dc in each dc around, join in 3rd ch of beg ch-3, fasten off.

Sleeve

Make 2

Rnd 1: Attach white/gold in 3rd sc of 4 skipped sc at underarm, ch 1, sc in same sc, sc in next sc, sc in each of next 10 chs, sc in each of next 2 sc, join in beg sc, turn. (14 sc)

Rnd 2: Ch 1, sc in each of next 2 sc, [2 sc in next sc] 10 times, sc in each of next 2 sc, join in beg sc, turn. (24 sc)

Rnds 3–7: Ch 1, sc in each sc around, join in beg sc, turn.

Rnd 8: Ch 1, sc in each of next 2 sc, [sc dec over next 2 sc] 5 times, sc in each of next 2 sc, join in beg sc, turn. (14 sc)

Rnd 9: Ch 1, sc in each of next 2 sc, [sc dec over next 2 sc] 5 times, sc in each of next 2 sc, join in beg sc, turn. (9 sc)

Rnds 10–25: Rep Rnd 3, at the end of Rnd 25, fasten off.

Rnd 26: Attach gold/gold, ch 1, sc in each sc around, join in beg sc, turn.

Rnd 27: Ch 1, 3 sc in each sc around, join in beg sc, fasten off.

Sleeve ruffle

Row 1: With gold/gold, ch 17, sc in 2nd ch from hook, sc in each rem ch across, turn.

Row 2: Ch 1, 3 sc in each sc across, fasten off. Sew sleeve ruffle to Rnd 10 of sleeve.

Front Panel

Row 1: With gold/gold, ch 7, sc in 2nd ch from hook, sc in each rem ch across, turn. (6 sc)

Row 2: Ch 1, sc in each sc across, turn.

Rows 3–7: Rep Row 2.

Row 8: Ch 1, 2 sc in first sc, sc in each sc across to last sc, 2 sc in last sc, turn. (8 sc)

Rows 9–17: Rep Row 2.

Row 18: Rep Row 8. (10 sc)

Rows 19–54: Rep Row 2, at the end of Row 54, fasten off.

Referring to photo for placement, glue panel to center front of dress.

Cut a 15½-inch length of sequins; glue around outer edge of front panel.

Glue a 7-inch length of

BARBIE® is a trademark owned by and used with permission of Mattel, Inc. © 2002 Mattel, Inc. All Rights Reserved.

gold ribbon down center front of panel. Place rem length of ribbon around base of bodice; sew at center front and each side.

Glue a 2-inch length of sequins centered down outer edge of each sleeve between sleeve ruffle and cuff.

Cut lace in half. Gather each half to fit around top edge of bodice from center back to just below sleeve on front; glue in place.

Sew 2 snap fasteners evenly sp down back opening.

Place dress on doll and tie gold ribbon in a bow at center back.

Cape

Note: *Thread 312 gold*

beads onto Spanish red thread.

Row 1: Beg at top with Spanish red, ch 19, sc in 2nd ch from hook, sc in each rem ch across, turn. (18 sc)

Row 2: Ch 3, 2 dc in same st, 3 dc in each rem st across, turn. (54 dc)

Row 3: Ch 3, dc in each st across, turn.

Row 4: Ch 3, dc in next st, [push up 1 bead, dc in each of next 2 sts] rep across, turn. (26 beads)

Row 5: Ch 3, dc in each dc across, turn.

Rows 6–27: Rep Rows 4 and 5.

Continued on page 157

Pastel Sunset Sling Purse

Design by Mary Jane Wood

Skill Level: Beginner

Size: 7 x 7¼ inches

Materials

► Lion Brand Kitchen worsted weight cotton: 2½ oz sherbet swirl #298, 2 oz pastel blue #106

► Crochet cotton size 10: 10 yds mauve

► Size G/6 crochet hook or size needed to obtain gauge

► Size F/5 crochet hook

► Size 7 steel crochet hook

► 19mm circle hook-and-loop tape

► Scrap of fiberfill

► Sewing needle and thread

► Tapestry needle

Women and children alike will smile with glee when you give them this perky little purse. With easy closure and a large, handy pocket on the back, you'll find it useful for a variety of occasions.

Gauge

With largest hook, 5 rnds and 7 sc sts = 1½ inches

Check gauge to save time.

Pattern Notes

Weave in loose ends as work progresses.

Join each rnd with a sl st unless otherwise stated.

Carry color not in use up side edge of purse.

Pattern Stitch

Popcorn (pc): 4 dc in indicated st, draw up a lp, remove hook, insert hook in first dc of 4-dc group, pick up dropped lp and draw through st on hook, ch 1 to lock.

Purse

Note: Do not join rnds unless otherwise stated; use a scrap of CC yarn to mark rnds.

Rnd 1 (RS): With largest hook and sherbet swirl, ch 2, 6 sc in 2nd ch from hook. (6 sc)

Rnd 2: Work 2 sc in each sc around. (12 sc)

Rnd 3: [Sc in next sc, 2 sc in next sc] rep around. (18 sc)

Rnd 4: [Sc in each of next 2 sc, 2 sc in next sc] rep around. (24 sc)

Rnd 5: [Sc in each of next 3 sc, 2 sc in next sc] rep around. (30 sc)

Rnd 6: [2 sc in next sc, sc in each of next 4 sc] rep around. (36 sc)

Rnd 7: With pastel blue, [sc in each of next 5 sc, 2 sc in next sc] rep around. (42 sc)

Rnd 8: [2 sc in next sc, sc in each of next 6 sc] rep around. (48 sc)

Rnd 9: With sherbet swirl, sc in each of next 4 sc, 2 sc in next sc, [sc in each of next 7 sc, 2 sc in next sc] 5 times, sc in next 3 sc. (54 sc)

Rnd 10: [Sc in each of next 8 sc, 2 sc in next sc] rep around. (60 sc)

Rnd 11: Sc in each sc around.

Rnd 12: Rep Rnd 11.

Rnds 13 & 14: With pastel blue, rep Rnd 11.

Rnds 15–18: With sherbet swirl, rep Rnd 11.

Rnd 19: With pastel blue, rep Rnd 11.

Rnd 20: [Sc in each of next 8 sc, sc dec over next 2 sc] rep around. (54 sc)

Rnds 21–23: With sherbet swirl, rep Rnd 11.

Rnd 24: [Sc in each of next 7 sc, sc dec over next 2 sc] rep around. (48 sc)

Rnds 25 & 26: With pastel blue, rep Rnd 11.

Rnd 27: With sherbet swirl, rep Rnd 11.

Rnd 28: [Sc in each of next 6 sc, sc dec over next 2 sc] rep around. (42 sc)

Rnd 29: Rep Rnd 11.

Rnd 30: Sc in each of next 42 sc, sl st in next st, fasten off sherbet swirl, turn.

Rnd 31 (WS): Draw up a lp of pastel blue, ch 1, sc in each of next 42 sc, join in beg sc, turn.

Rnd 32 (RS): Ch 1, sc in each of next 42 sc, join in beg sc, fasten off.

Flap

Row 1 (RS): Working in back lps this row only, attach sherbet swirl in any st of Rnd 32, ch 1, sc in same st, sc in each of next 20 sts, leaving rem sts unworked, turn. (21 sc)

Row 2 (WS): Ch 1, sc in each of next 21 sc, turn.

Row 3: Ch 1, sc in first sc, sc dec over next 2 sc, sc in each rem sc across, turn. (20 sc)

Row 4: Rep Row 3. (19 sc)

Rows 5 & 6: With pastel

blue, rep Row 3. (17 sc)

Rows 7–10: With sherbet swirl, rep Row 3. (13 sc)

Row 11: With pastel blue, ch 1, sc in first sc, sc dec over next 2 sc, hdc in each of next 2 sc, dc in next sc, tr in each of next 2 sc, dc in next sc, hdc in each of next 2 sc, sc in rem 2 sc, turn. (12 sts)

Row 12: Ch 1, sc in each of next 2 sts, hdc in each of next 2 sts, dc in each of next 4 sts, hdc in each of next 2 sts, sc in each of next 2 sts, fasten off. (12 sts)

Row 13 (RS): Attach pastel blue with a sl st in side edge of Row 1 of flap, sc in side edge of each of next 10 rows, sk next row, 12 sc across Row 12 of flap, sk side edge of Row 12, sc in side edge of each of next 10 rows, sl st in side edge of Row 1, fasten off.

If purse curls slightly, press with iron using a damp cloth.

Shoulder Strap

Row 1: With hook size F and pastel blue, leaving a slight length at beg for sewing, ch 2, sc in 2nd ch from hook, turn clockwise.

Row 2: Sc in first vertical lp (not under the horizontal lp), turn clockwise.

Row 3: Do not ch, sc under both vertical lps, turn clockwise.

Rep Row 3 until desired length, sl st in side edge of purse in Rnd 32, fasten off. Using care that strap is not twisted, with rem beg length, sew strap to opposite edge of Rnd 32 of purse.

Flower Button

Rnd 1: With steel hook size 7 and mauve cotton, ch 2, 6 sc in 2nd ch from hook, join in beg sc. (6 sc)

Rnd 2: Ch 3 (counts as first dc throughout), pc in same st as beg ch-3, [dc, pc] in each of next 5 sc, join in 3rd ch of beg ch-3.

(6 dc; 6 pc)

Rnd 3: Ch 3, 2 dc in top of pc, dc in next ch-1 sp, [dc in next dc, 2 dc in top of pc, dc in next ch-1 sp] rep around, join in 3rd ch of beg ch-3. (24 dc)

Rnd 4: Ch 3, dc in each dc around, join in 3rd ch of beg ch-3

Rnd 5: Ch 3, sk next dc, [dc dec over next 2 dc] 11 times, join in 3rd ch of beg ch-3, leaving a length of cotton, fasten off. (12 dc)

Stuff lightly with fiberfill. Sew button centered over Rows 11 and 12 of flap.

Sew hook-and-loop tape
Continued on page 157

Critter Finger Puppets

Designs by Michele Wilcox

Skill Level: Beginner

Size: 3 inches tall

Materials

▶ Worsted weight yarn: Small amounts each of brown, off-white, black, yellow, orange, blue, light gray, light gold, white, beige

▶ Size G/6 crochet hook or size needed to obtain gauge

▶ Polyester fiberfill

▶ Tapestry needle

Turn a rainy afternoon into a time of fun and enjoyment. Stitch one or all five of these clever puppets and let your children's imaginations run wild!

Gauge

4 sc = 1 inch; 4 sc rnds = 1 inch

Check gauge to save time.

Pattern Notes

Weave in loose ends as work progresses.

Do not join rnds unless otherwise indicated. Use a scrap of CC yarn to mark rnds.

Bear

Head & Body

Rnd 1 (RS): With brown, ch 2, 7 sc in 2nd ch from hook. (7 sc)

Rnd 2: 2 sc in each sc around. (14 sc)

Rnd 3: Sc in each sc around.

Rnds 4 & 5: Rep Rnd 3.

Rnd 6: Sc dec over next 2 sc, [sc in next sc, sc dec over next 2 sc] 4 times. (9 sc)

Stuff head with a small amount of fiberfill.

Rnd 7: [Sc in next sc, sc dec over next 2 sc] 3 times. (6 sc)

Rnd 8: Rep Rnd 2. (12 sc)

Rnds 9–14: Rep Rnd 3, at the end of Rnd 14, sl st in next st, fasten off.

Ear

Make 2

Rnd 1: With brown, ch 2, 6 sc in 2nd ch from hook, sl st to join in beg sc, leaving a length of yarn, fasten off. (6 sc)

Sew an ear to each side of head.

Snout

Rnd 1: With off-white, ch 2, 6 sc in 2nd ch from hook, sl st to join in beg sc. (6 sc)

Rnd 2: [Sc in next sc, 2 sc in next sc] rep around, sl st to join in beg sc, leaving a length of yarn, fasten off. (9 sc)

Sew snout to front of face, stuffing with fiberfill before closing.

Using photo as a guide, with black, embroider a French knot for nose and upside down Y for mouth centered under nose.

With black, embroider a French knot for each eye.

Arm

Make 2

Rnd 1: With brown, ch 2, 6 sc in 2nd ch from hook. (6 sc)

Rnds 2–5: Sc in each sc around, at the end of Rnd 5, sl st in next st, leaving a length of yarn, fasten off.

Sew an arm at each side of body over Rnd 8.

Duck

Head & Body

Rnds 1–14: With yellow, rep Rnds 1–14 of bear head and body.

Beak

Upper

Row 1: With orange, ch 4, sc in 2nd ch from hook, sc in next ch, 3 sc in last ch, working in rem lps on opposite side of foundation ch, sc in each of next 2 chs, fasten off. (7 sc)

Lower

Row 1: With orange, ch 3, sc in 2nd ch from hook, 3 sc in next ch, working in rem lps on opposite side of foundation ch, sc in next ch, leaving a length of yarn, fasten off. (5 sc)

Sew beak sections between Rnds 5 and 6 at center front of head.

With blue, embroider French knot eye between Rnds 4 and 5 at each side of beak.

With yellow, sew 3 lps to top of head.

Wing

Make 2

Row 1: With yellow, ch 6, sc in 2nd ch from hook, sc in each rem ch across, turn. (5 sc)

Row 2: Ch 1, sc dec over next 2 sc, sc in next sc, sc dec over next 2 sc, turn. (3 sc)

Row 3: Ch 1, draw up a lp in each sc across, yo, draw through all 4 lps on hook, fasten off. (1 sc)

Fold Row 1 in half and sew to side of body.

Mouse

Head & Body

Rnds 1–14: With light

gray, rep Rnds 1–14 of head and body of bear.

Snout

Row 1: With light gray, ch 10, sc in 2nd ch from hook, sc in each rem ch across, turn. (9 sc)

Row 2: Ch 1, [sc dec over next 2 sc] twice, sc in next sc, [sc dec over next 2 sc] twice, turn. (5 sc)

Row 3: Ch 1, sc dec over next 2 sc, sc in next sc, sc dec over next 2 sc, turn. (3 sc)

Rnd 4: Ch 1, draw up a lp in each sc across, yo, draw through all 4 lps on hook, fasten off.

Fold in half and sew side seam. Sew to front of head, stuffing with fiberfill before closing.

With black, embroider a French knot for each eye slightly above snout.

Using photo as a guide, with black, embroider a satin-st nose; embroider an upside down Y for mouth.

Arm
Make 2

Rnds 1–5: With light gray, rep Rnds 1–5 of bear. (6 sc)

Tail

Row 1: With light gray, ch 20, sl st in 2nd ch from hook, sl st in each rem ch across, leaving a length of yarn, fasten off.

Sew tail to center back of body Rnd 14.

Penguin

Head & Body

Rnds 1–14: With black, rep Rnds 1–14 of head and body of bear.

Arm
Make 2

Rnds 1–5: With black, rep Rnds 1–5 of bear. (6 sc)

Tummy

Row 1: With white, ch 6, hdc in 3rd ch from hook, hdc in next ch, sc in next ch, 3 sc in last ch, working on opposite side of foundation ch, sc in next ch, hdc in each of next 3 chs, leaving a length of yarn, fasten off.

Sew to center front bottom of body.

Wing
Make 2

Row 1: With black, ch 7, sc in 2nd ch from hook, sc in each rem ch across, turn. (6 sc)

Row 2: Ch 1, sc dec over next 2 sc, sc in each of next 2 sc, sc dec over next 2 sc, turn. (4 sc)

Row 3: Ch 1, [sc dec over next 2 sc] twice, turn. (2 sc)

Row 4: Ch 1, sc dec over next 2 sc, fasten off.

Fold Row 1 in half and sew to side of body.

Beak

Row 1: With light gold, ch 4, sc in 2nd ch from hook, sc in each of next 2 chs, turn. (3 sc)

Row 2: Ch 1, sc dec over next 2 sc, sc in next sc, turn. (2 sc)

Row 3: Ch 1, sc dec over next 2 sc, leaving a length of yarn, fasten off.

Fold piece in half and sew side seam; sew to front of head.

With blue, embroider a French knot eye on each side of beak.

Rabbit

Head & Body

Rnds 1–14: With beige, rep Rnds 1–14 of head and body of bear.

Arm

Make 2

Rnds 1–5: With beige, rep Rnds 1–5 of bear. (6 sc)

Facial Features

With brown, embroider French knot eyes between Rnds 3 and 4, spacing ½ inch apart; embroider a French knot nose centered between eyes. With brown, embroider an upside down Y centered below nose.

Ear

Make 2

Row 1: With beige, ch 4, sc in 2nd ch from hook, sc in each rem ch across, turn. (3 sc)

Row 2: Ch 1, sc in next sc, 2 sc in next sc, sc in next sc, turn. (4 sc)

Rows 3 & 4: Ch 1, sc in each sc across, turn.

Row 5: Ch 1, [sc dec over next 2 sc] twice, fasten off. Sew Row 1 to top of head.

Tail

With white, make a 1¼-inch pompom and sew to back bottom of body. ✄

Mr. Brown the Bear

Continued from page 133

Rnds 5–8: Rep Rnd 4. At the end of Rnd 8, fasten off brown.

Rnd 9: Attach yellow, rep Rnd 4.

Rnds 10–18: Rep Rnd 4.

Rnd 19: [Sc in each of next 3 sc, sc dec over next 2 sc] rep around. (12 sc)

Rnd 20: [Sc dec over next 2 sc] rep around, sl st in next st, leaving a length of yarn, fasten off. (6 sc)

Weave rem length through rem sts; sew arm to body.

Cuff

Make 2

Row 1: With yellow, ch 5, sc in 2nd ch from hook, sc in each rem ch across, turn. (4 sc)

Rows 2-16: Working in back lps only, ch 1, sc in each st across, turn, at the end of Row 16, leaving a length of yarn, fasten off.

Sew piece around arm, sewing ends tog at underside of arm.

Thumb

Make 2

Rnd 1: With brown, ch 2, 6 sc in 2nd ch from hook. (6 sc)

Rnds 2 & 3: Sc in each sc around. at the end of Rnd 3, sl st in next st, leaving a length of yarn, fasten off.

Stuff thumb with fiberfill; sew to upper side of hand. ✄

Ladybug Ball

Continued from page 141

Spot

Make 8

Rnd 1: With black, ch 2, 6 sc in 2nd ch from hook, join in beg sc. (6 sc)

Rnd 2: Ch 1, 2 sc in each sc around, join, leaving a length of yarn, fasten off. (12 sc)

Center Stripe

With black, ch 42, leaving a length of yarn, fasten off.

Finishing

With tapestry needle, starting at base of Rnd 9, sew stripe centered around ball, ending at opposite side of base of Rnd 9.

Sew 4 spots in place on back on each side of center stripe. ✄

Josephine's Coronation Gown

Continued from page 151

Row 28: Ch 3, dc in each st across, fasten off.

Top

Row 1: Attach Spanish red in rem lp on opposite side of foundation ch, ch 1, sc in each ch across, turn. (18 sc)

Row 2: Ch 1, sc in each sc across, turn.

Row 3: Ch 25, sk first 6 sc of Row 2, sc in each of next 6 sc, ch 25, sl st in last st of Row 2, do not turn.

Edging

Rnd 1 (RS): Ch 1, working across ends of rows, sc evenly sp down side edge of cape, 3 sc in corner st, sc in each st across bottom edge, 3 sc in corner st, sc evenly sp up side edge, sc in each ch and each sc of Row 3, join in beg sc, fasten off.

Row 2 (RS): Attach white/gold in side edge in line with Row 1 of top and edging, ch 1, sc in each sc around to opposite edge, working 3 sc in each center corner sc, fasten off.

BARBIE® is a trademark owned by and used with permission of Mattel, Inc. © 2002 Mattel, Inc. All Rights Reserved.

Row 3 (RS): Attach gold/gold in first sc of Row 5, ch 1, sc in each sc down side edge, 3 dc in center corner st, dc in each sc across bottom edge, 3 dc in center corner sc, sc in each rem sc of Row 5, fasten off.

Place cape on doll by slipping arms through ch-25 sps of top.

Crown

Row 1: With gold/gold, ch 41, sc in 2nd ch from hook, sc in each rem ch across, turn. (40 sc)

Row 2: Ch 1, sc in each of next 15 sts, hdc in next st, dc in each of next 2 sts, tr in each of next 4 sts, dc in each of next 2 sts, hdc in next st, sc in each of next 15 sts, turn.

Row 3: Ch 1, sc in each of next 15 sc, [ch 2, sc in next st] 10 times, ch 2, sc in each of next 15 sts, do not turn.

Row 4: Sc evenly sp across ends of rows, working in rem lps across opposite side of foundation ch, sc in each of next 15 chs, [ch 2, sc in next ch] 10 times, ch 2, sc in each of next 15 chs, fasten off.

Glue a 4½-inch length of sequins centered over Row 1 of crown. Arrange doll's hair as desired. Place crown around head and measure for fastener; sew snap fastener at center back. Place on doll.

If desired, use straight pins to attach rem 2 gold beads to doll's ears for earrings. ✄

Pastel Sunset Sling Purse

Continued from page 153

centered under flower button on opposite side of flap and in line for closure on purse.

Pocket

Row 1: Beg at top with larger hook and sherbet swirl, ch 14, sc in 2nd ch from hook, sc in each rem ch across, turn. (13 sc)

Row 2: Ch 1, sc in each sc across, turn.

Rows 3 & 4: Rep Row 2.

Rows 5 & 6: With pastel blue, rep Row 2.

Rows 7–10: With sherbet swirl, rep Row 2.

Rows 11 & 12: With pastel blue, rep Row 2.

Rows 13–16: With sherbet swirl, rep Row 2.

Row 17: With pastel blue, rep Row 2.

Row 18: Ch 1, sc dec over next 2 sc, sc in each sc across to last 2 sc, sc dec over next 2 sc, turn. (11 sc)

Rows 19 & 20: With sherbet swirl, rep Row 18. (7 sc)

Row 21: Ch 1, sc in each of next 2 sc, 2 sc in next sc, sc in next sc, 2 sc in next sc, sc in each of next 2 sc, turn. (9 sc)

Row 22: Ch 1, sc in first sc, sc dec over next 2 sc, sc in next sc, 2 sc in next sc, sc in next sc, sc dec over next 2 sc, sc in next sc, fasten off. (8 sc)

Rnd 23: Attach pastel blue in opposite side of foundation ch, ch 1, sc in same st as beg ch-1, [ch 1, sk next st, sc in next st] 6 times, sl st evenly sp around rem outer edge, join in beg sc, leaving a length of yarn, fasten off.

Position pocket centered on back of purse; with rem length, sew to purse. ✄

Fashion Favorites

From little floral pins, to ponchos and elegant wraps, to snuggly warm sweaters, this chapter provides a selection of fashion favorites for young and old alike!

Sweet Scallops Cardigan

Design by Melissa Leapman

Skill Level: Intermediate

Size: Finished bust measurement: 35 (40, 45, 49¾, 54½) inches

Instructions are given for smallest size, with larger sizes in parentheses. When only 1 number is given, it applies to all sizes.

Materials

► Plymouth Wildflower DK 51 percent cotton/49 percent acrylic yarn (1¾ oz per skein): 18 (19, 20, 21, 22) skeins salmon #52

► Size F/5 crochet hook or size needed to obtain gauge

► Size E/4 crochet hook

► 6 (¾-inch) buttons

► Tapestry needle

Gauge

With larger hook, 20 sts and 16 rows = 4 inches

Check gauge to save time.

Pattern Notes

Weave in loose ends as work progresses.

Ch 3 counts as first dc throughout.

Textured Pattern

Foundation row (RS): Sc in 4th ch from hook, dc in next ch, [sc in next ch, dc in next ch] rep across, turn.

Row 1: Ch 1, sc in first dc, [dc in next sc, sc in next dc] rep across, turn.

Row 2: Ch 3, [sc in dc, dc in sc] rep across, turn.

Rep Rows 1 and 2 for pattern.

Back

With larger hook, ch 87 (99, 111, 123, 135), work in textured pattern on 85 (97, 109, 121, 133) sts until piece measures approximately 12½ (13, 13, 13½, 14) inches from beg, ending with a WS row.

Armhole shaping

Sl st across first 9 sts, ch 3, continue in established pattern until 8 sts rem in row, turn, leaving rem sts unworked. (69, 81, 93, 105, 117 sts)

Continue even until piece measures approximately 20 (21, 21, 22, 23) inches from beg, ending with a WS row.

Neck shaping

With RS facing, work across next 17 (23, 29, 35, 41) sts, turn, leaving rem sts unworked.

Continue even until piece measures approximately 21 (22, 22, 23, 24) inches from beg, fasten off.

With RS facing, sk next 35 sts for neckline opening, attach yarn with sl st in next st and rep previous neck shaping.

Left Front

With larger hook, ch 45 (51, 57, 63, 69), work even in textured pattern on 43 (49, 55, 61, 67) sts until piece measures approximately 12½ (13, 13, 13½, 14) inches from beg, ending with a WS row.

Armhole shaping

Sl st across first 9 sts, ch 3, continue in textured pattern on 35 (41, 53, 59) sts until piece measures approximately 13 (14, 14, 15, 16) inches from beg, ending with a RS row

Neck shaping

Dec 1 st at neckline edge at beg of next row. (34, 40, 46, 52, 58 sts)

[Dec 1 st at neck edge every row] 8 times, [dec 1 st at neck edge every other row] 9 times. (17, 23, 29, 35, 41 sts)

Continue even until piece measures the same as back to shoulder, fasten off.

Right Front

Work as for left front until piece measures approximately 12½ (13, 13, 13½, 14) inches from beg, ending with a WS row.

Armhole shaping

Work in established pattern across row until 8 sts rem, turn, leaving rem sts unworked.

Complete right front as left front.

Sleeve
Make 2

With larger hook, ch 45 (45, 51, 51, 51), work textured pattern, inc 1 st each side every other row 9 (13, 8, 12, 20) times, then every 4th row 12 (11, 13, 11, 6) times. (85, 91, 91, 95, 101 sts)

Continue even until sleeve measures approximately 19 (20¼, 19½, 19½, 18½) inches from beg, fasten off.

Back Lower Border

Row 1: With RS facing and smaller hook, attach yarn with a sl st in first st, ch 2, working along opposite side of foundation ch,

Continued on page 163

Delicate Cardigan
Instructions begin on page 162

Sweet Scallops Cardigan

Delicate Cardigan

Design by Melissa Leapman
Photo on page 161

Skill Level: Intermediate

Size: Finished bust measurement: 38 (42, 46, 50) inches

Instructions are given for smallest size, with larger sizes in parentheses. When only 1 number is given, it applies to all sizes.

Materials

► Coats & Clark Lustersheen sport weight yarn (1¾ oz per ball): 15 (16, 17, 18) balls vanilla #7

► Size E/4 crochet hook or size needed to obtain gauge

► Size C/2 crochet hook

► 1-inch button

► Tapestry needle

Stitch this beautiful cardigan for yourself or to give as a gift. Its delicate border and simple style give it real appeal!

Gauge

With larger hook, 24 dc and 12 rows = 4 inches

Check gauge to save time.

Pattern Notes

Weave in loose ends as work progresses.

Ch 3 counts as first dc throughout.

Delicate Pattern

Foundation row (RS): 3 dc in 5th ch from hook, [sk next 2 chs, 3 dc in next ch] rep across, ending with sk next ch, dc in next ch, turn.

Pattern row: Ch 3, sk first 2 dc, [3 dc in next dc, sk next 2 dc] rep across, ending with sk next dc, dc in 3rd of turning ch-3, turn.

Back

Row 1: With larger hook, ch 115 (127, 139, 151), work in delicate pattern on 113 (125, 137, 149) sts until piece measures approximately 17½ inches from beg, ending with a WS row.

Armhole shaping

Sl st across first 6 sts, ch 3, sk next 2 dc, continue in pattern across row until 6 dc rem in row, ending row with dc in next dc, turn, leaving rem sts unworked. (101, 113, 125, 137) sts

Continue even until piece measures approximately 25 (25½, 26, 26½) inches from beg, ending with a WS row.

Neck shaping

With RS facing, ch 3, sk first 2 dc, *3 dc in next dc, sk next 2 dc, rep from * 8 (9, 10, 11) times, sk next 2 dc, dc in next dc, turn.

Continue even until piece measures approximately 26 (26½, 27, 27½) inches from beg, fasten off.

For 2nd neck shaping, with RS facing, sk center 41 dc for neck opening, attach yarn with a sl st in next dc, ch 3, complete the same as for first neck shaping.

Left Front

With larger hook, ch 58 (64, 70, 76), work even in delicate pattern on 56 (62, 68, 74) sts until piece measures approximately 17½ inches from beg, ending with a WS row.

Armhole shaping

Sl st in next 6 sts, ch 3, sk next 2 dc, continue in pattern to end of row.

Continue even on 50 (56, 62, 68) sts until piece measures approximately 23½ (24, 24½, 25) inches from beg, ending with a RS row.

Neck shaping

Row 1 (WS): Sl st in next 15 sts, ch 3, *sk next 2 dc, 3 dc in next dc, rep from * across, ending with sk next 2 dc, dc in 3rd ch of turning ch-3, turn.

Row 2: Ch 3, work in pattern until 5 sts rem on row, ending with sk next 2 dc, yo, insert hook in next dc, yo, draw up a lp, yo, draw through 2 lps on hook, sk next dc, yo, insert hook into 3rd ch of turning ch-3, draw up a lp, yo, draw through 2 lps on hook, yo, draw through all 3 lps on hook, turn.

Row 3: Ch 3, sk dec st and next dc, *3 dc in next dc, sk next 2 dc, rep from * across, ending with sk next 2 dc, dc in 3rd ch of turning ch-3, turn.

[Rep Rows 2 and 3] once, then work even until piece measures same as back, fasten off.

Right Front

Work the same as left front until piece measures approximately 17½ inches from beg, ending with a WS row, turn.

Armhole shaping

Work in established pattern until 8 sts rem in row, ending with sk next 2 dc, dc in next dc, turn leaving rem sts unworked.

Continue even on 50 (56, 62, 68) sts until piece measures approximately 23½ (24, 24½, 25) inches from beg, ending with a RS row.

Neck shaping

Row 1 (WS): Work in pattern until 17 sts rem in row, ending with sk next 2 dc, dc in next dc, leaving rem sts unworked, turn.

Row 2: Ch 2, sk first 3 sts, dc in next dc, [sk next 2

dc, 3 dc in next dc] rep across, ending with sk next 2 dc, dc in 3rd ch of turning ch-3, turn.

Row 3: Ch 3, work in pattern until 3 sts rem in row, ending with sk next dc, dc in next dc, leaving rem sts unworked, turn.

[Rep Rows 2 and 3] once, finish as for left front.

Sleeve
Make 2

With larger hook, ch 52 (58, 58, 64), work even in delicate pattern on 50 (56, 56, 62) sts for 2 rows.

Work next 2 rows with 2 dc in first dc, sk next dc, 3 dc in next dc, [sk next 2 dc, 3 dc in next dc] rep across, ending with sk next dc, 3 dc in top of turning ch-3, ch 3, turn. For next row, sk first dc, [3 dc in next dc, sk next 2 dc] rep across, ending with 3 dc in next dc, dc in 3rd of turning ch.

Work 3 (3, 2, 2) rows even.

Rep last 5 (5, 4, 4) rows 8 (8, 9, 9) more times. (104, 110, 116, 122 sts).

Continue even until sleeve measures approximately 19½ (19, 18, 17½) inches from beg, fasten off.

Lower Back Border

Row 1 (RS): With smaller hook, attach yarn with sl st in first st, working across opposite side of foundation ch, ch 1, sc in each ch across, turn. (113, 125, 137, 149 sts)

Row 2: Ch 3, sk first 2 sts, [3 dc in next sc, sk next 2 sc] rep across, ending with sk next sc, dc in last sc, turn.

Row 3: Ch 3, sk first 2 dc, [dc in next dc, ch 6, sl st in 3rd ch from hook, 3 dc around post of last dc made, sk next 2 dc] rep across, ending with dc in next dc, ch 6, sl st in 3rd ch from hook, 3 dc around post of last dc, sk next dc, dc in 3rd ch of turning ch-3, fasten off.

Lower Front Border

Row 1 (RS): With smaller hook, attach yarn in opposite side of foundation ch, ch 1, work 56 (62, 68, 74) sts across, turn.

Rows 2 & 3: Rep Rows 2 and 3 of lower back border.

Lower Sleeve Border

Row 1 (RS): With smaller hook, attach yarn with a sl st to first st, working across opposite side of foundation ch, ch 1, work 50 (56, 56, 62) sc across, turn.

Rows 2 & 3: Rep Rows 2 and 3 of lower back border.

Assembly
Sew shoulder seams; sew center top of sleeve at center shoulder seam. Sew side and sleeve seams.

Front Trim

Row 1 (RS): With smaller hook, attach yarn to lower right front edge, ch 1, sc evenly sp up right front, around neckline and down left front, turn.

Row 2: Ch 1, sc in each sc up left front, around neckline and down right front, turn.

Row 3: Ch 1, sc in each sc up right front to top neckline corner, ch 5 (buttonhole lp), sc in each rem sc around neckline and down left front, fasten off. Sew button opposite buttonhole lp. ✄

Sweet Scallops Cardigan

Continued from page 160

sk next 2 chs, *[{dc, ch 1} 4 times, dc] in next ch, sk next 5 chs, rep from * across, ending with [{dc, ch 1} 4 times, dc] in next ch, sk next 2 chs, hdc in last ch, turn.

Row 2: Ch 1, sc in first st, *[sc in next ch-1 sp, ch 3] 3 times, sc in next ch-1 sp, rep from * across, ending row with sc in 2nd of turning ch-2, turn.

Row 3: Ch 3, sk first 2 sc, sk next ch-3 sp, sk next sc, *[{dc, ch 1} 4 times, dc] in next ch-3 sp, sk next 2 ch-3 sps, rep from * across, ending with dc in last sc, turn.

Rep Rows 2 and 3 until border measures approximately 2 inches from beg, ending with Row 3, fasten off.

Front Lower Border
Make 2

Work as for back lower border.

Sleeve Lower Border
Make 2

Work as for back lower border.

Assembly

Sew shoulder seams; sew center top of sleeve at center shoulder seam and sew sleeve and side seams.

Front Borders

Row 1 (RS): With smaller hook, attach yarn to lower right front edge, ch 1, sc evenly sp up right front, around neckline and down left front, working 2 sc at beg of each front neck shaping and dec 1 sc at beg of each back neck shaping, turn.

Row 2: Ch 1, sc in each sc, inc at each front neckline and dec at each back neck shaping to keep work flat, turn.

Rep Row 2 until border measures ½ inch from beg, then place 6 markers along right front, making the first and last ¼ inch from upper and lower edges.

Continue to rep Row 2 and make buttonholes with ch 3, sk next 3 sts at each of the 6 marker st.

Continue in sc, working 3 sc in each ch-3 sp. When border measures approximately 1 inch, fasten off.

Sew buttons opposite buttonholes. ✄

Crocheted Flower Pin

Design by Sue Childress

Skill Level: Beginner

Size:
Flower: 3 inches in diameter

Leaf: 2 inches in length

Materials
- ► Trendsetter Yarns Sunshine (95 yds per ball): 30 yds pink
- ► Grignasco cotton size 5 (200 yds per ball): 5 yds dark green
- ► Size D/3 crochet hook or size needed to obtain gauge
- ► 1-inch pin back
- ► Hot-glue gun
- ► ½-inch rhinestone shank button

Flower pins are a revived fashion favorite. Make a number of them to coordinate with your wardrobe or to give as gifts!

Gauge
Work evenly and consistently

Pattern Note
Weave in loose ends as work progresses.

Flower
Rnd 1: With pink, ch 4, 19 dc in 3rd ch from hook, join in 4th ch of beg ch-4. (20 dc)

Rnd 2: Working in back lps this rnd only, ch 1, sc in same st as beg ch, [ch 3, sc in next st] rep around, do not join. (20 ch-3 sps)

Rnd 3: Working in rem front lps of Rnd 1, [ch 3, sc in next st] rep around, do not join. (20 ch-3 sps)

Rnd 4: Working around post of dc sts of Rnd 1, [ch 3, sc around post of next dc] rep around, sl st to join in first ch of ch-3 of Rnd 4, fasten off.

Leaf
Rnd 1: With dark green, ch 10, hdc in 3rd ch from hook, hdc in each of next 2 chs, 2 dc in each of next 2 chs, tr in each of next 2 chs, 6 tr in last ch, working on opposite side of foundation ch, tr in each of next 2 chs, 2 dc in each of next 2 chs, hdc in each of next 3 chs, join in top of beg ch, fasten off.

Finishing
Glue button to center front of flower; glue leaf in place on underside of flower; glue pin back to center back of flower. ✄

Flower Barrettes

Designs by Jo Hanna Dzikowski

Skill Level: Beginner

Size: 2¼ inches long

Materials

- ⅛-inch-wide satin ribbon: 10 yds cream, 5 yds avocado
- ⅛-inch-wide metallic ribbon: 10 yds gold
- Size C/2 crochet hook or size needed to obtain gauge
- 3 (5mm) yellow pearl beads
- 3 gold 2¼-inch barrettes
- Hot-glue gun
- Sewing needle and thread needle

Gauge

2 = ½ inch; 2 rows = ½ inch
Check gauge to save time.

Pattern Notes

Weave in loose ends as work progresses.

Join rnds with a sl st unless otherwise stated.

Barrette Base

Make 1 each, avocado, metallic gold and cream

Row 1: Ch 4, sc in 2nd ch from hook, sc in each rem ch across, turn. (3 sc)

Rows 2–10: Ch 1, sc in each sc across, turn.

Row 11: Ch 1, sc in first sc, ch 2, sk next sc, sc in last sc, fasten off.

Rose Bud No. 1

Make 1 each metallic gold and cream

Rnd 1: Ch 4, sl st to join to form a ring, [ch 3, 2 dc in ring, sl st in ring] 5 times, fasten off. (5 petals)

Rose Bud No. 2

Make 1

Rnd 1: With cream, ch 4, sl st to join to form a ring, ch 1, 8 sc in ring, join in beg sc. (8 sc)

Rnd 2: Working in back lps only, [ch 6, sl st in same st, ch 6, sl st in next st] rep around, fasten off.

Finishing

Open barrette, sl ch-2 sp of

These pretty flower barrettes are as fun as they are functional. Each one takes less than an hour so you can make as many as you want!

avocado base onto back end of barrette. Cover top of barrette with glue and press base in place. Sew bead to center of cream rose bud No. 1 and glue rose to center of barrette. Rep in same manner with rem piece, attaching metallic base with cream rose bud No. 2 and cream base with metallic flower. ✂

Fingerless Bridal Gloves

Design by Shirley Patterson

Skill Level: Beginner

Size: 3½ inches across palm

Materials

▶ Crochet cotton size 10: 350 yds white

▶ Size 6 steel crochet hook or size needed to obtain gauge

▶ 2 yellow ribbon roses

▶ 2 white rubber bands slightly smaller than wrist

▶ Tapestry needle

Something old, something new. … These fingerless bridal gloves would make a unique gift for the new bride!

Gauge

4 dc cls = 1 inch; 4 cl rnds = 1 inch

Check gauge to save time.

Pattern Notes

Weave in loose ends as work progresses.

Join rnds with a sl st unless otherwise stated.

When rnd begins with a 3-dc cl, beg ch-2 does not count as a st.

Gloves are worked from fingers toward wrist.

For larger glove size use steel hook size 6.

To achieve a proper fit, measure width of palm, then work a swatch of 3-dc cl sts and measure how many cl sts per inch.

Pattern Stitches

3-dc cl: [Yo hook, insert hook in indicated st, yo, draw up a lp, yo, draw through 2 lps on hook] 3 times, yo, draw through all 4 lps on hook.

2-tr cl: Ch 4, [yo hook twice, insert hook in same st as beg ch-4, yo, draw up a lp, {yo, draw through 2 lps on hook} twice] twice, yo, draw through all 3 lps on hook, ch 4, sl st in same st as 2-tr cl.

Glove

Make 2

Rnd 1: Ch 60, using care not to twist ch, join to form a ring, ch 2, 3-dc cl in same ch as beg ch-2, ch 1, sk 1 ch, [3-dc cl in next ch, ch 1, sk 1 ch] rep around, join in top of first 3-dc cl. (30 cls; 30 ch-1 sps)

Rnd 2: Sl st into next ch-1 sp, ch 2, 3-dc cl in same ch-1 sp, ch 1, [3-dc cl in next ch-1 sp, ch 1] rep around, join in top of first 3-dc cl. (30 cls; 30 ch-1 sps)

Rnds 3–6: Rep Rnd 2.

Rnd 7: Rep Rnd 2, ending with join in top of first 3-dc cl, do not sl st into ch-1 sp.

Note: At this point, try on for sizing, placing foundation ch at approximately the base of knuckles just before finger openings. Glove should fit just to the beg of thumb. Add or subtract a rnd as needed.

Thumb opening

Row 8: Ch 3 (counts as first dc throughout), [3-dc cl in next ch-1 sp, ch 1] 26 times, dc in top of next 3-dc cl, leaving rem sts unworked, turn. (26 cls)

Row 9: Ch 3, 3-dc cl in ch-1 sp between dc and next 3-dc cl, ch 1, [3-dc cl in next ch-1 sp, ch 1] 25 times, dc in 3rd ch of turning ch-3, turn. (26 cls)

Rnd 10: Ch 3, 3-dc cl in ch-1 sp between dc and next 3-dc cl, ch 1, [3-dc cl in next ch-1 sp, ch 1] 25 times, dc in 3rd ch of beg ch-3, ch 7, join in top of first 3-dc cl of this rnd.

Rnd 11: Sl st into next ch-1 sp, ch 2, 3-dc cl in same ch-1 sp as beg ch-2, ch 1, [3-dc cl in next ch-1 sp, ch 1] 25 times, sk next dc, [3-dc cl in ch-7 sp, ch 1, sk 1 ch] 4 times, join in top of first cl. (30 cls; 30 ch-1 sps)

Rnds 12 & 13: Rep Rnd 2.

Rnd 14: Ch 1, sc in top of each 3-dc cl and in each ch-1 sp around, join in beg sc. (60 sc)

Rnd 15: Holding rubber band next to Rnd 14 and working over band and into sts, ch 1, sc in each sc around, join in beg sc. (60 sc)

Edging

Rnd 16: Work 2-tr cl in same st as joining, sl st in next 2 sts, [2-tr cl, sl st in next 2 sts] rep around, fasten off. (30 tr cls)

Foundation Trim

Rnd 1: Attach cotton in opposite side of foundation ch, ch 1, [sc in each of next 3 sc, ch 3, sl st in top of last sc] rep around, join in beg sc, fasten off.

Thumb Trim

Rnd 1: Attach cotton at Rnd 8 along side, ch 2, [3-dc cl, ch 1] 15 times evenly sp around thumb opening, join in top of first cl. (15 cls; 15 ch-1 sps)

Rnd 2: Ch 1, working in each cl and each ch-1 sp, [sc in each of next 3 sts, ch 3, sl st in top of last sc] rep around, join in beg sc, fasten off.

Finishing

Press gloves as needed. Sew ribbon rose to Rnd 14 of each glove in line with ring finger. ✂

Pearly Purse

Design by Sue Childress

Skill Level: Intermediate

Size: 4¼ x 4½ inches

Materials

► Grignasco cotton size 5 (50 grams per ball): 125 yds white #1

► Size B/1 crochet hook or size needed to obtain gauge

► 108 (6mm) pearl beads

► 2½ x 3½-inch silver purse frame

► 18-inch silver chain

► Tapestry needle

first hdc throughout), 2 hdc in next dc, *[sk next dc, 5 dc in next dc, pearl, sk next dc, sc in next dc] 4 times, sk next dc, 5 dc in next dc, hdc in each of next 2 dc *, 3 hdc in next dc, hdc in each of next 2 dc, 5 dc in next dc, pearl, sk next dc, sc in next dc, [sk next dc, 5 dc in next dc, pearl, sk next dc, sc in next dc] 3 times, sk 1 dc, 5 dc in next dc, hdc in each of next 2 hdc, 2 hdc in next dc, join in 2nd ch of beg ch-2.

Rnd 3: Ch 2, hdc in each of next 2 hdc, *[sk next 2 dc, pearl, sc in next dc, 5 dc in next sc] 4 times, sc in center dc, sk next 2 dc *, hdc in each of next 7 hdc, rep from * to *, hdc in each of next 4 hdc, join in 2nd ch of beg ch-2.

Rnd 4: Ch 2, hdc in each of next 2 hdc, *[5 dc in next sc, pearl, sc in 3rd dc] 4 times, 5 dc in next sc *, hdc in each of next 7 hdc, rep from * to *, hdc in

Continued on page 186

Gauge

[5 dc, sc, 5 dc] = 1½ inches; 3 pattern rows = 1 inch

Check gauge to save time.

Pattern Notes

Weave in loose ends as work progresses.

Join rnds with a sl st unless otherwise stated.

Pattern Stitch

Pearl: Push up a pearl bead, hold in front of work and work into indicated st.

Purse

Thread beads onto cotton.

Rnd 1: Ch 20, 3 dc in 4th ch from hook, dc in each of next 15 chs, 7 dc in last ch, working on opposite side of foundation ch, dc in each of next 15 chs, 3 dc in same ch as first 3 dc, join in top of beg ch. (44 dc)

Rnd 2: Ch 2 (counts as

Mesh Snoods

Designs by Shirley Patterson

Skill Level: Beginner

Size: One size fits all

Materials

▶ Crochet cotton size 10: 75 yds each white and ecru

▶ Metallic thread size 5: 35 yds each gold and silver

▶ Sizes 3 and 5 steel crochet hooks or size needed to obtain gauge

▶ 4–6-inch barrette for each snood

▶ Tapestry needle

Gauge

Gold metallic flower = 2 inches; silver metallic flower = 1¾ inches

Check gauge to save time.

Pattern Notes

Weave in loose ends as work progresses.

Join rnds with a sl st unless otherwise stated.

Pattern Stitches

Shell: [2 dc, ch 2, 2 dc] in indicated ch sp.

When a rnd begins with a shell, replace first dc with ch 3.

Sc shell: [2 sc, ch 2, 2 sc] in indicated ch sp.

P: Ch 3, sl st in top of last st.

Gold Metallic Snood

Flower

Rnd 1: With larger hook and gold metallic, ch 6, [hdc, ch 3] 5 times in first ch of ch-6, join in 3rd ch of beg ch-6. (6 hdc; 6 ch-3 sps)

Rnd 2: Ch 1, [sc, hdc, 3 dc, hdc, sc] in each ch-3 sp around, join in beg sc. (6 petals)

Rnd 3: Working behind petals of previous rnd, [sl st in vertical strand of st between petals, ch 4] rep around, join in beg st. (6 ch-4 sps)

Rnd 4: Sl st into ch sp, ch 1, [sc, hdc, 5 dc, hdc, sc] in each ch-4 sp around, join in beg sc.

Rnd 5: Working behind petals of previous rnd, [sl st in vertical strand of st between petals, ch 5] rep around, join in beg st. (6 ch-5 sps)

Rnd 6: Sl st into ch sp, ch 1, [sc, hdc, 7 dc, hdc, sc] in each ch-5 sp around, join in beg sc.

Rnd 7: Working behind petals of previous rnd, [sl st in vertical strand of st between petals, ch 6] rep around, join in beg st.

Rnd 8: Sl st into ch sp, ch 1, [sc, hdc, 9 dc, hdc, sc] in each ch-6 sp around, join in beg sc, fasten off.

Snood

Rnd 9: With larger hook, attach white cotton to center dc at center of any petal on flower, ch 1, sc in same dc as beg ch, ch 9, [sc in center dc of next petal, ch 9] 5 times, join in beg sc. (6 sc; 6 ch-9 sps)

Rnd 10: Ch 3, *[dc, ch 3, dc] in sc, sk next 2 chs, [dc, ch 3, dc] in next ch, sk next 3 chs, [dc, ch 3, dc] in next ch, sk next 2 chs, rep from * 3 times, **[sc, ch 3, sc] in next sc, sk next 2 chs, [sc, ch 3, sc] in next ch, sk next 3 chs, [sc, ch 3, sc] in next ch, sk next 2 chs] rep from **, sk beg ch-3, join in top of first dc.

Rnd 11: Sl st into ch-3 sp, [shell in ch-3 sp, {ch 5, sc in next ch sp} twice, ch 5] 4 times, [sc shell in next ch-3 sp, {ch 3, sc in next ch sp} twice, ch 2] twice,

join in top of beg shell.

Rnd 12: Sl st into ch-2 sp of shell, [shell in ch-2 sp of shell, {ch 5, sc in next ch sp, p} 3 times, ch 5] 4 times, [sc shell in ch-2 sp of next shell, {ch 3, sc in next ch sp, p} 3 times, ch 3] twice, join in top of beg shell.

Rnd 13: Sl st into ch-2 sp of shell, [shell in ch-2 sp of shell, {ch 5, sc in next ch sp, p} 4 times, ch 5] 4 times, [sc shell in ch-2 sp of next shell, {ch 3, sc in next ch sp, p} 4 times, ch 3] twice, join in top of beg shell.

Rnd 14: Sl st into ch-2 sp of shell, [shell in ch-2 sp of shell, {ch 5, sc in next ch sp, p} 5 times, ch 5] 4 times, [sc shell in ch-2 sp of next shell, {ch 3, sc in next ch sp, p} 5 times, ch 3] twice, join in top of beg shell.

Rnd 15: Sl st into ch-2 sp of shell, [shell in ch-2 sp of shell, {ch 5, sc in next ch sp, p} 6 times, ch 5] 4 times, [sc shell in ch-2 sp of next shell, {ch 3, sc in next ch sp, p} 6 times, ch 3] twice, join in top of beg shell.

Rnd 16: Sl st into ch-2 sp of shell, [shell in ch-2 sp of shell, {ch 5, sc in next ch sp, p} 7 times, ch 5] 4 times, [sc shell in ch-2 sp of next shell, {ch 3, sc in next ch sp, p} 7 times, ch 3] twice, join in top of beg shell.

Rnd 17: Sl st into ch-2 sp of shell, ch 1, [sc in ch-2 sp of shell, p, ch 3, {dc in next ch sp, p, ch 3} rep across until ch-2 sp of next shell] rep around, join in beg sc, fasten off.

Finishing

Thread tapestry needle with double strand of cotton 18 inches in length.

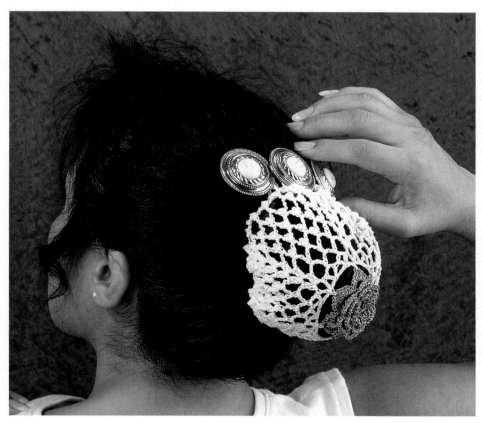

Weave through ch sps of Rnd 17; secure ends and weave into piece.

Thread tapestry needle with a long length of white cotton doubled. Open the barrette and securely sew sc st area of 2nd and 3rd dc shells of Rnd 17 to barrette. This will position the small shells at the bottom of the snood.

Silver Metallic Snood

Flower

Rnds 1–8: With smaller hook and silver metallic thread, rep Rnds 1–8 of flower for gold metallic snood.

Snood

Rnd 9: With smaller hook, attach ecru at back between dc sts of Rnd 8 in ch st of Rnd 7, ch 1, sc in same sp as beg ch, ch 7, [sc at center back between dc of Rnd 8 in ch st of Rnd 7, ch 7] rep around, join in beg sc. (6 ch-7 sps)

Rnd 10: Ch 1, [sc, hdc, 11 dc, hdc, sc] in each ch-7 sp around, join in beg sc.

Rnd 11: Sl st across to first dc of 11-dc group, ch 1, [sc in first dc, p, ch 5, sk next 4 sts, sc in next dc, p, ch 5, sk next 4 sts, sc in next dc, p, ch 5] rep around, join in beg sc. (18 ch-5 sps)

Rnds 12–23: Sl st into center of ch-5 sp, ch 3 (counts as first dc throughout), p, ch 5, [dc in next ch sp, p, ch 5] 11 times, [sc in next ch sp, p, ch 5] 5 times, sc in last ch-5 sp, p, ch 2, dc in beg dc.

Rnd 24: Ch 1, 3 sc over same sp as beg ch-1, sc in next dc, [5 sc in next ch-5 sp, sc in next dc or sc] rep around, ending with 2 sc in same ch sp as beg 3-sc group, join in beg sc, fasten off.

Finishing

Thread tapestry needle with a 36-inch-long double strand of ecru cotton. Weave through ch sps of Rnd 23; pull to desired opening. Knot ends to secure and weave ends into Rnd 24; fasten off.

Thread tapestry needle with a double length of ecru cotton. Open barrette and position sc sts of Rnds 12–23 at bottom edge and center dc sts of Rnd 23 at center of barrette and sew in place. ✂

Love Knot Wrap

Design by Diane Poellot

Skill Level: Intermediate

Size: 23 x 72 inches

Materials

► Caron Simply Soft worsted weight yarn: 10 oz off-white #9702

► Size J/10 crochet hook or size needed to obtain gauge

► Tapestry needle

Like a silken web, this wrap is intriguing with its delicate stitch—a perfect accessory for those cool summer evenings!

Gauge

Love knot = 1 inch

Check gauge to save time.

Pattern Notes

Weave in loose ends as work progresses.

Join rnds with a sl st unless otherwise stated.

Pattern Stitch

Love knot (lk): Draw up a lp approximately ¾ inch,

sc over back strand of lp.

Wrap

Row 1: Ch 2, sc in 2nd ch from hook, 28 lks, turn.

Row 2: Sc in 4th sc from hook, 2 lks, [sk next sc, sc in next sc, 2 lks] rep across, turn.

Row 3: 3 lks, sc in next sc, [2 lks, sk next sc, sc in next sc] rep across, turn.

Rows 4–72: Rep Row 3,

at the end of Row 72, do not turn.

Edging

Rnd 1: Ch 3, 2 lks, dc in same st (for corner), working across long edge, 1 lk, dc in next sc, [2 lks, sk next sc, dc in next sc] rep across to corner, [dc, 2 lks, dc] in corner, working

across short end, 1 lk, dc in next sc, [2 lks, sk next sc, dc in next sc] rep across to corner, [dc, 2 lks, dc] in corner, continue in same manner on rem 2 sides, join in top of beg ch-3.

Rnd 2: Ch 1, sc in same st as beg ch, [lk, sc in sc of next lk] rep around, join in beg sc, fasten off. ✄

Bobbles Sweater & Hat

Designs by Ann E. Smith

Skill Level: Beginner

Size: 8–10 small, (12–14 medium, 16–18 large) Instructions are given for smallest size with larger sizes in parentheses. When only 1 number is given, it applies to all sizes.

Materials

► Lion Brand Jiffy Quick & Easy Mohair-Look yarn (115 yds per skein: 10 (11, 13) skeins Daytona #354

► Size K/10½ crochet hook or size needed to obtain gauge

► Size J/10 crochet hook

► 6 (1-inch) clear toggle buttons

► Tapestry needle

Gauge

In body pattern with larger hook, 15 sts = 6 inches; 12 rows = 4 inches

Check gauge to save time.

Pattern Note

Weave in loose ends as work progresses.

Body Pattern

Row 1 (WS): Ch 1, sc in each of first 3 sts, [working in back lp of next st only, {sl st, ch 3, sl st} (for bobble), sc in each of next 3 sts] rep across, turn.

Row 2: Ch 1, sc in each of first 3 sc, [sc in rem lp behind bobble, sc in each of next 3 sc] rep across, turn.

Rows 3 & 4: Ch 1, sc in each sc across, turn.

Row 5: Ch 1, sc in first sc, *working in back lp only of next sc, [sl st, ch 3, sl st] (for bobble) **, sc in each of next 3 sc, rep from * across, ending last rep at **, sc in last sc, turn.

Row 6: Ch 1, sc in first sc, *sc in rem lp behind bobble **, sc in each of next 3 sc, rep from * across, ending last rep at **, sc in last sc, turn.

Rows 7 & 8: Rep Rows 3 and 4.

Rep Rows 1–8 for body pattern.

This sweater and hat will provide warmth in the cold of winter and makes a great Christmas gift!

Sweater

Body

Row 1 (WS): With larger hook, beg at lower edge above border, ch 84 (92, 100), sc in 2nd ch from hook, sc in each rem ch across, turn. (83, 91, 99 sc)

Row 2: Ch 1, sc in each sc across, turn.

Rep Rows 1–8 of body pattern until piece measures approximately 13 (14½, 16) inches from beg, ending with a WS row.

Right Front

Work in established pattern across next 19 (21, 23) sts, leaving rem sts unworked.

Continue in pattern, [dec 1 sc at armhole edge every row] 3 times. Work even on rem 16 (18, 20) sts to approximately 17 (19, 21) inches from beg, ending with a RS row.

Neck shaping

Work in pattern across, leaving last 4 (6, 6) sts unworked.

Continue in pattern on rem 12 (13, 14) sts to approximately 20 (22, 24) inches from beg, ending with a RS row, fasten off.

Back

With RS facing, attach yarn with sl st in first st next to right front, ch 1, sc in same st as joining, work in established pattern across next 44 (48, 52) sts. (45, 49, 53 sts)

[Dec 1 sc each edge every row] 3 times. Work even on rem 39 (43, 47) sts to same length as right front, ending with a RS row, fasten off.

Left Front

With RS facing, attach yarn with sl st in first st next to back, ch 1, sc in same st as joining, work in established pattern across rem 18 (20, 22) sts. (19, 21, 23 sts)

Continue in pattern, [dec 1 sc at armhole edge every row] 3 times. (16, 18, 20 sts)

To reverse neck shaping, sl st in next 5 (6, 7) sts, ch 1, beg in same st as beg ch, work in pattern across rem 12 (13, 14) sts.

Complete as for right front.

Sleeve
Make 2

Row 1 (WS): Beg at lower edge above cuff with larger hook, ch 20 (24, 24), sc in 2nd ch from hook, sc in each rem ch across, turn. (19, 23, 23 sc)

Row 2: Ch 1, sc in each sc across, turn.

Beg body pattern, including new sts into pattern as they accumulate, [inc 1 st each edge every 4th row] 5 (1, 3) times and then [every 6th row] 3 (6, 5) times. (35, 37, 39 sts)

Continued on page 187

Poncho Perfection

Design by Melissa Leapman

Skill Level: Beginner

Size: One size fits all

Materials

▶ Brown Sheep Co. Cotton Fleece 80 percent pima cotton, 20 percent merino wool worsted weight yarn (215 yds per skein): 11 skeins blue paradise #CW765

▶ Size G/6 crochet hook or size needed to obtain gauge

▶ Size F/5 crochet hook

▶ Scrap of CC yarn or 4 markers

▶ Tapestry needle

Gauge

With larger hook, 4 dc = 1 inch; square = 8¼ inches
Check gauge to save time.

Pattern Notes

Weave in loose ends as work progresses.

Join rnds with a sl st unless otherwise stated.

Pattern Stitch

Triple dec: *Yo hook, insert hook back to front to back again around vertical post of next st, yo, draw up a lp, yo, draw through 2 lps on hook *, yo hook, insert hook front to back to front again around vertical post of next st, yo, draw up a lp, yo, draw through 2 lps on hook, rep from * to *, yo, draw through all 4 lps on hook.

Square

Make 24

Rnd 1 (RS): With larger hook, ch 7, join to form a ring, ch 3 (counts as first dc throughout), 23 dc in ring, join in 3rd ch of beg ch-3. (24 dc)

Rnd 2: Ch 1, sc in same st as beg ch, ch 9, sk next 2 dc, [sc in next dc, ch 9, sk next 2 dc] rep around, join in beg sc. (8 ch-9 lps)

Rnd 3: Sl st into 5th ch of ch-9, ch 3, 6 dc in same ch as beg ch, [7 dc in 5th ch of next ch-9 sp] rep around, join in 3rd ch of beg ch-3. (56 dc)

Rnd 4: Sl st into 4th dc of 7-dc group, ch 1, sc in same dc, ch 9, [sc in 4th dc of next 7-dc group, ch 9] rep around, join in beg sc. (8 ch-9 lps)

Rnd 5: Sl st into next ch sp, ch 3, [5 dc, ch 3, 6 dc] in same ch-9 sp, *9 dc in next ch-9 sp **, [6 dc, ch 3, 6 dc] in next ch-9 sp, rep from * around, ending last rep at **, join in 3rd ch of beg ch-3. (4 ch-3 sps; 84 dc)

Rnd 6: Ch 3, dc in each of next 5 dc, *[2 dc, ch 3, 2 dc] in next ch-3 sp **, dc in each of next 21 dc, rep from * around, ending last rep at **, dc in each of next 15 dc, join in 3rd ch of beg ch-3. (4 ch-3 sps; 100 dc)

Rnd 7: Ch 3, dc in each of next 7 dc, *[2 dc, ch 3, 2 dc] in next ch-3 sp **, dc in each of next 25 dc, rep from * around, ending last rep at **, dc in each of next 17 dc, join in 3rd ch of beg ch-3. (4 ch-3 sps; 116 dc)

Rnd 8: Ch 3, dc in each of next 9 dc, *[2 dc, ch 3, 2 dc] in next ch-3 sp **, dc in each of next 29 dc, rep from * around, ending last rep at **, dc in each of next 19 dc, join in 3rd ch of beg ch-3, fasten off. (4 ch-3 sps; 132 dc)

Assembly

With RS facing, working in back lps only, whip-stitch squares tog in rows of 5 squares each, omitting center square of 3rd row for neckline opening.

Neckline Ribbing

Rnd 1 (RS): With smaller hook, attach yarn in first dc beyond corner ch-3 sp, ch 3 (counts as first dc throughout), dc in each of next 32 dc, dc in corner ch-3 sp, [dc in each of next 33 dc, dc in corner ch-3 sp] rep around, join in top of beg ch-3. (136 dc)

Note: Place a marker on each dc worked in corner ch-3 sp.

Rnd 2: Ch 2 (counts as first dc of ribbing throughout), [fpdc around next st, bpdc around next st] rep around, join in 2nd ch of beg ch-2.

Rnd 3: Ch 2, *[fpdc around fpdc, bpdc around bpdc] rep around until 1 st before marker, triple dec over next 3 sts, rep from * around, join in 2nd ch of beg ch-2.

Rnd 4: Rep Rnd 3, fasten off.

Outer Edging

Rnd 1 (RS): With smaller hook, attach yarn in first dc after any corner ch-3 sp, ch 3 (counts as first dc throughout), dc in each dc, dc in each corner sp of straight edge and dc in each joining of squares around working [2 dc, ch 3, 2 dc] in each of the 4 corner ch-3 sp, join in 3rd ch of beg ch-3. (177 dc each side edge)

Rnd 2: Ch 2, *[fpdc around next st, bpdc around next st] rep across to corner ch-3 sp, [2 dc, ch 3, 2 dc] in corner ch-3 sp,

Continued on page 186

Tweed Hat & Purse

Designs by Sue Childress

Skill Level: Beginner

Size:

Hat: 21 inches in diameter

Purse: 8 x 9 inches plus handle

Materials

► Madil Cotton Cable Euro Yarns sport weight (50 grams per ball): 1 ball each red #562 (A), purple #557 (B), gold #565 (C), green #563 (D) and turquoise #574 (E)

► Trendsetter Yarns String-Along Yarn (20 grams per ball): 2 balls charm #1000

► Size C/2 crochet hook or size needed to obtain gauge

► Glue

► Tapestry needle

Gauge

6 sts = 1 inch

Check gauge to save time.

Pattern Notes

Weave in loose ends as work progresses.

Join rnds with a sl st unless otherwise stated.

Hat

Rnd 1: With E, ch 4, sl st to join to form a ring, ch 3 (counts as first dc throughout), 11 dc in ring, join in 3rd ch of beg ch-3. (12 dc)

Rnd 2: Ch 3, dc in same st as beg ch, 2 dc in each rem dc around, join in 3rd ch of beg ch-3. (24 dc)

Rnd 3: Ch 3, 2 dc in next dc, [dc in next dc, 2 dc in next dc] rep around, join in 3rd ch of beg ch-3. (36 dc)

Rnd 4: Ch 3, 2 dc in next dc, [dc in next dc, 2 dc in next dc] rep around, join in 3rd ch of beg ch-3. (54 dc)

Rnd 5: Ch 3, dc in next dc, 2 dc in next dc, [dc in each of next 2 dc, 2 dc in next dc] rep around, join in 3rd ch of beg ch-3. (72 dc)

Rnd 6: Ch 3, dc in each of next 2 dc, 2 dc in next dc, [dc in each of next 3 dc, 2 dc in next dc] rep around, join in 3rd ch of beg ch-3. (90 dc)

Rnd 7: Ch 3, dc in same st as beg ch-3, dc in each of next 4 dc, [2 dc in next dc, dc in each of next 4 dc] rep around, join in 3rd ch of beg ch-3. (108 dc)

Rnd 8: Ch 3, [dc in each of next 14 dc, 2 dc in next dc] 7 times, dc in each of next 2 dc, join in 3rd ch of beg ch-3. (115 dc)

Rnd 9: Ch 3, bpdc around each dc around, join in 3rd ch of beg ch-3, fasten off.

Rnd 10: Attach 1 strand each C and charm in any dc, ch 3, dc in each dc around, join in 3rd ch of beg ch-3, drop charm, do not fasten off.

Rnd 11: Continuing with C only, ch 3, dc in each dc around, join in 3rd ch of beg ch-3, fasten off C.

Note: Rnds 10 and 11 establish pattern for hat, continue in the following color sequence.

Rnd 12: With B and charm, rep Rnd 10.

Rnd 13: With B only, rep Rnd 11.

Rnd 14: With D and charm, rep Rnd 10.

Rnd 15: With D only, rep Rnd 11.

Rnd 16: With A and charm, rep Rnd 10.

Rnd 17: With A only, rep Rnd 11, do not fasten off A.

Rnd 18: Ch 1, [sc in each of next 6 dc, sc dec over next 2 dc] 14 times, sc in each of next 3 sc, join in beg sc, fasten off A.

Rnd 19: Attach C, ch 1, [sc in each of next 5 sc, sc dec over next 2 sc] 14 times, sc in each of next 3 sc, join in beg sc, fasten off C. (87 sc)

Rnd 20: Attach B, ch 1, sc in each sc around, join in beg sc, fasten off.

Rnd 21: Attach D, rep Rnd 20.

Purse

Rnd 1: With D, ch 33, 3 dc in 4th ch from hook, dc in each of next 28 chs, 7 dc in last ch, working on opposite side of foundation ch, dc in each of next 28 dc, 3 dc in same st as beg dc, join in top of beg ch. (70 dc)

Rnd 2: Ch 3 (counts as first dc throughout), 2 dc in each of next 3 dc, dc in each of next 28 dc, 2 dc in each of next 3 dc, dc in next dc, 2 dc in each of next 3 dc, dc in each of next 28 dc, 2 dc in each of next 3 dc, join in 3rd ch of beg ch-3. (82 dc)

Rnd 3: Ch 3, bpdc around each dc around, join in 3rd ch of beg ch-3.

Rnd 4: Ch 3, dc in each dc around, join in 3rd ch of beg ch-3.

Rnd 5: With charm and D held tog, ch 3, dc in each dc around, join in 3rd ch of beg ch-3.

Rnd 6: Ch 3, dc in each dc around, join in 3rd ch

of beg ch-3, drop charm, do not fasten off.

Rnd 7: Ch 3, dc in each dc around, join in 3rd ch of beg ch-3, fasten off D.

Rnd 8: With C and charm, ch 3, dc in each dc around, join in 3rd ch of beg ch-3.

Rnd 9: Ch 3, dc in each dc around, join in 3rd ch of beg ch-3, drop charm, do not fasten off.

Rnd 10: With C only, ch 3, dc in each dc around, join in 3rd ch of beg ch-3, fasten off C.

Rnds 11–16: With A and charm, rep Rnd 8.

Rnd 17: With A, rep Rnd 10.

Rnds 18 & 19: With B and charm, rep Rnd 8. At the end of Rnd 19, fasten off charm.

Rnd 20: With B, rep Rnd 10.

Rnd 21: Attach E, ch 1, sc in each dc around, join in beg sc.

Rnd 22: Ch 1, sc in each sc around, join in beg sc, fasten off.

Handle

Note: Make 2 each purple, green, turquoise; make 2 each holding gold and charm tog; make 1 red.

Ch 100, fasten off. Holding all chs tog, knot all ends tog at one end. Separate 1 red ch; twist all rem chs tog. Wrap separate red ch around bundle of chs several times to opposite end; knot all ends tog. Sew ends of handle to inside of purse; glue ends to secure. ✂

Sugar & Spice Pullover

Design by Shirley Zebrowski

Skill Level: Beginner

Size: Child's sizes 2 (4, 6, 8)
Chest: 24 (26, 28, 30) inches
Sleeve length: 6½ (8½, 9½, 10) inches

Materials

► Worsted weight yarn: 7 (9, 10, 11) oz pink/gray tweed

► Size H/8 crochet hook or size needed to obtain gauge

► 5 (¾-inch) pink buttons

► Tapestry needle

Gauge

12 sts = 4 inches
Check gauge to save time.

Pattern Notes

Weave in loose ends as work progresses.

Join rnds with a sl st unless otherwise stated.

Front & Back

Make 2

Row 1: Ch 36 (39, 42, 45), dc in 2nd ch from hook, [sc in next ch, dc in next ch] rep across, turn. (35, 38, 41, 44 sts)

Row 2: Ch 1, sc in dc, [dc in sc, sc in dc] rep across, turn.

Row 3: Ch 2 (counts as first dc), [sc in next dc, dc in next sc] rep across, turn.

Rep Rows 2 and 3 for pattern until piece measures 13½ (15½, 17½, 19½) inches.

First shoulder shaping

Rows 1 & 2: Work in pattern across 11 (12, 13, 14) sts, turn. At the end of Row 2, fasten off.

Second shoulder shaping

Row 1: Sk next 13 (14, 15, 16) sts for neck opening, attach yarn in next st, work in pattern across, turn.

Row 2: Work in pattern across, fasten off.

Sleeve

Make 2

Row 1: Ch 20, (21, 23, 25), dc in 2nd ch from hook, [sc in next ch, dc in next ch] rep across, turn. (19, 20, 22, 24 sts)

Work pattern Rows 2 and 3, inc 1 st in pattern each side edge every 3rd row until 32 (33, 35, 38) sts. Work even in pattern until sleeve measures 6½ (8½, 9½, 10) inches, fasten off.

Pocket

Make 2

Row 1: Ch 12, dc in 2nd ch from hook, [sc in next ch, dc in next ch] rep across, turn. (11 sts)

Work pattern Rows 2 and 3 until pocket measures 4 inches, leaving a length of yarn, fasten off.

Assembly

Sew shoulder seams. Sew center top of sleeve centered over shoulder seam. Sew sleeve and side seams. Sew pockets to front 1½ inches from front bottom of sweater.

Neckline Trim

Rnd 1 (RS): Attach yarn at center back neckline, ch 1, sc evenly sp around neckline opening, join in beg sc.

Rnds 2 & 3: Ch 1, sc in each sc around, join in beg sc, at the end of Rnd 3, fasten off.

Finishing

Sew 3 buttons down center front of sweater. Sew 1 button to inside edge of sweater below pocket.

Use natural sps of pocket to button. ✂

Get ready for school and fall weather with this long pullover. The two front pockets are great for warming little hands or bringing along a little treat!

Rainbow Poncho Set

Designs by Margret Willson

Skill Level: Beginner

Size:

Girl's: Fits sizes 4–10

Doll: Fits 16–18 inch dolls

Materials

► Worsted weight yarn (3½ oz per skein): 2 skeins purple, 1 skein each blue, green, yellow, orange and red

► Size H/8 crochet hook or size needed to obtain gauge

► Tapestry needle

Little girls love to play dress up with their dolls, and this colorful set includes a poncho pattern for 16–18-inch dolls.

Gauge

Rnds 1 and 2 = 2½ inches
Check gauge to save time.

Pattern Notes

Weave in loose ends as work progresses.

Join rnds with a sl st unless otherwise stated.

Pattern Stitches

6-dc dec: *[Yo hook, insert hook in next sp, yo, draw up a lp, yo, draw through 2 lps on hook] twice in same sp, rep from * twice in each of next 2 sps, yo, draw through all 7 lps on hook.

4-dc dec: *[Yo hook, insert hook in next sp, yo, draw up a lp, yo, draw through 2 lps on hook] twice in same sp *, sk dec on previous rnd, rep from * to * once, yo, draw through all 5 lps on hook.

Granny Squares

Make 16 for girl's and 4 for doll

Rnd 1 (RS): With red, ch 4, join to form a ring, ch 3 (counts as first dc through-out), 2 dc in ring, ch 3, [3 dc in ring, ch 3] 3 times, join in 3rd ch of beg ch-3, fasten off.

Rnd 2: Attach orange in any ch-3 sp, ch 3, [2 dc, ch 3, 3 dc] in same ch-3 sp, 3 dc in next sp between 3-dc groups, [{3 dc, ch 3, 3 dc} in next corner ch-3 sp, 3 dc in next sp between 3-dc groups] rep around, join in 3rd ch of beg ch-3, fasten off.

Rnd 3: Attach yellow in any corner ch-3 sp, ch 3, [2 dc, ch 3, 3 dc] in same ch-3 sp, 3 dc in next sp between 3-dc groups, [{3 dc, ch 3, 3 dc} in corner ch-3 sp, 3 dc in each sp between 3-dc groups] rep around, join in 3rd ch of beg ch-3, fasten off.

Rnd 4: With green, rep Rnd 3.

Rnd 5: With blue, rep Rnd 3.

Rnd 6: With purple, rep Rnd 3.

Assembly

Using diagram as a guide and working in back lps only, whipstitch granny squares tog for each doll and girl's poncho.

Doll Bottom Trim

Rnd 1: Attach purple in any dc on bottom edge, ch 1, sc in each st around bottom edge, working 3 sc in each of the 2 corner ch-3 sps, join in beg sc, fasten off.

Girl's Bottom Trim

Rnd 1: Attach purple in center back ch-3 sp at bottom edge, ch 3 (counts as first dc throughout), [2 dc, ch 3, 3 dc] in same ch-3 sp, 3 dc in each sp between dc groups to center front ch-3 sp, [3 dc, ch 3, 3 dc] in center front ch-3 sp, work 3 dc in each sp between dc groups to center back, join in 3rd ch of beg ch-3.

Rnds 2 & 3: Sl st into corner ch-3 sp, ch 3, [2 dc, ch 3, 3 dc] in center back corner ch-3 sp, 3 dc in each sp between dc groups to center front ch-3 sp, [3 dc, ch 3, 3 dc] in center front corner ch-3 sp, 3 dc in each sp between dc groups to center back, join in 3rd ch of beg ch-3, at the end of Rnd 3, fasten off.

Doll & Girl's Neckline Trim

Rnd 1: Attach purple in sp

Continued on page 186

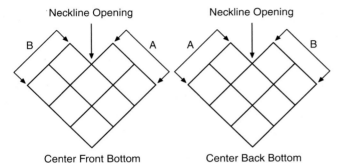

Neckline Opening

B   A   A   B

Center Front Bottom   Center Back Bottom

Girl's Poncho

A

A

Center Front

Doll's Poncho

Bright Bows Beach Bag

Design by Dot Drake

Skill Level: Beginner

Size: 11 x 12 inches

Materials

▶ Coats & Clark Red Heart Kids worsted weight yarn: 5 oz each yellow #2320, turquoise #2850, pink #2734 and 4 oz bikini #2945

▶ Size G/6 crochet hook or size needed to obtain gauge

▶ Size F/5 crochet hook

▶ Tapestry needle

This cheerful bag with its colorful bows will be a summer favorite. Large enough to pack a towel and bathing suit, it's great for the beach; or pack a sketchpad and pencils and head for the park!

Gauge

With G hook, Rnds 1–8 = 7 inches in diameter; 4 sc and 4 sc rnds = 1 inch

Check gauge to save time.

Pattern Notes

Weave in loose ends as work progresses.

Join rnds with sl st unless otherwise stated.

Pattern Stitch

Curl: 2 sc in 2nd ch from hook, 2 sc in each rem ch across.

Bag

Rnd 1 (WS): With pink, ch 4, 11 dc in 4th ch from hook, join in 4th ch of beg ch-4. (12 dc)

Rnd 2: Ch 2 (counts as first hdc throughout), hdc in same st as beg ch-2, 2 hdc in each dc around, join in 2nd ch of beg ch-2. (24 hdc)

Rnd 3: Ch 2, hdc in same st as beg ch, hdc in next hdc, [2 hdc in next hdc, hdc in next hdc] rep around, join in 2nd ch of beg ch-2. (36 hdc)

Rnd 4: Ch 2, hdc in same st as beg ch, hdc in each of next 2 hdc, [2 hdc in next hdc, hdc in each of next 2 hdc] rep around, join in 2nd ch of beg ch-2. (48 hdc)

Rnd 5: Ch 2, hdc in same st as beg ch, hdc in each of next 3 hdc, [2 hdc in next hdc, hdc in each of next 3 hdc] rep around, join in 2nd ch of beg ch-2. (60 hdc)

Rnd 6: Ch 2, hdc in same st as beg ch, hdc in each of next 4 hdc, [2 hdc in next hdc, hdc in each of next 4 hdc] rep around, join in 2nd ch of beg ch-2. (72 hdc)

Rnd 7: Ch 2, hdc in same st as beg ch, hdc in each of next 5 hdc, [2 hdc in next hdc, hdc in each of next 5 hdc] rep around, join in 2nd ch of beg ch-2. (84 hdc)

Rnd 8: Ch 2, hdc in same st as beg ch, hdc in each of next 6 hdc, [2 hdc in next hdc, hdc in each of next 6 hdc] rep around, join in 2nd ch of beg ch-2. (96 hdc)

Rnd 9: Ch 1, working in front lps this rnd only, sc in each st around, join in beg sc.

Rnd 10: Ch 1, [sc in next sc, tr in next sc] rep around, join in beg sc.

Rnd 11: Ch 4 (counts as first tr throughout), sc in next tr, [tr in next sc, sc in next tr] rep around, join in 4th ch of beg ch-4.

Rnd 12: Ch 1, [sc in tr, tr in sc] rep around, join in beg sc.

Rnds 13 & 14: Rep Rnds 11 and 12, at the end of Rnd 14, fasten off.

Rnd 15: Attach yellow, rep Rnd 11.

Rnd 16: Rep Rnd 12.

Rnds 17 & 18: Rep Rnds 11 and 12.

Rnd 19: Ch 2, hdc in each st around, join in 2nd ch of beg ch-2, fasten off.

Rnd 20: Attach turquoise, ch 1, sc in each st around, join in beg sc. (96 sc)

Rnds 21–57: Ch 1, sc in each sc around, join in beg sc.

Rnd 58: Ch 4 (counts as first dc, ch-1), sk next sc, [dc in next sc, ch 1, sk 1 sc] rep around, join in 3rd ch of beg ch-4. (48 dc; 48 ch-1 sps)

Rnd 59: Ch 1, sc in same st as beg ch, sc in next ch-1 sp, [sc in next dc, sc in next ch-1 sp] rep around, join in beg sc, fasten off.

Rnd 60: Attach bikini at side edge of bag, ch 1, *[sc in each of next 7 sc, ch 20, curl] twice, sc in each of next 7 sc, ch 30, curl **, sc in each of next 7 sc, ch 40, curl, sc in each of next 7 sc, ch 30, curl, rep from * around, ending last rep at **, sc in each of next 5 sc, join in beg sc, fasten off.

Tie

Make 2

With turquoise, ch 134, fasten off. Tie a knot in each end of tie. Fold bag in half, weave first tie through dc sts of Rnd 58 across front; weave 2nd tie through dc sts of Rnd 58

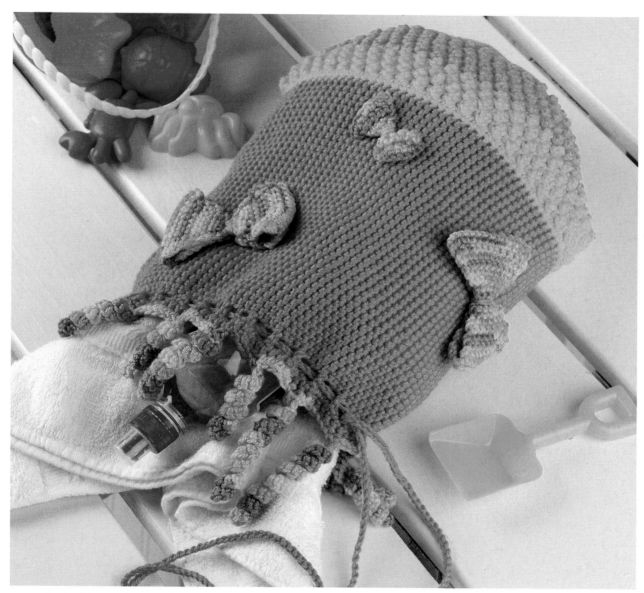

across back. Knot ends of ties tog at each end.

Large Bow
Make 3

Row 1: With bikini, ch 5, sc in 2nd ch from hook, sc in each rem ch across, turn. (4 sc)

Row 2: Ch 1, sc in each sc across, turn.

Rows 3–6: Ch 1, 2 sc in first sc, sc in each rem sc across to last sc, 2 sc in last sc, turn. (12 sc)

Rows 7 & 8: Rep Row 2.

Rows 9–12: Ch 1, sc dec over next 2 sc, sc in each rem sc across to last 2 sc, sc dec over last 2 sc, turn. (4 sc)

Rows 13–23: Rep Rows 2–12, at the end of Row 23, fasten off.

Sew opposite side of foundation ch to Row 23. Holding narrow sections tog, wrap bikini yarn several times around center, secure and fasten off. Sew bows as desired on bag.

Small Bow
Make 2

Row 1: With bikini, ch 7, sc in 2nd ch from hook, sc in each rem ch across, turn. (6 sc)

Row 2: Ch 1, sk first sc, sc in each of next 4 sc, turn. (4 sc)

Row 3: Ch 1, sk first sc, sc in each of next 2 sc, turn. (2 sc)

Row 4: Ch 1, sc in each of next 2 sc, turn.

Row 5: Ch 1, 2 sc in each sc across, turn. (4 sc)

Row 6: Ch 1, 2 sc in first sc, sc in each of next 2 sc, 2 sc in next sc, fasten off. (6 sc)

Sew bows as desired to bag. ✂

Chenille Heart Pin

Design by Lori Zeller

Skill Level: Beginner

Size: 2½ x 2¾ inches

Materials

- ► Chenille yarn: Small amount red
- ► Crochet cotton size 10: 10 yds white
- ► Size F/5 crochet hook or size needed to obtain gauge
- ► Size B/1 crochet hook
- ► 4 inches (⅛-inch-wide) white ribbon
- ► ½-inch gold heart-shaped shank button
- ► ¾-inch pin back
- ► Hot-glue gun

Ever an expression of love, this beautiful heart pin would make a wonderful gift anytime!

Gauge

With larger hook, 4 sc = 1 inch; 4 sc rows = 1 inch

Check gauge to save time.

Pattern Notes

Weave in loose ends as work progresses.

Join rnds with a sl st unless otherwise stated.

Heart

Make 2

Row 1: With larger hook and red yarn, ch 2, 2 sc in 2nd ch from hook, turn. (2 sc)

Row 2: Ch 1, 2 sc in each sc across, turn. (4 sc)

Row 3: Ch 1, 2 sc in first sc, sc in each of next 2 sc, 2 sc in last sc, turn. (6 sc)

Row 4: Ch 1, sc in each of next 3 sc, ch 1, sc in each of next 3 sc, turn.

Row 5: Ch 1, sc in each of next 3 sc, 2 sc in ch-1 sp, sc in each of next 3 sc, turn. (8 sc)

Row 6: Ch 1, sc in each sc across, turn.

First lobe

Row 7: Ch 1, sc in each of next 4 sc, turn. (4 sc)

Row 8: Ch 1, [dec 1 sc over next 2 sc] twice, fasten off. (2 sc)

Second lobe

Row 7: Attach red in next unworked sc of Row 6, ch 1, sc in same st as beg ch, sc in each of next 3 sc, turn. (4 sc)

Row 8: Ch 1, [dec 1 sc over next 2 sc] twice, fasten off. (2 sc)

Rnd 9: Holding both hearts tog and working through both thicknesses, attach red in opposite side of foundation ch of Row 1, ch 1, [sc, ch 2, sc] in same st as beg ch-1, sc in end of each of next 8 rows, 2 sc in each of next 2 sc, sc in end of next 2 rows on inside of each lobe, 2 sc in each of next 2 sc, sc in end of each of next 8 rows, join in beg sc, fasten off. (30 sc; 1 ch-2 sp)

Edging

Rnd 10: With smaller hook, attach white cotton in ch-2 sp at bottom of heart, ch 1, [sc, ch 3, sc] in same ch-2 sp, ch 3, [sc in next sc, ch 3] rep around, join in beg sc, fasten off.

Finishing

Fold ribbon into a bow and glue to center front of heart over Row 6. Glue heart-shaped button over center of bow. Glue pin back to back of heart. ✄

Floral Lapel Pins

Designs by Lori Zeller

Skill Level: Beginner

Size:

Pink Flower: 1½ inches in diameter

White Flower: 1¾ inches in diameter

Materials

► Crochet cotton size 10: 30 yds white, 20 yds pink, 5 yds each mint green and green

► Size 5 steel crochet hook or size needed to obtain gauge

► 2 (¾-inch) pin backs

► 2 (⅝-inch) round flat white buttons

► Hot-glue gun

► Tapestry needle

Flower pins are back in style and with these simple patterns you can make any number of them to match your wardrobe!

Gauge

Rnd 1 = ⅝ inch in diameter; 5 dc = ½ inch

Check gauge to save time.

Pattern Notes

Weave in loose ends as work progresses.

Join rnds with a sl st unless otherwise stated.

Pink Flower

Rnd 1: With white, ch 6, join to form a ring, ch 3 (counts as first dc throughout), 17 dc in ring, join in 3rd ch of beg ch-3, fasten off. (18 dc)

Rnd 2: Attach pink in any dc, ch 1, 2 sc in each dc around, join in beg sc. (36 sc)

Rnd 3: Working in front lps only, ch 1, sc in same st as joining, sl st in next st, sc in next st, [sc, ch 4, sc] in next st, [sc in next st, sl st in next st, sc in next st, {sc, ch 4, sc} in next st] rep around, join in beg sc. (9 petals)

Rnd 4: Working in rem back lps of Rnd 2, sl st in st behind first sc of Rnd 3, sl st in next st, sk next st, 8 dc in next st, [sk next st, sl st in next st, sk next st, 8 dc in next st] rep around, ending with last sl st in 2nd sl st of rnd, fasten off. (9 petals)

Leaf

Make 2

Rnd 1: With green, ch 9, dc in 4th ch from hook, dc in each of next 2 chs, hdc in next ch, sc in next ch, [sl st, ch 1, sl st] in last ch, working on opposite side of foundation ch, sc in next ch, hdc in next ch, dc in each of next 4 chs, join in top of beg ch-9, leaving a length of cotton, fasten off.

White Flower

Rnd 1: With white, ch 6, join to form a ring, ch 3 (counts as first dc throughout), 17 dc in ring, join in 3rd ch of beg ch-3. (18 dc)

Rnd 2: Working in front

lps this rnd only, ch 1, sc in same st as beg ch, ch 2, [sc in next st, ch 2] rep around, join in beg sc.

Rnd 3: Sl st into ch-2 sp, ch 3, 2 dc in same ch-2 sp, sc in next ch-2 sp, [3 dc in next ch-2 sp, sc in next ch-2 sp] rep around, join in 3rd ch of beg ch-3. (9 petals)

Rnd 4: Working in rem back lps of Rnd 1, sc in first st, ch 3, [sc in next st, ch 3] rep around, join in beg sc.

Rnd 5: Sl st into ch-3 sp, ch 1, sc in same ch-3 sp, 5 dc in next ch-3 sp, [sc in next ch-3 sp, 5 dc in next ch-3 sp] rep around, join in beg sc, fasten off.

Leaf
Make 2
Rnd 1: With mint green, rep Rnd 1 of leaf for pink flower.

Finishing
Sew leaves to back of each flower as desired. Glue a button to center of Rnd 1 of each flower. Glue pin to back of flower. ✄

Pearly Purse
Continued from page 167

each of next 4 hdc, join in 2nd ch of beg ch-2.

Rnd 5: Ch 2, hdc in each of next 2 hdc, *[pearl, sc in 3rd dc of next 5-dc group, 5 dc in next sc] 4 times, pearl, sc in 3rd dc of next 5-dc group *, hdc in each of next 7 hdc, rep from * to *, hdc in each of next 4 hdc, join in 2nd ch of beg ch-2.

Rnds 6–13: Rep Rnds 4 and 5, at the end of Rnd 13, turn.

Divide for front & back
Row 1: Sl st in next hdc, ch 2, hdc in each of next 8 sts, dc in each of next 15 sts, hdc in each of next 9 sts, turn.

Row 2: Ch 2, hdc in each of next 9 sts, dc in each of next 11 sts, hdc in each of next 10 sts, turn.

Row 3: Ch 2, hdc in each of next 5 sts, dc in each of next 5 sts, tr in each of next 8 sts, dc in each of next 5 sts, hdc in next 6 sts, sl st down side of rows to Rnd 13.

Rep Rows 1–3 on opposite side edge.

Rnd 4: Ch 1, sc evenly sp around outer edge of top opening, working 2 sc over posts of side edge of rows, join in beg sc, fasten off.

Finishing
Sew Rnd 4 to purse frame; attach chain to purse frame. ✄

Poncho Perfection
Continued from page 174

rep from * around, join in 2nd ch of beg ch-2.

Rnd 3: Ch 2, *[fpdc around fpdc, bpdc around bpdc] rep across to corner sts, maintain pattern of fpdc and bpdc on corner sts, work [2 dc, ch 3, 2 dc] in corner ch-3 sp, rep from * around, join in 2nd ch of beg ch-2, fasten off. ✄

Rainbow Poncho Set
Continued from page 180

at shoulder between dc groups, ch 3 (counts as first dc throughout), 2 dc in same sp, *3 dc in each sp to within 1 sp of corner, 6-dc dec over next 3 sps, rep from * around, working 3 dc in each sp between dc groups, join in 3rd ch of beg ch-3.

Rnd 2: Sl st into next sp between dc groups, ch 3, 2 dc in same sp, *3 dc in each sp to within 1 sp of dec sts, 4 dc dec, rep from * around, working 3 dc in each rem sp between dc groups, join.

Note: For doll only, fasten off at the end of Rnd 2.

Rnd 3: Rep Rnd 2, fasten off. ✄

Bobbles Sweater & Hat

Continued from page 172

Continue in established pattern on 35 (37, 39) sts to approximately 14½ (15, 15) inches from beg, ending with a WS row.

Sleeve shaping

[Dec 1 st each edge every row] 3 times. (29, 31, 33 sts)

Continue in established pattern on 29 (31, 33) sts to approximately 15½ (16, 16½) inches from beg, ending with a RS row, fasten off.

Assembly

Sew shoulder seams; set in sleeves and sew sleeve seams.

Body Band

Row 1 (RS): With smaller hook, attach yarn with sl st in corner of lower right front edge, ch 1, work 54 (60, 66) sc evenly sp up front edge to neck, 3 sc in corner st, sc in each of next 3 (4, 5) sc, sc dec over next 2 sts, 6 sc evenly sp along side of neck, sc dec over next 2 sts, 14 (16, 18) sc across back neck, sc dec over next 2 sts, 6 sc evenly sp along side of neck, sc dec over next 2 sts, sc in each of next 3 (4, 5) sc, 3 sc in corner st, work 54 (60, 66) sc down left front, turn.

Row 2: Working in front lps this row only, ch 1, sc in each st around, turn.

Row 3: Ch 3 (counts as first dc), dc in each sc around, working 3 dc in each corner and dc dec

over next 2 sc at each neck and shoulder dec in the same area as Row 1 (4 dec sts), turn.

Row 4: Rep Row 2, fasten off.

Row 5 (RS): Working in rem free lps of Row 1 with smaller hook attach yarn in right front bottom, sl st in each rem lp of Row 1 to opposite edge, sl st in each st across bottom edge of band to rem free lp of Row 3.

Row 6 (RS): Working in rem free lps of Row 3, sl st in each st to opposite edge, fasten off.

Sew buttons evenly sp up left front of sweater and use natural sps between dc sts of Row 3 for buttonholes.

Hat

Note: Do not join rnds on hat unless otherwise indicated; use a scrap of CC yarn to mark rnds.

Rnd 1: Beg at crown with larger hook, ch 2, 8 sc in 2nd ch from hook. (8 sc)

Rnd 2: 2 sc in each sc around. (16 sc)

Rnd 3: [Sc in next sc, 2 sc in next sc] rep around. (24 sc)

Rnd 4: *Working in front lp only of next sc, [sl st, ch 3, sl st] (for bobble), sc in each of next 3 sc, rep from * around. (6 bobbles)

Rnd 5: [Sc in rem back lp behind bobble, 2 sc in next sc, sc in next sc, 2 sc in next sc] 6 times. (36 sc)

Rnd 6: Sc in each of next 3 sc, [bobble in front lp only of next sc, sc in each of next 5 sc] rep around to last 3 sts, bobble in next sty, sc in each of next 2 sc.

Rnd 7: Sc in each of next 2 sc, *2 sc in next sc, sc in rem lp behind bobble, 2 sc in next sc **, sc in each of next 3 sc, rep from * around, ending last rep at **, sc in next sc. (48 sc)

Rnd 8: Sc in each of next 5 sc, [bobble in front lp only of next sc, sc in each of next 7 sc] rep around to last 3 sc, bobble in front lp only of next sc, sc in each of next 2 sc.

Rnd 9: Sc in each of next 3 sc, *2 sc in next sc, sc in rem lp behind bobble, 2 sc in next sc **, sc in each of next 5 sc, rep from * around, ending last rep at **, sc in each of next 4 sc. (60 sc)

Rnd 10: [Sc in each of next 9 sc, bobble in front lp only of next sc] rep around.

Rnd 11: [2 sc in next sc, sc in each of next 7 sc, 2 sc in next sc, sc in rem lp behind bobble] rep around. (72 sc)

Rnd 12: Sc in next sc, *bobble in front lp only of next st **, sc in each of next 3 sc, rep from * around, ending last rep at **, sc in each of next 2 sc.

Rnd 13: Sc in next sc, *sc in rem lp behind bobble **, sc in each of next 3 sc, rep from * around, ending last rep at **, sc in each of next 2 sc.

Rnd 14: [Sc in each of next 3 sc, bobble in front lp only of next sc] rep around.

Rnd 15: [Sc in each of next 3 sc, sc in rem lp behind bobble] rep around.

Rnd 16: Working in front lps only, sl st in each st around.

Rnd 17: Working in rem back lps of rnd before last, sc in each st around.

Rnd 18: [Sc in each of next 5 sc, sk next sc] rep around. (60 sc)

Rnd 19: Sc in each sc around.

Rnd 20: [Sc in next sc, bobble in front lp only of next st] rep around.

Rnd 21: [Sc in next sc, sc in rem lp behind bobble] rep around.

Rnds 22 & 23: Rep Rnd 19.

Rnds 24–29: Rep Rnds 16 and 17.

Rnd 30: [Sl st in next sc, ch 1] rep around, ending with sl st in beg sl st, fasten off. ✀

General Instructions

Please review the following information before working the projects in this book. Important details about the abbreviations and symbols used are included.

Hooks

Crochet hooks are sized for different weights of yarn and thread. For thread crochet, you will usually use a steel crochet hook. Steel crochet-hook sizes range from size 00 to 14. The higher the number of the hook, the smaller your stitches will be. For example, a size 1 steel crochet hook will give you much larger stitches than a size 9 steel crochet hook. Keep in mind that the sizes given with the pattern instructions were obtained by working with the size thread or yarn, and hook given in the materials list. If you work with a smaller hook, depending on your gauge, your project size will be smaller; if you work with a larger hook, your finished project's size will be larger.

Gauge

Gauge is determined by the tightness or looseness of your stitches, and affects the finished size of your project. If you are concerned about the finished size of the project matching the size given, take time to crochet a small section of the pattern and then check your gauge. For example, if the gauge called for is 10 dc = 1 inch, and your gauge is 12 dc to the inch, you should switch to a larger hook. On the other hand, if your gauge is only 8 dc to the inch, you should switch to a smaller hook.

If the gauge given in the pattern is for an entire motif, work one motif and then check your gauge.

Understanding Symbols

As you work through a pattern, you'll quickly notice several symbols in the instructions. These symbols are used to clarify the pattern for you: brackets [], curlicue brackets {}, asterisks *. Brackets [] are used to set off a group of instructions worked a number of times. For example, "[ch 3, sc in ch-3 sp] 7 times" means to work the instructions inside the [] seven times. Brackets [] also set off a group of stitches to be worked in one stitch, space or loop. For example, the brackets [] in this set of instructions, "Sk 3 sc, [3 dc, ch 1, 3 dc] in next st" indicate that after skipping 3 sc, you will work 3 dc, ch 1 and 3 more dc all in the next stitch.

Occasionally, a set of instructions inside a set of brackets needs to be repeated, too. In this case, the text within the brackets to be repeated will be set off with curlicue brackets {}. For example, "[Ch 9, yo twice, insert hook in 7th ch from hook and pull up a loop, sk next dc, yo, insert hook in next dc and pull up a loop, {yo and draw through 2 lps on hook} 5 times, ch 3] 8 times." In this case, in each of the eight times you work the instructions included in brackets, you will work the section included in curlicue brackets five times.

Asterisks * are also used when a group of instructions is repeated. They may either be used alone or with brackets. For example, "*Sc in each of the next 5 sc, 2 sc in next sc, rep from * around, join with a sl st in beg sc" simply means you will work the instructions from the first * around the entire round. "*Sk 3 sc, [3 dc, ch 1, 3 dc] in next st, rep from * around" is an example of asterisks working with brackets. In this set of instructions, you will repeat the instructions from the asterisk around, working the instructions inside the brackets together. ❤

Buyer's Guide

When looking for a specific material, first check your local craft stores and yarn shops. If you are unable to locate a product, contact the manufacturers listed below for the closest retail source in your area.

❤ **Brown Sheep Co.**
100662 County Rd. 16
Mitchell, NE 69357
(308) 635-2198

❤ **Caron International**
Customer Service
P.O. Box 222
Washington, NC 27889
(800) 868-9194

❤ **Coats & Clark**
Consumer Service
P.O. Box 12229
Greenville, SC 29612-0229
(800) 648-1479
www.coatsandclark.com

❤ **Patons Yarns**
Box 40
Listowel, Ontario
N4W 3H3 Canada
(519) 291-3780
www.patonsyarns.com

❤ **DMC Corp.**
Hackensack Ave. Bldg. 10A
South Kearny, NJ 07032
(800) 275-4117
www.dmc-usa.com

❤ **Lion Brand Yarn Co.**
34 W. 15th St.
New York, NY 10011
(800) 795-5466
www.lionbrand.com

❤ **Trendsetter Yarns**
16742 Stagg St. Ste. 104
Van Nuys, CA 91406-1641
(800) 446-2425

STITCH GUIDE

Front Loop (a)
Back Loop (b)

Chain (ch)
Yo, draw lp through hook.

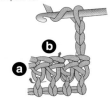

Slip Stitch Joining
Insert hook in beg ch, yo, draw lp through.

Front Post/Back Post Dc
Fpdc (a): Yo, insert hook from front to back and to front again around the vertical post (upright part) of next st, yo and draw yarn through, yo and complete dc.
Bpdc (b): Yo, reaching over top of piece and working on opposite side (back) of work, insert hook from back to front to back again around vertical post of next st, yo and draw yarn through, yo and complete dc.

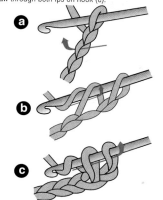

Single Crochet (sc)
Insert hook in st (a), yo, draw lp through (b), yo, draw through both lps on hook (c).

Half-Double Crochet (hdc)
Yo, insert hook in st (a), yo, draw lp through (b), yo, draw through all 3 lps on hook (c).

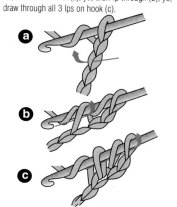

DECREASING

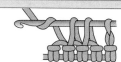

Single Crochet Decrease
Dec 1 sc over next 2 sts as follows: Draw up a lp in each of next 2 sts, yo, draw through all 3 lps on hook.

Double Crochet Decrease
Dec 1 dc over next 2 sts as follows: [Yo, insert hook in next st, yo, draw up lp on hook, yo, draw through 2 lps] twice, yo, draw through all 3 lps on hook.

Double Crochet (dc)
Yo, insert hook in st (a), yo, draw lp through (b), [yo, draw through 2 lps] twice (c, d).

Treble Crochet (tr)
Yo hook twice, insert hook in st (a), yo, draw lp through (b), [yo, draw through 2 lps on hook] 3 times (c, d, e).

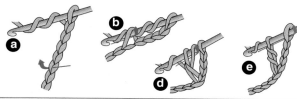

SPECIAL STITCHES

Chain Color Change (ch color change)
Yo with new color, draw through last lp on hook.

Double Crochet Color Change (dc color change)
Drop first color, yo with new color, draw through last 2 lps of st.

Reverse Single Crochet (reverse sc)
Working from left to right, insert hook in next st to the right (a), yo, draw up lp on hook, complete as for sc (b).

Stitch Abbreviations
The following stitch abbreviations are used throughout this publication.

beg ....begin(ning)
bl(s) ....block(s)
bpdc.......................................back post dc
ch(s)...chain(s)
cl(s)...cluster(s)
CC.......................................contrasting color
dc......................................double crochet
dec...decrease
dtr.......................................double treble crochet
fpdc......................................front post dc
hdc....................................half-double crochet
inc...increase
lp(s)..loop(s)
MC...main color
p...picot
rem....................................remain(ing)
rep...repeat
rnd(s)..round(s)
RS................................right side facing you
sc.....................................single crochet
sk...skip
sl st...slip stitch
sp(s)...space(s)
st(s)...stitch(es)
tog...together
tr.......................................treble crochet
trtr....................................triple treble crochet
WS.............................wrong side facing you
yo...yarn over

Crochet Hooks
METRIC	US
.60mm	14 steel
.75mm	12 steel
1.00mm	10 steel
1.25mm	8 steel
1.50mm	7 steel
1.75mm	5 steel
2.00mm	B/1
2.50mm	C/2
3.00mm	D/3
3.50mm	E/4
4.00mm	F/5
4.50mm	G/6
5.00mm	H/8
5.50mm	I/9
6.00mm	J/10

Yarn Conversion
OUNCES TO GRAMS
1	28.4
2	56.7
3	85.0
4	113.4

GRAMS TO OUNCES
25	⅞
40	1⅜
50	1¾
100	3½

Crochet Abbreviations
US	INTL
sc—single crochet	dc—double crochet
dc—double crochet	tr—treble crochet
hdc—half-double crochet	htr—half treble crochet
tr—treble crochet	dtr—double treble crochet
dtr—double treble crochet	trip—triple treble crochet
sk—skip	miss

YARNS
Bedspread weight	No. 10 cotton or Virtuoso
Sport weight	3-ply or thin DK
Worsted weight	Thick DK or Aran

Check tension or gauge to save time.

Special Thanks

Carol Alexander
Blushing Rose Valance, Frosty Morn, Hearts & Flowers Delight, Mini Victorian Dresser Box, Rose Pocket Place Mats

Belinda Carter
Nawina Pillow

Sue Childress
Braided-Look Oval Rug, Tweed Hat & Purse, Crocheted Flower Pin, Pansy Teacup Pincushion Set, Pearly Purse, Pretty 'n' Pink Floral Basket

Kathryn Clark
Easter Egg Frames

Paula Clark
Votive Cup Holders

Donna Collinsworth
Patchwork Heart Rug

Margaret Dick
Playpen Pad Cover

Dot Drake
Bitty Mouse & Pansy Pig Puppets, Bright Bows Beach Bag

Jo Hanna Dzikowski
Flower Barrettes, Tea Rose Trellis

Darla Fanton
Raspberry Sherbet Afghan, Reversible Baby Bib, Rustic Ripple

Nazanin Fard
Baby Layette

Valmay Flint
Scalloped Pineapple Doily

Norma Gale
Victorian Picture Frames

Gloria Graham
Sachet

Lauri Grammer
Blooming Hearts Gift Set

Christine Grazioso
Bounteous Blue

Anne Halliday
Blue Skies, Spring Flowers; Visions of Autumn; Rings in Hexagon Motifs; Spiraling Bars & Squares

Tammy Hildebrand
Beaded Potpourri Bowl, Li'l Bear's Outfit

Melissa Leapman
Delicate Cardigan, Poncho Perfection, Sweet Scallops Cardigan

Peggy Longshore
Chevron Ripple Baby Afghan

Jo Ann Maxwell
Curlicue Dress

Beverly Mewhorter
Baby's Hat & Mitten Set, Cleopatra Fashion Doll Gown, Josephine's Coronation Gown, Pretty Roses Blender Cover, Victorian Rose Teddy Bear

Shirley Patterson
Rainbow Knots Baby Afghan, Fingerless Bridal Gloves, Mesh Snoods

Maggie Petsch
Swan Bonbon Dish, Three Napkin Rings

Diane Poellot
Baby's First Football, Love Knot Wrap

Susan Peak
Crocus in the Snow

Josie Rabier
Lacy Lamp Shade Cover, Tabletop Ecru Doily

Sandy Scoville
Bookmarks for Book Lovers

Ruth Shepherd
Imagination Edging, Pointing the Way Edging

Ann E. Smith
Ombre Blocks Cardigan, Red Hooded Jacket, Bobbles Sweater & Hat, Hooded Cardigan, Red & White Layette

Martha Stein
Tulip Garden

Rena Stevens
Climbing Flowers

Angela Tate
Double Aran, Aran Squares

Vicky Tignanelli
Nursery Rhyme Dolls

Sharon Valiant
Christening Bonnet, Scallop Edging

Michele Wilcox
Critter Finger Puppets, Flower Basket Guest Towel Set, Flowered Squares Baby Afghan, Ladybug Ball, Mr. Brown the Bear

Margret Willson
Easy Ombre Afghan, Rainbow Poncho Set

Mary Jane Wood
Pastel Sunset Sling Purse

Shirley Zebrowski
Suger & Spice Pullover

Lori Zeller
Chenille Heart Pin, Kitchen Dress-Ups, Floral Lapel Pins

Notes